'Professor Sir David Omand deconstructs then reconstructs an important mode of thinking, spy thought, for those of us who deal with strategy, information, misinformation and disinformation. He leaves the reader with a powerful framework to help us face the realpolitik of the world' Professor Michael Mainelli, Alderman and Sheriff of the City of London

'*How Spies Think* is a masterclass in miniature form, offering the enduring lessons of a consequential life in service as keys to success in any profession facing the challenges and opportunities of an uncertain future' Chris Inglis, former Deputy Director of the NSA

'A tour de force. David Omand equips the reader with powerful intelligence techniques to survive in the new digital age. He lightens it with a fascinating selection of anecdotes, some firsthand, to illustrate his themes. And he makes an overwhelming case for rationality as the best response to a world of fake news and cyberattacks. Essential reading' Richard Wilson, former Head of the Home Civil Service

'With today's political reality trumping political fiction, we rely now for mystery on the world of spies, espionage and secret intelligence. In this fascinating and revealing book David Omand, after a lifetime in that shadowy world, pulls back the curtain on spying triumphs, the occasional disasters, but also the important lessons for all of us from these dark but essential arts. It is a true eye-opener on a world which outsiders only guess about' Lord George Robertson, former UK Defence Secretary and Secretary General of NATO

'A fascinating book about how to think. Not just about intelligence but also about disinformation, distortion, subversion and all the other perils of a digital age. There cannot be anybody in Britain who can match David Omand's broad experience in seeking, assessing and using secret intelligence. This personal experience produces his careful and thorough analytical rules' David Wilson, Baron Wilson of Tillyorn, former Governor of Hong Kong

'Britain's spooks are world-renowned. This brilliant book lets us in on one of the secrets of their success – how to use rigorous analysis to separate fact from fake. It's a skill that can help us all to make better choices in our lives' Peter Ricketts, former British National Security Adviser

ABOUT THE AUTHOR

David Omand was the first UK Security and Intelligence Coordinator, responsible to the Prime Minister for the professional health of the intelligence community, national counter-terrorism strategy and 'homeland security'. He served for seven years on the Joint Intelligence Committee. He was Permanent Secretary of the Home Office from 1997 to 2000, and before that Director of GCHQ.

How Spies Think

Ten Lessons in Intelligence

DAVID OMAND

PENGUIN BOOKS

PENGUIN BOOKS

UK | USA | Canada | Ireland | Australia
India | New Zealand | South Africa

Penguin Books is part of the Penguin Random House group of companies
whose addresses can be found at global.penguinrandomhouse.com.

Penguin
Random House
UK

First published by Viking 2020
Published with a new preface in Penguin Books 2021

002

Printed and bound in Great Britain by Clays Ltd, Elcograf S.p.A.

The authorized representative in the EEA is Penguin Random House Ireland, Morrison Chambers,
32 Nassau Street, Dublin D02 YH68

A CIP catalogue record for this book is available from the British Library

ISBN: 978-0-241-38519-7

www.greenpenguin.co.uk

MIX
Paper from
responsible sources
FSC® C018179

Penguin Random House is committed to a
sustainable future for our business, our readers
and our planet. This book is made from Forest
Stewardship Council® certified paper.

For Keir, Robert, Beatrice and Ada,
in the hope that you will grow up in a better world

Contents

Contents

Preface to the paperback edition

So much has happened in less than a year since this book was first published in autumn 2020 that the least I owe the reader is an updating preface to introduce the paperback edition. Time seems to have speeded up for world events, while slowing down for those of us shielding for the last year from the COVID-19 pandemic and watching, as if in slow motion, a series of extraordinary events unfold. It is no comfort to me that all the themes in this book have been illustrated in primary colours over that short period.

I started writing this book after seeing how the Brexit referendum and the 2016 US Presidential election were being reflected on social media. What I was horrified to see was a rising tide of half-truths and distortions designed to try to persuade us online of what we ought to think and want. Not to mention seeing some downright falsehoods and deceptions, coming not only from Russia, aimed at creating a hostile atmosphere, widening divisions in our societies and increasingly setting us at each other's throats. The failed insurrection of the supporters of President Trump, their storming of Congress and his historic impeachment by Congress for the second time have illustrated one of the key lessons of the book – the power of social media to mobilize the energy of individuals for causes, good or ill. The failure of that attempt to overturn the legitimate outcome of the US election does nevertheless give me confidence that I am justified in ending the book on a note of optimism over the strength of democracy provided we look after it. But it has been a close-run thing in the US.

Ironically, Facebook's founder, Mark Zuckerberg, had changed the company's mission statement the year after the 2016 US election from 'making the world more open and connected' to a more action-oriented appeal to 'give people the power to build community and bring the world closer together'. An admirable sentiment but, as so often happens, one that was to be realized in an unforeseen way. The sections of the Republican community that had so passionately supported Donald Trump's election in 2016 used social media to come even closer together, but only to end up violently contesting the 2020 election result on the basis of the President's baseless claim that it was being stolen, a case where social media had induced the transition from 'I would like it to be true' to, with constant repetition, 'It might be true', which, despite proof to the contrary, slid too easily for the Trump base into 'For me, it is as good as true – and I will act believing it to be true.' More than three years after Facebook's change of mission statement, some of those groups have done exactly what Mark Zuckerberg envisioned: they have bound themselves together for a passionately held common cause. But their 'something greater than ourselves' wasn't what Zuckerberg had had in mind: a seditious movement upsetting the peaceful transfer of power following a fair and certified election in the United States. As I explain in the book, we must now recognize that sedition and subversion have gone digital.

Only time will tell whether the social media giants will acknowledge that the problem lies deep in the very architecture of their platforms. They have been built to encourage the personalized advertising technology that pays for the platform, based on identifying groups of users with similar opinions and characteristics from their personal data, including from their internet usage. A *Wall Street Journal* article from May 2020 reported an alarming finding from Facebook's own researchers. According to a 2016 internal Facebook study, '64 percent of all extremist group joins are due to our recommendation tools . . . Our recommendation systems grow the problem.' One user found that the more he posted deranged Trumpist messages, the more followers Facebook sent his way, and soon he was effectively hosting a group based on election denial, with tens of thousands of members. Thereby hangs the myth of 'the steal' of the Presidency by Joe Biden – a conspiracy still believed by millions of heavily armed US voters. That story has not ended.

I remind us in the book why so much online content works at an emotional not a rational level. It is a toxic combination when the inherent characteristics of the business model of the Internet combine with our human psychological vulnerability when online. We are targeted with the political messages that the algorithms have revealed are most likely to trigger our emotional response, just as we are targeted by marketing for specific products and services that the algorithms have concluded we ought to have an interest in – without our realizing how we are being manipulated. I was struck recently by the words of Jimmy Wales, co-creator of Wikipedia: 'If you think about advertising-driven social media, the real incentive is to show you as many ads as possible . . . and it's driven them to create addictive products. It's driven them, in many cases, to prioritize agitation and argumentation, in a negative sense, over education and learning and thoughtfulness.'

It is worth re-emphasizing that the Internet is a marvellous, life-enhancing invention. We are dependent on the Internet for our future economic and social development. It is as well that the COVID-19 pandemic did not strike us twenty years ago when we would not have had the apps that have helped us to video call loved ones, to work from home, to provide online education and to allow us to purchase food and goods online. We have nevertheless been forcibly reminded that the Internet has a dark side. Twitter finally banished President Trump from its platform after he appeared to have incited the mob to march on Congress, and that appears to have led to a marked decline in offensive tweets, although there is some evidence that these have moved to other niche platforms used by the far right. It is a good sign that Facebook is stepping up its content moderation and agreeing to be bound by the decisions reached by an independent oversight board of lawyers, journalists, human rights advocates and other academics. Those who wield power in cyberspace have to accept their heavy social responsibility.

As I describe in the book, social media allows the microtargeting of political messages tailored to the feelings of different audiences having, as we have seen, a transformational impact on traditional politics. I am not naive about the old practice of politics. You cannot be a Permanent Secretary of a major department of state in Whitehall without understanding the sometimes brutal realities of the democratic process. Social media provides a powerful persuasive tool and as such will be used in the contest that is the competition for power. The sensible public has always understood that traditional political debate has its political swagger and exaggeration. And we have always known that personal ambitions and bitter political rivalries are inseparable from the contest that is democratic politics. But we should not have to suffer those who blur, or even deny, the very nature of truth. No one is entitled to their own alternative facts, and I have been gratified by the way that readers of the earlier edition of this book have responded to endorse that message.

Another internet concern tackled in the book through the lens of intelligence is the prevalence of conspiracy stories spread by social media. Recent months have seen telling examples swirling around COVID-19 and drawing in long-term anti-vaxxers, with potentially disastrous consequences for those who act on these conspiratorial ideas, and causing harm for all of us. We have had unfounded claims that the vaccines will cause mutations in the RNA sequence of those who take it. And of government ambitions to control the lives of citizens through forced vaccinations, alleging that those who do not take the vaccine will lose their jobs and their children be barred from school, or even that they will be kept from going out in public. We have had fantasist stories both that COVID-19 is a hoax and that it is a US bioweapon gone rogue. There has been a media campaign in Russia falsely denigrating the Oxford University / AstraZeneca vaccine as being dangerous to humans (labelling it 'the monkey vaccine'). We still see Russian media trying to erode Western public confidence by highlighting the few recorded cases of side effects from the approved vaccines. Then last year we had the home-grown conspiracy story spread on social media that emissions from 5G mobile-phone masts can cause COVID-19, leading to attacks on mobile-phone masts in some major cities in England. That baseless claim capitalized on years of conspiracy beliefs that mobile phones cause a range of medical harms. Combating falsehoods that mislead the public on the facts about disease and health measures has become an important role for public health. Again, the gravity of the pandemic and the reputational damage the social media platforms are suffering have triggered them into adding warnings to posts about the disease from their platforms, removing the most dangerous of them and de-platforming the worst offenders.

I have been much encouraged by the many comments posted by those who have read the book and who have found it helpful to use my model of analysis to help them understand the experience of COVID-19. A good example comes from the anticipated emergence of different natural mutations of the virus as it infected more and more people. We must be grateful for the past investment in UK bioscience that provided the capability to gene-sequence viral samples from many patients. Therefore, the scientists in the UK were quick to detect signs of increasing numbers of people infected with a particular new variant in Kent and spreading elsewhere. In the language of my model, they had *situational awareness* to answer questions about the 'what and where' of events. Then came the essential step of providing scientific *explanation* of what was being observed, in terms of a mutation on that part of the virus called the spike protein, giving the variant a selective advantage and making the virus more transmissible. With sufficient data and that sound explanation, the modellers were then able to provide ministers with useable *estimates* of likely increased transmissibility and to apply that modelling to the likely consequential increase in the R number over time. It matters, of course, in the modellers' forecasts what they have assumed about future public compliance with lockdown or the transmissibility of a new variant. Disagreements between professionals often boil down to disagreement about the appropriateness of assumptions to use in the model. I describe in the book how that same analytic progression is used by intelligence analysts assembling the basis for warning assessments for the National Security Council – for example, of signs of hostile activity around the world in cyberspace or that could affect our interests and the safety of the public.

But I warn in the book that while we are so closely focused on examining current threats we may find an unwelcome and unexpected surprise comes and hits us on the back of the head. So let me emphasize here the value of what I term *strategic notice* of possible future developments of concern. Strategic notice helps contingency planning, answering important questions of the 'How could we best prepare for whatever might appear next?' type, or even 'How could we pre-empt this risk so that it never comes to test us?'

With strategic notice we may be able to mitigate the risk: for example, by commissioning relevant research or investing in greater resilience. To develop the COVID-19 example, we had plenty of strategic notice of a new coronavirus pandemic (it was top of the risk matrix in my time as UK Security and Intelligence Coordinator, although we assessed it was most likely to be in the form of a mutated flu virus). The good news is that there was then significant investment in the research capability to develop and test vaccines much faster than ever before. We see the beneficial results today. The bad news was that despite the strategic notice there was not the investment in related resilience, so when this particular pandemic arrived, the UK did not have stocks of protective clothing and masks even to cover the immediate needs of health and care-home workers (nor up-to-date plans of how to acquire more, quickly) and did not have rehearsed plans to expand rapidly existing local track-and-trace systems. Another important lesson of intelligence is that by paying heed to strategic notice we do not have to be so surprised by surprise. Taken together, those outputs from rational analysis form the SEES model: situational awareness; explanation; estimation and modelling; and finally strategic notice.

The appearance of new, more dangerous variants of the disease and the increasing heartbreak from its economic ravages and divisive social and educational effects have led to public questioning of how far politicians have been, as they claim, 'following the science'. The tension between rational analysis and political mandate is another key theme of the book that has been exposed in recent events.

In government, professional analysts and policymakers inhabit largely different domains (in part a deliberate organizational arrangement to reduce the risk of perceptions of political bias creeping into professional assessment). The inhabitants of these domains therefore need to take the trouble to understand each other and how far to expose any remaining disagreements, such as we see reported today in arguments over measures to restrict the spread of COVID-19 disease, such as closing schools. The processes of analysis and its complexities can seem abstract and remote from the people-dominated world of the politician; but analysts too often see policy driven by magical thinking, believing that the announced objective or target will be achieved without assurance that the real-world mechanisms and resources are on the ground capable of securing it. Sometimes there can be specific 'warning failures' that fall into the cracks between adequate foreknowledge and appropriately swift precautionary action: hearing the words but not listening to the message. Misunderstanding can arise because professionals and policymakers have failed sufficiently to probe each other's position. The answer you get from professionals does depend on the precise question you asked. When I was Permanent Secretary in the Home Office, my brilliant chief lawyer, the late Dame Juliet Wheldon, used to insist that I not ask her what the law says but to tell her honestly what I needed to achieve so she could then give me her professional judgement as to whether it could be achieved within the law, and if so how. For law, substitute science.

In the book I describe the risks of hostile activity in cyberspace, but I did not imagine that threat would be so dramatically highlighted by Russia being caught recently conducting one of largest cyber-espionage campaigns ever (codename SolarWinds) against the United States. I warn in the book that subversion and sedition have now gone digital. I was not surprised that the Russian intelligence agencies would try to silence and discredit President Putin's principal domestic critic, Alexei Navalny. But I confess to being taken aback that they would resort to old-fashioned murder to remove him and that, even after the exposure of their bungled attempt to murder Sergei Skripal and his daughter in Salisbury in 2018, they would choose to do this by using the illegal nerve agent Novichok, bringing even more international condemnation on their heads. I was not surprised, however, that it was the open-source intelligence group Bellingcat, working with investigative journalists, that was able to pin this on the FSB, Russia's domestic-security agency. Clever intelligence gathering and analysis in the digital age are not confined to secret agencies.

I must thank all those who have read the book and fed back to me their wide experience of decisionmaking under uncertainty. The CEO of a major British FTSE company told me he had read the book and it had already changed the way he thought about pending decisions on major contracts and customer relationships. He sent copies of the book to all his senior managers with the injunction to use the SEES model, and to apply its lessons to negotiation and forming lasting partnerships based on demonstrating a record of trustworthiness. Likewise, the MD of a cybersecurity company has told me he has sent copies of the book to all his contacts with a similar message. I am glad of this direct evidence that the SEES model is being of practical use in answering the question of what we need to know to take solid evidence-based decisions.

I have kept the description of the SEES model as it was in the first edition. But I was struck by the comments of one correspondent who felt I could have been clearer that, in arguing for more rationality in the taking of decisions, I was not trying to banish the feelings which drive big decisions and motivate genuine political engagement. I am happy to use this preface to reassure on that point and to expand on my thinking. I do not wish to be read as being secretly tempted to want government handed over to the modern equivalent of Plato's unelected guardians. The cost–benefit analyst does not always know best. Understanding well what is, does not tell us what we ought to strive for.

It is the same when it comes to making a big personal decision. We have to bring together in our own head two different qualities of thought: on the one hand, rational analysis of the situation we are in and the options open; and, on the other hand, understanding what our ambitions are for what we want to achieve by our choice, or what outcomes we fear and wish to avoid and what our values tell us we should do. Both kinds of thought, the dispassionate and the impassioned, the 'what is' and the values-driven 'what we hope will be', need to be understood and integrated if we are to make sound decisions. However imperfectly, it is what I have tried to do myself facing difficult choices. One personal example was deciding to seek another senior post after only just surviving treatment for the life-threatening cancer that had forced me to stand down in 2001 as Permanent Secretary to the Home Office. I had to balance the professional medical advice I had been given of the continuing risks with a sense of continuing duty and, I confess, a residual ambition to make a difference. I ended up accepting the Prime Minister's offer that I become the first UK Security and Intelligence Coordinator in the Cabinet Office, a tough assignment but one that I have never regretted taking.

Much of the problem I describe with the use of social media today is that it reduces the analytic input in favour of the emotional. On social media we can feel our emotional responses being heightened. The motivations (including aspects that were previously unconscious to us) that lead us to feel we want to make a decision surface more vividly into our mind. At the level of advertising, for example, we experience too readily mimetic desire, wanting what other people want (or social media influencers induce us to want). We all can suffer too in our thinking from the cognitive biases that I describe in Chapter 5. We may, for example, have been selective about the facts we chose to emphasize as important, or we may have been attracted by explanations of events with which we felt most comfortable and ignored those that ran counter to our instincts. It can be a dangerous combination when we undervalue the use of rational analysis and when we do not realize that the analysis itself is less objective than we believe it to be.

Bringing these types of thinking, rational analysis and personal desires, together inside a single mind has always been hard. I hope that this book will encourage readers to find ways of using the method I describe to arrive at results for their own decisions that feel right to them but are grounded firmly in reality. But a warning message that the book offers is to take extra care to check that rational analysis has its proper place. Achieving that is getting harder now we are in the digital age of social media.

David Omand
February 2021

Introduction

*Why we need these lessons in seeking independence
of mind, honesty and integrity*

Westminster, March 1982. 'This is very serious, isn't it?' said Margaret Thatcher. She frowned and looked up from the intelligence reports I had handed her. 'Yes, Prime Minister,' I replied, 'this intelligence can only be read one way: the Argentine Junta are in the final stages of preparing to invade the Falkland Islands, very likely this coming Saturday.'

It was the afternoon of Wednesday, 31 March 1982.

I was the Principal Private Secretary to the Defence Secretary, John Nott. We were in his room in the House of Commons drafting a speech when an officer from the Defence Intelligence Staff rushed down Whitehall with a locked pouch containing several distinctive folders. I knew immediately from the red diagonal crosses on their dark covers that they contained top secret material with its own special codeword (UMBRA), denoting that they came from the Government Communications Headquarters (GCHQ).

The folders contained decrypted intercepts of Argentine naval communications. The messages showed that an Argentine submarine had been deployed on covert reconnaissance around the Falklands capital, Port Stanley, and that the Argentine Fleet, which had been on exercises, was reassembling. A further intercept referred to a task force said to be due to arrive at an unstated destination in the early hours of Friday, 2 April. From their analysis of the coordinates of the naval vessels, GCHQ had concluded that its destination could only be Port Stanley.[1]

John Nott and I looked at each other with but one thought, loss of the Falkland Islands would bring a major existential crisis for the government of Margaret Thatcher: the Prime Minister must be told at once. We hurried down the Commons corridor to her room and burst in on her.

The last assessment she had received from the UK Joint Intelligence Committee (JIC) had told her that Argentina did not want to use force to secure its claim to the sovereignty of the Falkland Islands. However, the JIC had warned that if there was highly provocative action by the British towards Argentine nationals, who had landed illegally on the British South Atlantic island of South Georgia, then the Junta might use this as a pretext for action. Since the UK had no intention of provoking the Junta, the assessment was wrongly inter-preted in Whitehall as reassuring. That made the fresh intelligence reports all the more dramatic. It was the first indi-cation that the Argentine Junta was ready to use force to impose its claim.

The importance for us of being able to reason

The shock of seeing the nation suddenly pitched into the Falklands crisis is still deeply etched in my memory. It demon-strated to me the impact that errors in thinking can have. This is as true for all life as it is for national statecraft. My objective in writing this book therefore is an ambitious one: I want to empower people to make better decisions by learning how intelligence analysts think. I will provide lessons from our past to show how we can know more, explain more and anticipate more about what we face in the extraordinary age we now live in.

There are important life lessons in seeing how intelligence analysts reason. By learning what intelligence analysts do when they tackle problems, by observing them in real cases from recent history, we will learn how they order their thoughts and how they distinguish the likely from the unlikely and thus make better judgements. We will learn how to test alternative explanations methodically and judge how far we need to change our minds as new information arrives. Sound thinkers try to understand how their unconscious feelings as individuals, as members of a group and within an institution might affect their judgement. We will also see how we can fall victim to conspiracy thinking and how we can be taken in by deliberate deception.

We all face decisions and choices, at home, at work, at play. Today we have less and less time to make up our minds than ever before. We are in the digital age, bombarded with contradictory, false and confusing information from more sources than ever. Information is all around us and we feel compelled to respond at its speed. There are influential forces at play ranged against us pushing specific messages and opinions through social media. Overwhelmed by all this information, are we less, or more, ignorant than in previous times? Today more than ever, we need those lessons from the past.

Looking over the shoulder of an intelligence analyst

Over the centuries, generals naturally learned the advantage that intelligence can bring. Governments today deliberately equip themselves with specialist agencies to access and analyse information that can help them make better decisions.[2] Britain's Secret Intelligence Service (MI6) runs human agents overseas. The Security Service (MI5) and its law enforcement partners investigate domestic threats and conduct surveillance on suspects. The Government Communications Headquarters (GCHQ) intercepts communications and gathers digital intelligence. The armed forces conduct their share of intelligence gathering in their operations overseas (including photographic intelligence from satellites and drones). It is the job of the intelligence analyst to fit all the resulting pieces together. They then produce assessments that aim to reduce the ignorance of the decisionmakers. They find out what is happening, they explain why it is happening and they outline how things might develop.[3]

The more we understand about the decisions we have to take, the less likely it is that we will duck them, make bad choices or be seriously surprised. Much of what we need can come from sources that are open to anyone, provided sufficient care is taken to apply critical reasoning to them.

Reducing the ignorance of the decisionmaker does not necessarily mean simplifying. Often the intelligence assessment has to warn that the situation is more complicated than they had previously thought, that the motives of an adversary are to be feared and that a situation may develop in a bad way. But it is better to know than not. Harbouring illusions on such matters leads to poor, or even disastrous, decisions. The task of the intelligence officer is *to tell it as it is* to government. When you make decisions, it is up to you to do the same to yourself.

The work of intelligence officers involves stealing the secrets of the dictators, terrorists and criminals who mean us harm. This is done using human sources or technical means to intrude into the privacy of personal correspondence or conversations. We therefore give our intelligence officers a licence to operate by ethical standards different from those we would hope to see applied in everyday life, justified by the reduction in harm to the public they can achieve.[4] Authoritarian states may well feel that they can dispense with such considerations and encourage their officers to do whatever they consider necessary, regardless of law or ethics, to achieve the objectives they have been set. For the democracies such behaviours would quickly undermine confidence in both government and intelligence services. Consequently, intelligence work is carefully regulated under domestic law to ensure it remains necessary and proportionate. I should therefore be clear. This book does not teach you how to spy on others, nor should it encourage you to do so. I want, however, to show that there are lessons from the *thinking* behind secret intelligence from which we can all benefit. This book is a guide to thinking straight, not a manual for bad behaviour.

Nor does thinking straight mean emotionless, bloodless calculation. 'Negative capability' was how the poet John Keats described the writer's ability to pursue a vision of artistic beauty even when it led to uncertainty, confusion and intellectual doubt. For analytic thinkers the equivalent ability is tolerating the pain and confusion of not knowing, rather than imposing ready-made or omnipotent certainties on ambiguous situations or emotional challenges. To think clearly we must have a scientific, evidence-based approach which nevertheless holds a space for the 'negative capability' needed to retain an open mind.[5]

Intelligence analysts like to look ahead, but they do not pretend to be soothsayers. There are always going to be surprise outcomes, however hard we try to forecast events. The winner of the Grand National or the Indy 500 cannot be known in advance. Nor does the favourite with the crowds always come out in front. Events sometimes combine in ways that seem destined to confound us. Importantly, risks can also provide opportunities if we can use intelligence to position ourselves to take advantage of them.

Who am I to say this?

Intelligence agencies prefer to keep quiet about successes so that they can repeat them, but failures can become very public. I have included examples of both, together with a few glimpses from my own experience – one that spans the startling development of the digital world. It is sobering to recall that in my first paid job, in 1965, in the mathematics department of an engineering company in Glasgow, we learned to write machine code for the early computers then available using five-character punched paper tape for the input. Today, the mobile device in my pocket has immediate access to more processing power than there was then in the whole of Europe. This digitization of our lives brings us huge benefits. But it is also fraught with dangers, as we will examine in Chapter 10.

In 1969, fresh out of Cambridge, I joined GCHQ, the British signals intelligence and communications security agency, and learned of their pioneering work applying mathematics and computing to intelligence. I gave up my plans to pursue a doctorate in (very) theoretical economics, and the lure of an offer to become an economic adviser in HM Treasury. I chose instead a career in public service that would take me into the worlds of intelligence, defence, foreign affairs and security. In the Ministry of Defence (MOD), as a policy official, I used intelligence to craft advice for ministers and the Chiefs of Staff. I had three tours in the Private Office of the Secretary of State for Defence (serving six of them, from Lord Carrington in 1973 to John Nott in 1981) and saw the heavy burden of decision-making in crisis that rests at the political level. I saw how valuable good intelligence can be, and the problems its absence causes. When I was working as the UK Defence Counsellor in NATO Brussels it was clear how intelligence was shaping arms control and foreign policy. And as the Deputy Under Secretary of State for Policy in the MOD I was an avid senior customer for operational intelligence on the crisis in the former Yugoslavia. In that role I became a member of the Joint Intelligence Committee (JIC), the most senior intelligence assessment body in the UK, on which I served for a total of seven years.

When I left the MOD to go back to GCHQ as its Director in the mid-1990s, computing was transforming the ability to process, store and retrieve data at scale. I still recall the engineers reporting triumphantly to me that they had achieved for the first time stable storage of a terabyte of rapidly accessible data memory – a big step then although my small laptop today has half as much again. Even more significantly, the Internet had arrived as an essential working domain for professionals, with the World Wide Web gaining in popularity and Microsoft's new Hotmail service making email a fast and reliable form of communication. We knew digital technology would eventually penetrate into every aspect of our lives and that organizations like GCHQ would have to change radically to cope.[6]

The pace of digital change has been faster than predicted. Then, smartphones had not been invented and nor of course had Facebook, Twitter, YouTube and all the other social media platforms and apps that go with them. What would become Google was at that point a research project at Stanford. Within this small part of my working lifetime, I saw those revolutionary developments, and much more, come to dominate our world. In less than twenty years, our choices in economic, social and cultural life have become dependent on accessing networked digital technology and learning to live safely with it. There is no way back.

When I was unexpectedly appointed Permanent Secretary of the Home Office in 1997, it brought close contact with MI5 and Scotland Yard. Their use of intelligence was in investigations to identify and disrupt domestic threats, including terrorist and organized crime groups. It was in that period that the Home Office drew up the Human Rights Act and legislation to regulate and oversee investigatory powers to ensure a continual balancing act between our fundamental rights to life and security and the right to privacy for our personal and family life. My career as a Permanent Secretary continued with three years in the Cabinet Office after 9/11 as the first UK Security and Intelligence Coordinator. In that post, rejoining the JIC, I had responsibility for ensuring the health of the British intelligence community and for drawing up the first UK counter-terrorism strategy, CONTEST, still in force in 2020 as I write.

I offer you in this book my choice of lessons drawn from the world of secret intelligence both from the inside and from the perspective of the policymaker as a user of intelligence. I have learned the hard way that intelligence is difficult to come by, and is always fragmentary and incomplete, and is sometimes wrong. But used consistently and with understanding of its limitations, I know it shifts the odds in the nation's favour. The same is true for you.

SEES: a model of analytical thinking

I am now a visiting professor teaching intelligence studies in the War Studies Department at King's College London, at

Sciences Po in Paris and also at the Defence University in Oslo. My experience is that it really helps to have a systematic way of unpacking the process of arriving at judgements and establishing the appropriate level of confidence in them. The model I have developed – let me call it by an acronym that recalls what analysts do as they look at the world, the *SEES* model – leads you through the four types of information that can form an intelligence product, derived from different levels of analysis:

- **Situational awareness** of what is happening and what we face now.
- **Explanation** of why we are seeing what we do and the motivations of those involved.
- **Estimates** and forecasts of how events may unfold under different assumptions.
- **Strategic notice** of future issues that may come to challenge us in the longer term.

There is a powerful logic behind this four-part SEES way of thinking.

Take as an example the investigation of far-right extremist violence. The first step is to find out as accurately as possible what is going on. As a starting point, the police will have had crimes reported to them and will have questioned witnesses and gathered forensic evidence. These days there is also a lot of information available on social media and the Internet, but the credibility of such sources will need careful assessment. Indeed, even well-attested facts are susceptible to multiple interpretations, which can lead to misleading exaggeration or underestimation of the problem.

We need to add meaning so that we can explain what is really going on. We do that in the second stage of SEES by constructing the best explanation consistent with the available evidence, including an understanding of the motives of those involved. We see this process at work in every criminal court when prosecution and defence barristers offer the jury their alternative versions of the truth. For example, why are the fingerprints of an accused on the fragments of a beer bottle used for a petrol bomb attack? Was it because he threw the bottle, or is the explanation that it was taken out of his recycling box by the mob looking for material to make weapons? The court has to test these narratives and the members of the jury have then to choose the explanation that they think best fits the available evidence. The evidence rarely speaks for itself. In the case of an examination of extremist violence, in the second stage we have to arrive at an understanding of the causes that bring such individuals together. We must learn what factors influence their anger and hatred. That provides the explanatory model that allows us to move on to the third stage of SEES, when we can estimate how the situation may change over time, perhaps following a wave of arrests made by the police and successful convictions of leading extremists. We can estimate how likely it is that arrest and conviction will lead to a reduction in threats of violence and public concern overall. It is this third step that provides the intelligence feedstock for evidence-based policymaking.

The SEES model has an essential fourth component: to provide strategic notice of longer-term developments. Relevant to our example we might want to examine the further growth of extremist movements elsewhere in Europe or the impact on such groups were there to be major changes in patterns of refugee movements as a result of new conflicts or the effects of climate change. That is just one example, but there are very many others where anticipating future developments is essential to allow us to prepare sensibly for the future.

The four-part SEES model can be applied to any situation that concerns us and where we want to understand what has happened and why and what may happen next, from being stressed out at a situation at work to your sports team losing badly. SEES is applicable to any situation where you have information, and want to make a decision on how best to act on it.

We should not be surprised to find patterns in the different kinds of error tending to occur when working on each of the four components of the SEES process. For example:

- Situational awareness suffers from all the difficulties of assessing what is going on. Gaps in information exist and often evoke a reluctance to change our minds in the face of new evidence.
- Explanations suffer from weaknesses in understanding others: their motives, upbringing, culture and background.
- Estimates of how events will unfold can be thrown out by unexpected developments that were not considered in the forecast.
- Strategic developments are often missed due to too narrow a focus and a lack of imagination as to future possibilities.

The four-part SEES approach to assessment is not just applicable to affairs of state. At heart it contains an appeal to rationality in all our thinking. Our choices, even between unpalatable alternatives, will be sounder as a result of adopting systematic ways of reasoning. That includes being able to distinguish between what we know, what we do not know and what we think may be. Such thinking is hard. It demands integrity.

Buddhists teach that there are three poisons that cripple the mind: anger, attachment and ignorance.[7] We have to be conscious of how emotions such as anger can distort our perception of what is true and what is false. Attachment to old ideas with which we feel comfortable and that reassure us that the world is predictable can blind us to threatening developments. This is what causes us to be badly taken by surprise. But it is ignorance that is the most damaging mental poison. The purpose of intelligence analysis is to reduce such ignorance, thereby improving our capacity to make sensible decisions and better choices in our everyday lives.

On that fateful day in March 1982 Margaret Thatcher had immediately grasped what the intelligence reports were telling her. She understood what the Argentine Junta appeared to be planning and the potential consequences for her premiership. Her next words demonstrated her ability to use that insight: 'I must contact President Reagan at once. Only he can persuade Galtieri [General Leopoldo Galtieri, the Junta's leader] to call off this madness.' I was deputed to ensure that the latest GCHQ intelligence was being shared with the US authorities, including the White House. No. 10 rapidly prepared a personal message from Thatcher to Reagan asking him to speak to Galtieri and to obtain confirmation that he would not authorize any landing, let alone any hostilities, and warning that the UK could not acquiesce in any invasion. But the Argentine Junta stalled requests for a Reagan conversation with Galtieri until it was much too late to call off the invasion.

Only two days later, on 2 April 1982, the Argentine invasion and military occupation of the Islands duly took place. There was only a small detachment of Royal Marines on the Islands and a lightly armed ice patrol ship, HMS *Endurance*, operating in the area. No effective resistance was possible. The Islands were too far away for sea reinforcements to arrive within the two days' notice the intelligence had given us, and the sole airport had no runway capable of taking long-distance troop-carrying aircraft.

We had lacked adequate situational awareness from intelligence on what the Junta was up to. We had failed to understand the import of what we did know, and therefore had not been able to predict how events would unfold. Furthermore, we had failed over the years to provide strategic notice that this situation was one that might arise, and so had failed to take steps that would have deterred an Argentine invasion. Failures in each of the four stages of SEES analysis.

All lessons to be learned.

How this book is organized

The four chapters in the first part of this book are devoted to the aforementioned SEES model. Chapter 1 covers how we can establish situational awareness and test our sources of information. Chapter 2 deals with causation and explanation, and how the scientific method called Bayesian inference, allows us to use new information to alter our degree of belief in our chosen hypothesis. Chapter 3 explains the process of making estimates and predictions. Chapter 4 describes the advantage that comes from having strategic notice of long-term developments.

There are lessons from these four phases of analysis in how to avoid different kinds of error, failing to see what is in front of us, misunderstanding what we do see, misjudging what is likely to follow and failing to have the imagination to conceive of what the future may bring.

Part Two of this book has three chapters, each drawing out lessons in how to keep our minds clear and check our reasoning.

We will see in Chapter 5 how cognitive biases can subconsciously lead us to the wrong answer (or to fail to be able to answer the question at all). Being forewarned of those very human errors helps us sense when we may be about to make a serious mistake of interpretation.

Chapter 6 introduces us to the dangers of the closed-loop conspiratorial mindset, and how it is that evidence which ought to ring alarm bells can too often be conveniently explained away.

The lesson of Chapter 7 is to beware deliberate deceptions and fakes aimed at manipulating our thinking. There is misinformation, which is false but circulated innocently; malinformation, which is true but is exposed and circulated maliciously; and disinformation, which is false, and that was known to be false when circulated for effect. The ease with which digital text and images can be manipulated today makes these even more serious problems than in the past.

Part Three explores three areas of life that call for the intelligent use of intelligence.

The lessons of Chapter 8 are about negotiating with others, something we all have to do. The examples used come from extraordinary cases of secret intelligence helping to shape perceptions of those with whom governments have to negotiate, and of how intelligence can help build mutual trust – necessary for any arms control or international agreement to survive – and help uncover cheating. We will see how intelligence can assist in unravelling the complex interactions that arise from negotiations and confrontations.

Chapter 9 identifies how you go about establishing and maintaining lasting partnerships. The example here is the successful longstanding '5-eyes' signals intelligence arrangement between the US, the UK, Canada, Australia and New Zealand, drawing out principles that are just as applicable to business and even to personal life.

The lesson of Chapter 10 is that our digital life provides new opportunities for the hostile and unscrupulous to take advantage of us. We can end up in an echo chamber of entertaining information that unconsciously influences our choices, whether over products or politics. Opinion can be mobilized by controlled information sources, with hidden funding and using covert opinion formers. When some of that information is then revealed to be knowingly false, confidence in democratic processes and institutions slowly ebbs away.

The concluding chapter, Chapter 11, is a call to shake ourselves awake and recognize that we are all capable of being exploited through digital technology. The lessons of this book put together an agenda to uphold the values that give legitimacy to liberal democracy: the rule of law; tolerance; the use of reason in public affairs and the search for rational explanations of the world around us; and our ability to make free and informed choices. When we allow ourselves to be over-influenced by those with an agenda, we erode our free will and that is the gradual erosion of an open society. Nobody should be left vulnerable to the arguments of demagogues or snake oil salesmen. The chapter and the book ends therefore on an optimistic note. We can learn the lessons of how to live safely in this digital world.

PART ONE

*An analyst SEES: four lessons
in ordering our thoughts*

I

Lesson 1: Situational awareness
Our knowledge of the world is always fragmentary and incomplete, and is sometimes wrong

London, 11 p.m., 20 April 1961. In room 360 of the Mount Royal Hotel, Marble Arch, London, four men are waiting anxiously for the arrival of a fifth. Built in 1933 as rented apartments and used for accommodation by US Army officers during the war, the hotel was chosen by MI6 as a suitably anonymous place for the first face-to-face meeting of Colonel Oleg Penkovsky of Soviet military intelligence, the GRU, with the intelligence officers who would jointly run him as an in-place agent of MI6 and CIA. When Penkovsky finally arrived he handed over two packets of handwritten notes on Soviet missiles and other military secrets that he had smuggled out of Moscow as tokens of intent. He then talked for several hours explaining what he felt was his patriotic duty to mother Russia in exposing to the West the adventurism and brinkmanship of the Soviet leader, Nikita Khrushchev, and the true nature of what he described as the rotten two-faced Soviet regime he was serving.[1]

The huge value of Penkovsky as a source of secret intelligence came from the combination of his being a trained intelligence officer and his access to the deepest secrets of the Soviet Union – military technology, high policy and personalities. He was one of the very few with his breadth of access allowed to visit London, tasked with talent spotting of possible sources for Soviet intelligence to cultivate in Western business and scientific circles.

Penkovsky had established an acquaintance with a frequent legitimate visitor to Moscow, a British businessman, Greville Wynne, and entrusted him with his life when he finally asked Wynne to convey his offer of service to MI6. From April 1961 to August 1962 Penkovsky provided over 5500 exposures of secret material on a Minox camera supplied by MI6. His material alone kept busy twenty American and ten British analysts, and his 120 hours of face-to-face debriefings occupied thirty translators, producing 1200 pages of transcript.

At the same time, on the other side of the Atlantic, intelligence staffs worried about the military support being provided by the Soviet Union to Castro's Cuba. On 14 October 1962 a U2 reconnaissance aircraft over Cuba photographed what looked to CIA analysts like a missile site under construction. They had the top secret plans Penkovsky had passed to MI6 showing the typical stages of construction and operation for Soviet medium-range missile sites. In the view of the CIA, without this information it would have been very difficult to identify which type of nuclear-capable missiles were at the launch sites and track their operational readiness. On 16 October President Kennedy was briefed on the CIA assessment and shown the photographs. By 19 October he was told a total of nine such sites were under construction and had been photographed by overflights. On 21 October the British Prime Minister, Harold Macmillan, was informed by President Kennedy that the entire US was now within Soviet missile range with a warning time of only four minutes. Macmillan's response is recorded as 'now the Americans will realize what we here in England have lived through these past many years'. The next day, after consultation with Macmillan, the President instituted a naval blockade of Cuba.[2]

The Cuban missile crisis is a clear example of the ability intelligence has to create awareness of a threatening situation, the first component of the SEES model of intelligence analysis. The new evidence turned US analysts' opinion on its head. They had previously thought the Soviets would not dare to attempt introducing nuclear missile systems in the Western hemisphere. Now they had a revised situational awareness of what the United States was facing.

There is a scientific way of assessing how new evidence should alter our beliefs about the situation we face, the task of the first stage of the SEES method. That is the Bayesian approach to inference, widely applied in intelligence analysis, modern statistics and data analysis.[3] The method is named after the Rev. Thomas Bayes, the eighteenth-century Tunbridge Wells cleric who first described it in a note on probability found among his papers after his death in 1761.

The Bayesian approach uses *conditional probability* to work backwards from seeing evidence to the most likely causes of that evidence existing. Think of the coin about to be tossed by a football referee to decide which side gets to pick which goal to attack in the first half of the game. To start with it would be rational to estimate that there is a 50 per cent probability that either team will win the toss. But what should we think if we knew that in every one of the last five games involving our team and the same referee we had lost the toss? We would probably suspect foul play and reduce our belief that we stand an even chance of winning the toss this time. That is what we describe as the conditional probability, *given* that we now know the outcome of previous tosses. It is different from our prior estimate. What Bayesian inference does in that case is give us a scientific method of starting with the evidence of past tosses to arrive at the most likely cause of those results, such as a biased coin.

Bayesian inference helps us to revise our degree of belief in the likelihood of any proposition being true *given* our learning of evidence that bears on it. The method applies even when, unlike the coin-tossing example, we only have a subjective initial view of the likelihood of the proposition being true. An example would be the likelihood of our political party winning the next election. In that case it might then be new polling evidence that causes us to want to revise our estimate. We can ask ourselves how far the new evidence helps us discriminate between alternative views of the situation or, as we should term them, *alternative hypotheses*, about what the outcome is likely to be. If we have a number of alternatives open to us, and the evidence is more closely associated with one of them than the alternatives, then it points us towards believing more strongly that that is the best description of what we face.

The Bayesian method of reasoning therefore involves adjusting our *prior* degree of belief in a hypothesis on receipt of new evidence to form a *posterior* degree of belief in it ('posterior' meaning after seeing the evidence). The key to that re-evaluation is to ask the question: if the hypothesis was actually true how likely is it that we would have been able to see that evidence? If we think that evidence is strongly linked to the hypothesis being true, then we should increase our belief in the hypothesis.

The analysts in the Defense Intelligence Agency in the Pentagon had originally thought it was very unlikely that the Soviet Union would try to introduce nuclear missiles into Cuba. That hypothesis had what we term a low prior probability.

We can set this down precisely using notation that will come in handy in the next chapter. Call the hypothesis that nuclear missiles would be introduced N. We can write their prior degree of belief in N as a *prior probability* $p(N)$ lying between 0 and 1. In this case, since they considered N very unlikely, they might have given $p(N)$ a probability value of 0.1, meaning only 10 per cent likely.

The 14 October 1962 USAF photographs forced them to a very different awareness of the situation. They saw evidence, E, consistent with the details Penkovsky had provided of a Soviet medium-range nuclear missile installation under construction. The analysts suddenly had to face the possibility that the Soviet Union was introducing such a capability into Cuba by stealth. They needed to find the *posterior probability* $p(N|E)$ (read as the reassessed probability of the hypothesis N *given* the evidence E where the word 'given' is written using the vertical line $|$).

The evidence in the photographs was much more closely associated with the hypothesis that these were Soviet nuclear missile launchers than any alternative hypothesis. Given the evidence in the photographs, they did not appear to be big trucks carrying large pipes for a construction site, for instance. The chances of the nuclear missile hypothesis being true given the USAF evidence will be proportionate to $p(E|N)$, which is the likelihood of finding that evidence on the assumption that N is true. That likelihood was estimated as much greater than the overall probability that such photographs might have been seen in any case (which we can write as $p(E)$). The relationship between the nuclear missile hypothesis and the evidence seen, that of $p(E|N)$ to $p(E)$, is the factor we need to convert the prior probability $p(N)$ to the posterior probability that the decisionmaker needs, $p(N|E)$.

The Rev. Bayes gave us the rule to calculate what the posterior probability is:

$$p(N \mid E) = p(N) . [p(E \mid N)/p(E)]$$

Or, the new likelihood of something being the case given the evidence is found by adjusting what you thought was likely (before you saw the evidence) by how well the new evidence supports the claim of what could be happening.

This is the only equation in this book. Despite wanting to talk as plainly as possible, I've included it because it turns words into precise calculable conditional likelihoods which is what so much of modern data science is about. In the next chapter we examine how we can apply Bayes's great insight to work backwards, inferring from observations what are the most likely causes of what we see.

The example of the Cuban missile crisis shows Bayesian logic in action to provide new situational awareness. For example, if the analysts had felt that the photographs could equally well have been of a civil construction site and so the photographs were equally likely whether or not N was true (i.e. whether or not these were nuclear missile launchers) then $p(E \mid N)$ would be the same as $p(E)$, and so the factor in Bayes's rule is unity and the posterior probability is no different from the prior. The President would not be advised to change his low degree of belief that Khrushchev would dare try to introduce nuclear missiles into Cuba. If, on the other hand, E would be much more likely to be seen in cases where N is true (which is what the Penkovsky intelligence indicated), then it is a strong indicator that N is indeed true and $p(E \mid N)$ will be greater than $P(E)$. So $p(N \mid E)$ therefore rises significantly. For the Pentagon analysts $p(N \mid E)$ would have been much nearer to 1, a near certainty. The President was advised to act on the basis that Soviet nuclear missiles were in America's backyard.

Kennedy's key policy insight in 1962 was recognition that Khrushchev would only have taken such a gamble over Cuba having been persuaded that it would be possible to install the missiles on Cuba covertly, and arm them with nuclear warheads before the US found out. The US would then have discovered that the Soviet Union was holding at immediate risk the entire Eastern seaboard of the US, but would have been unable to take action against Cuba or the missiles without running unacceptable risk. Once the missiles had been discovered before they were operational, it was then the Soviet Union that was carrying the risk of confrontation with the naval blockade Kennedy had ordered. Kennedy privately suggested a face-saving ladder that Khrushchev could climb down (by offering later withdrawal of the old US medium-range missiles based in Turkey), which Khrushchev duly accepted. The crisis ended without war.

The story of President Kennedy's handling of the Cuban missile crisis has gone down as a case study in bold yet responsible statecraft. It was made possible by having situational awareness – providing the what, who, where and when that the President needed based on Penkovsky's intelligence on technical specifications about Soviet nuclear missiles, their range and destructive power, and how long they took to become operational after they were shipped to a given location. That last bit of intelligence persuaded Kennedy that he did not need to order air strikes to take out the missile sites immediately. His awareness of the time he had gave him the option of trying to persuade Khrushchev that he had miscalculated.

Bayesian inference is central to the SEES method of thinking. It can be applied to everyday matters, especially where we may be at risk of faulty situational awareness. Suppose you have recently been assigned to a project that looks, from the outside, almost impossible to complete successfully on time and in budget. You have always felt well respected by your line manager, and your view of the situation is that you have been given this hard assignment because you are considered highly competent and have an assured future in the organization. However, at the bottom of an email stream that she had forgotten to delete before forwarding, you notice that your manager calls you 'too big for your boots'. Working backwards from this evidence you might be wise to infer that it is more likely your line manager is trying to pull you down a peg or two, perhaps by getting you to think about your ability to work with others, by giving you a job that will prove impossible. Do try such inferential reasoning with a situation of your own.

Most intelligence analysis is a much more routine activity than the case of the Cuban missile crisis. The task is to try to piece together what's going on by looking at fragmentary information from a variety of sources. The Bayesian methodology is the same in weighing information in order to be able to answer promptly the decisionmakers' need to know what is happening, when and where and who is involved.

When data is collected in the course of intelligence investigations, scientific experiments or just in the course of web browsing and general observation, there is a temptation to expect that it will conform to a known pattern. Most of the data may well fit nicely. But some may not. That may be because there are problems with the data (source problems in intelligence, experimental error for scientists) or because the sought-for pattern is not an accurate enough representation of reality. It may be that the bulk of the observations fit roughly the expected pattern. But more sensitive instruments or sources with greater access may also be providing data that reveals a new layer of reality to be studied. In the latter case, data that does not fit what has been seen before may be the first sighting of a new phenomenon that cries out to be investigated, or, for an intelligence officer, that could be the first sign that there is a deception operation being mounted. How to treat such 'outliers' is thus often the beginning of new insights. Nevertheless, it is a natural human instinct to discard or explain away information that does not fit the prevailing narrative. 'Why spoil a good story' is the unconscious thought process. Recognizing the existence of such cases is important in learning to think straight.

Penkovsky had quickly established his bona fides with MI6 and the CIA. But our judgements depend crucially on assessing how accurate and reliable the underlying information base is. What may be described to you as a fact about some event of interest deserves critical scrutiny to test whether we really do know the 'who, what, where and when'. In the same way, an intelligence analyst would insist when receiving a report from a human informant on knowing whether this source had proved to be regular and reliable, like Penkovsky, or was a new untested source. Like the historian who discovers a previously unknown manuscript describing some famous event in a new way, the intelligence officer has to ask searching questions about who wrote the report and when, and whether they did so from first-hand knowledge, or from a sub-source, or even from a sub-sub-source with potential uncertainty, malicious motives or exaggeration being introduced at each step in the chain. Those who supply information owe the recipient a duty of care to label carefully each report with descriptions to help the analyst assess its reliability. Victims of village gossip and listeners to *The Archers* on BBC Radio 4 will recognize the effect.

The best way to secure situational awareness is when you can see for yourself what is going on, although even then be aware that appearances can be deceptive, as optical illusions demonstrate. It would always repay treating with caution a report on a social media chat site of outstanding bargains to be had on a previously unknown website. Most human eye-witness reporting needs great care to establish how reliable it is, as criminal courts know all too well. A good intelligence ex-ample where direct situational awareness was hugely helpful comes from the Falklands conflict. The British authorities were able to see the flight paths of Argentine air force jets setting out to attack the British Task Force because they had been detected by a mountaintop radar in Chile, and the Chilean government had agreed their radar picture could be accessed by the UK.

Experienced analysts know that their choice of what deserves close attention and what can be ignored is a function of their mental state at the time.[4] They will be influenced by the terms in which they have been tasked but also by how they may have unconsciously formulated the problem. The analysts will have their own prejudices and biases, often from mem-ories of previous work. In the words of the tradecraft primer for CIA officers: 'These are experience based constructs of assumptions and expectations both about the world in general and more specific domains. These constructs strongly influ-ence what information analysts will accept – that is, data that are in accordance with analysts' unconscious mental models are more likely to be perceived and remembered than informa-tion that is at odds with them.'[5] Especial caution is needed therefore when the source seems to be showing you what you had most hoped to see.

The interception and deciphering of communications and the product of eavesdropping devices usually have high credibility with intelligence analysts because it is assumed those involved do not realize their message or conversation is not secure and therefore will be speaking honestly. But that need not be the case, since one party to a conversation may be trying to deceive the other, or both may be participating in an attempt to deceive a third party, such as the elaborate fake communications generated before the D-Day landings in June 1944 to create the impression of a whole US Army Corps stationed near Dover. That, combined with the remarkable double agent operation that fed back misleading information to German intelligence, provided the basis of the massive deception operation mounted for D-Day (Operation Fortitude). The main purpose was to convince the German High Command that the landings in Normandy were only the first phase with the main invasion to follow in the Pas de Calais. That intelligence-led deception may have saved the Normandy landings from disaster by persuading the German High Command to hold back an entire armoured division from the battle.

Unsubstantiated reports (at times little more than rumour) swirl around commercial life and are picked up in the business sections of the media and are a driver of market behaviour. As individuals, the sophisticated analysts of the big investment houses may well not be taken in by some piece of market gossip. But they may well believe that the average investor will be, and that the market will move and thus as a consequence they have to make their investment decisions as if the rumour is true. It was that insight that enabled the great economist John Maynard Keynes to make so much money for his alma mater, King's College Cambridge, in words much quoted today in the marketing material of investment houses: 'successful investing is anticipating the anticipation of others'.[6] Keynes described this process in his General Theory as a beauty contest:

> It is not a case of choosing those which, to the best of one's judgment, are really the prettiest, nor even those which average opinion genuinely thinks the prettiest. We have reached the third degree where we devote our intelligences to anticipating what average opinion expects the average opinion to be. And there are some, I believe, who practise the fourth, fifth and higher degrees.[7]

The Penkovsky case had a tragic ending. His rolls of film had to be delivered by dead drop in the teeth of Soviet surveillance using methods later made famous by John le Carré's fictional spies, including the mark on the lamppost to indicate there was material to pick up. That task fell to Janet Chisholm, the wife of Penkovsky's SIS case officer working under diplomatic cover in the Moscow Embassy. She had volunteered to help and was introduced to Penkovsky during one of his official visits to London. It was no coincidence therefore that her children were playing on the pavement of Tsvetnoy Boulevard while she watched from a nearby bench, at the exact moment Oleg Penkovsky in civilian clothes walked past. He chatted to the children and offered them a small box of sweets (that he had been given for that purpose during his meeting in London) within which were concealed microfilms of documents that Penkovsky knew would meet London's and Washington's urgent intelligence requirements. Similar drops of film followed. She was, however, later put under routine surveillance and by mischance she was seen making a 'brush contact' with a Russian who the KGB could not immediately identify but who triggered further investigations. That and other slips made by Penkovsky led finally to his arrest. His go-between, the British businessman Greville Wynne, was then kidnapped during a business trip to Budapest, and put on show trial in Moscow alongside Penkovsky. Both were found guilty. Penkovsky was severely tortured and shot. Wynne spent several years in a Soviet prison until exchanged in 1964 in a spy swop for the convicted KGB spy Gordon Lonsdale (real name Konon Molody) and his cut-outs, an antiquarian bookseller and his wife, Peter and Helen Kroger, who had helped him run a spy ring against the UK Admiralty research establishment at Portland.

The digital revolution in information gathering

Today a Penkovsky could more safely steal secret missile plans by finding a way of accessing the relevant database. That is true for digital information of all kinds if there is access to classified networks. Digital satellite imagery provides global coverage. The introduction of remotely piloted aircraft with high-resolution cameras provides pin-sharp digitized imagery for operational military, security and police purposes, as well as for farming, pollution control, investigative journalism and many other public uses. At any incident there are bound to be CCTV cameras and individuals with mobile phones (or drones) that have high-resolution cameras able to take video footage of the event – and media organizations such as broadcasters advertise the telephone numbers to which such footage can be instantly uploaded. Every one of us is potentially a reconnaissance agent.

There is the evident risk that we end up with simply too much digital data to make sense of. The availability of such huge quantities of digitized information increases the import-ance of devising artificial intelligence algorithms to sort through it and highlight what appears to be important.[8] Such methods rely upon applying Bayesian inference to learn how best to search for the results we want the algorithms to detect. They can be very powerful (and more reliable than a human would be) if the task they are given is clear-cut, such as check-ing whether a given face appears in a large set of facial images or whether a specimen of handwriting matches any of those in the database. But these algorithms are only as reliable as the data on which they were trained, and spurious correlations are to be expected. The human analyst is still needed to examine the selected material and to add meaning to the data.[9]

At the same time, we should remember that the digital world also provides our adversaries with ample opportunities to operate anonymously online and to hack our systems and steal our secrets. Recognition of these cyber-vulnerabilities has led the liberal democracies to give their security and intelli-gence agencies access to powerful digital intelligence methods, under strict safeguards, to be able to search data in bulk for evidence about those who are attacking us.

One side effect of the digitization of information is the dem-ocratization of situational awareness. We can all play at being intelligence analysts given our access to powerful search engines. Anyone with a broadband connection and a mobile device or computer has information power undreamed of in previous eras. There is a new domain of open-source intelli-gence, or OSINT. We use this ourselves when trying to decide which party to vote for in an election and want to know what each candidate stands for, or ascertaining the level of property prices in a particular area, or researching which university offers us the most relevant courses. The Internet potentially provides the situational awareness that you need to make the right decision. But like intelligence officers you have to be able to use it with discrimination.

The tools available to all of us are remarkable. Catalogues of image libraries can be searched to identify in fractions of a second a location, person, artwork or other object. Google Images has indexed over 10 billion photographs, drawings and other images. By entering an address almost anywhere in the world, Google Street View will enable you to see the building and take a virtual drive round the neighbourhood with maps providing directions and overlays of information. The position of ships and shipping containers can be displayed on a map, as can the location of trains across much of Europe.

With ingenuity and experience, an internet user can often generate situational awareness to rival that of intelligence agencies and major broadcasting corporations. The not-for-profit organization Bellingcat[10] is named after Aesop's fable in which the mice propose placing a bell around the neck of the cat so that they are warned in good time of its approach but none will volunteer to put the bell on it. Bellingcat publishes the results of non-official investigations by private citizens and journalists into war crimes, conditions in war zones and the activities of serious criminals. Its most recent high-profile achievement was to publish the real identities of the two GRU officers responsible for the attempted murder of the former MI6 agent and GRU officer Sergei Skripal and his daughter in Salisbury and the death of an innocent citizen.

It requires practice to become as proficient in retrieving situational information from the 4.5 billion indexed pages of the World Wide Web (growing by about one million documents a day) and the hundreds of thousands of accessible databases. Many sites are specialized and may take skill and effort, and the inclination to find (a location map of fishing boats around the UK, for example, should you ever want to know, can be found at fishupdate.com).

Although huge, the indexed surface web accessible by a search engine is estimated to be only 0.03 per cent of the total Internet. Most of the Internet, the so-called deep web, is hidden from normal view, for largely legitimate reasons since it is not intended for casual access by an average user. These are sites that can only be accessed if you already know their location, such as corporate intranets and research data stores, and most will be password-protected. In addition to the deep web, a small part of the Internet is the so-called 'dark web' or 'dark net' with its own indexing, which can only be reached if specialist anonymization software such as Tor is being used to hide the identity of the inquirer from law enforcement.[11] The dark net thus operates according to different rules from the rest of the Internet that has become so much a part of all of our daily lives. An analogy for the deep web would be the many commercial buildings, research laboratories and government facilities in any city that the average citizen has no need to access, but when necessary can be entered by the right person with the proper pass. The dark net, to develop that cityscape analogy, can be thought of like the red-light district in a city with a small number of buildings (sometimes very hard to find), where access is controlled because the operators want what is going on inside to remain deeply private. At one time, these would have been speakeasies, illegal gambling clubs, flophouses and brothels, but also the meeting places of impoverished young artists and writers, political radicals and dissidents. Today it is where the media have their secure websites which their sources and whistleblowers can access anonymously.

I guess we have all cursed when clicking on the link for a web page we wanted brought up the error message '404 Page Not Found'. Your browser communicated with the server, but the server could not locate the web page where it had been indexed. The average lifespan of a web page is under 100 days so skill is needed in using archived web material to retrieve sites that have been mislabelled, moved or removed from the web. Politicians may find it useful that claims they make to the electorate can thus quickly disappear from sight, but there are search methods that can retrieve old web pages and enable comparison with their views today.[12] Most search engines use asterisks to denote wild cards, so a query that includes 'B*n Lad*n' will search through the different spellings of his name such as Ben Laden, Bin Laden (the FBI-preferred spelling), Bin Ladin (the CIA-preferred spelling) and so on. Another useful lesson is the use of the tilde, the ~ character on the keyboard. So prefacing a query term with ~ will result in a search for synonyms as well as the specific query term, and will also look for alternative endings. Finally, you can ask the search to ignore a word by placing a minus in front of it, as –query. The meta-search engine Dogpile will return answers taken from other search engines, including from Google and Yahoo.

The order in which results are presented to you after entering a search query into a search engine can give a misleading impression of what is important. The answers that are returned (miraculously in a very small fraction of a second) may have been selected in a number of different ways. The top answer may be as a result of *publicity-based search* – a form of product placement where a company, interest group or political party has paid to have its results promoted in that way (or has used one of the specialist companies that offer for a fee to deliver that result to advertisers). A search on property prices in an area will certainly flag up local estate agents who have paid for the marketing advantage of appearing high up on the page. The answers will also take account of the accumulated knowledge in the search database of past answers, and also which answers have been most frequently clicked for further information (a *popularity-based* search, thus tapping into a form of 'wisdom of the crowd'). This can be misleading. While it may be interesting to see the results of a search for information about university courses that has been sorted by what were the most popular such searches, it is hardly helpful if what you want to know about is all the courses available that match your personal interests.

Finally, and perhaps most disturbingly, the suggested answers to the query may represent a sophisticated attempt by the algorithm to conduct *a personalized search* by working out what it is that the user is most likely to want to know (in other words, inferring why the question is being asked) from the user's previous internet behaviour and any other personal information about the individual accessible by the search engine. Two different people entering the same search terms on different devices will therefore get a different ranking of results. My query '1984?' using the Google Chrome browser and the Google search engine brings up George Orwell's dystopian novel along with suggestions of how I can most conveniently buy or download a copy. Helpfully, the Wikipedia entry on the book is also high up on the first page of the 1.49 billion results I am being offered (in 0.66 seconds). The same query using the Apple Safari browser and its search engine brings up first an article about the year 1984 telling me it was a leap year. And a very different past browsing history might highlight references to the assassination of Indira Gandhi in 1984, or news that the release of the forthcoming film

Wonder Woman 1984 has been postponed to 2020. Internet searching is therefore a powerful tool for acquiring the components of situational awareness. That is, for as long as we can rely on an open Internet. If the authorities were to have insisted that the search algorithms did not reference Orwell's book in response to queries from their citizens about 1984 then we would indeed have entered Orwell's dystopian world. That, sadly, is likely to be the ambition of authoritarian regimes that will try to use internet technology for social control.

Conclusions: lessons in situational awareness

In this chapter, we have been thinking about the first stage of SEES, the task of acquiring what I have termed *situational awareness*, knowing about the here and now. Our knowledge of the world is always fragmentary and incomplete, and is sometimes wrong. But something has attracted our attention and we need to know more. It may be because we have already thought about what the future may bring and had strategic notice of areas we needed to monitor. Or it may be that some unexpected observation or report we have received triggers us to focus our attention. There are lessons we can learn about how to improve our chances of seeing clearly what is going on when answering questions that begin with 'who, what, where and when'.

We should in those circumstances:

- Ask how far we have access to sufficient sources of information.
- Understand the scope of the information that exists and what we need to know but do not.

- Review how reliable the sources of information we do have are.
- If time allows, collect additional information as a cross-check before reaching a conclusion.
- Use Bayesian inference to use new information to adjust our degree of belief about what is going on.
- Be open and honest about the limitations of what we know, especially in public, and be conscious of the public reactions that may be triggered.
- Be alive to the possibility that someone is deliberately trying to manipulate, mislead, deceive or defraud us.

2

Lesson 2: Explanation
Facts need explaining

Belgrade, Sunday, 23 July 1995. It was getting dark when our
military aircraft landed on an airfield just outside the Serbian
capital. We were met by armed Serbian security officers and
quickly hustled into cars, watched over cautiously by a diplomat from the British Embassy. After what seemed an endless
drive into the country we arrived at a government guest house.
Our mission was to deliver in person an ultimatum to its occu-
pant, General Ratko Mladić, the commander of the Bosnian
Serb Army, the man who became infamous as the 'butcher of
Srebrenica'.[1]

Two days before, at a conference in London, the international community had united to condemn in the strongest
terms the actions of Mladić's Bosnian Serb Army in overrun-
ning the towns of Srebrenica and Zepa. These towns had
been placed under the protection of the United Nations as
'safe areas', where the Bosnian Muslim population could
shelter from the civil war raging around them. Sadly, there
had been insufficient understanding in the UN of the ethnic-
cleansing activities of Mladić and his army, and thus no
proper plans made about how the safe areas were to be
defended from him. The UN peacekeeping force in Bosnia,
UNPROFOR, was small and lightly armed, and in accordance with UN rules wore blue-painted helmets and rode in

white-painted vehicles. They were not a fighting force that could combat the Bosnian Serb Army when it defied the UN. The full extent of the genocidal mass killings and use of rape as a weapon of war by troops under Mladić's command in Bosnia was not then known, but enough evidence had emerged from Srebrenica to force a reluctant London Conference and NATO international community that enough was enough. Any further interference with the remaining safe areas would be met by the use of overwhelming air power. The purpose of the mission to Belgrade was to confront Mladić with the reality of that threat and make him desist from further aggression.

Leading the delegation were the three airmen who controlled NATO air power over Bosnia: the Commander of the US Air Force in Europe along with his British and French opposite numbers. I was the Deputy Under Secretary of State for Policy in the Ministry of Defence in London and I was acting as adviser to Air Chief Marshal Sir William Wratten, Commander-in-Chief of the RAF's Strike Command, a man with a formidable reputation as the architect of British bombing strategy during the first Gulf War. I was there with my opposite numbers from the Ministry of Defence in Paris and the Office of the Secretary of Defense in the Pentagon (my friend Joe Kruzel, who was tragically to die on duty later in Bosnia when his armoured vehicle rolled off a narrow pass). One of our tasks was to use the opportunity to try to understand the motivations of Mladić, the 'why and what for' of his actions, and whether he was likely to be deterred by the formal NATO warning from the air commanders of the US, UK and France.

When we arrived at the guest house we were escorted to the dining room and invited to sit at one side of a long table already set with traditional sweetmeats and glasses of plum brandy. Mladić entered in jovial mood with his army jacket around his shoulders hanging unbuttoned, accompanied by the head of his secret police. We had been forewarned that in soldier-to-soldier company he was likely to be bluffly affable, one of the reasons his men adored him. We had therefore resolved on the flight that we would all refuse to accept the hospitality he was bound to offer, an act that we guessed would cause offence and thus jolt Mladić into recognizing this was not a friendly visit. That ploy worked.

Mladić became visibly agitated, defiantly questioning whether the three air forces could pose any real threat to his army given the puny use of NATO air power up to that point. The air commanders had wisely chosen to wear their leather jackets and aviator sunglasses, and not their best dress uniforms. They menacingly described the massive air power they could command and delivered their blunt ultimatum: further attacks against the safe areas would not be tolerated, and substantial air actions would be mounted, 'if necessary at unprecedented levels'. The atmosphere in the room grew frosty.

Explanations and motives

In the Introduction I described understanding and explanation as the second component of my SEES model of intelligence analysis. Intelligence analysts have to ask themselves why the people and institutions that they are observing are acting as they appear to be, and what their motives and objectives are. That is what we were trying to establish in that visit to Mladić. That's as true for you in everyday life as it is for intelligence analysts. The task is bound to be all the harder if the analysis is being done at a distance by those brought up in a very different culture from that of the intelligence target. Motives are also easily misread if there is projective identification of some of your own traits in your adversary. This can become dangerous in international affairs when a leader accuses another of behaviour of which they themselves are guilty. That may be a cynical ploy. But it may also be a worrying form of self-deception. The leader may be unconsciously splitting off his own worst traits in order to identify them in the other, allowing the leader then to live in a state of denial believing that they do not actually possess those traits themselves. I'm sure you recognize a similar process in your office every day, too.

If it is the actions of a military leader that are under examination then there may be other objective factors explaining his acts, including the relative capabilities of his and opposing forces, the geography and terrain, and the weather as well as the history, ethnology and cultural anthropology of the society being studied. There are bound to be complexities to unravel where it may be the response to perceived policies and actions by other states, or even internal opposition forces within the society, that provide the best explanation along with an understanding of the history that has led to this point. From the outset of the Bosnian conflict, reports from the region spoke of excesses by the different factions fighting each other, a common feature of civil wars. Such evidence was available. But it was not clear at first what the deeper motivations were that would eventually drive the troops of Ratko Mladić to the horrifying extremes of genocide.

The choice of facts is not neutral, nor do facts speak for themselves

One possible reason we may wrongly understand *why* we see what we do is because we have implicitly, or explicitly, chosen to find a set of facts that supports an explanation we like and not another. We saw in the preceding chapter that even situational awareness cannot be divorced from the mindset of the analyst. The action of selection of what to focus on is unlikely to be a fully neutral one. This is a problem with which biographers and historians have always had to grapple. As the historian E. H. Carr wrote: 'By and large, the historian will get the kind of facts he wants. History means interpretation.'[2]

Reality is what it is. We cannot go back in time to change what we have observed. More correctly, then, for our purposes reality is what it *was* when we made our observations. Reality will have changed in the time it has taken us to process what we saw. And we can only perceive some of what is out there. But we can make a mental map of reality on which we locate the facts that we think we know, and when we got to know them. We can place these facts in relation to each other and, via our memory, fill in some detail from our prior knowledge. Then we look at the whole map and hope we recognize the country outlined.

More often than not, facts can bear different meanings. Therein lies the danger of mistakes of interpretation. A shopkeeper facing a young man asking to buy a large meat cleaver has to ask herself, gang member or trainee butcher? Let me adapt an example that Bertrand Russell used in his philosophy lectures to illustrate the nature of truth.[3] Imagine a chicken farm in which the chickens conduct an espionage operation on the farmer, perhaps by hacking into his computer. They discover that he is ordering large quantities of chicken food. The Joint Intelligence Committee of chickens meets. What do they conclude? Is it that the farmer has finally recognized that they deserve more food; or that they are being fattened up for the kill? Perhaps if the experience of the chickens has been of a happy outdoor life, then their past experience may lead them to be unable to conceive of the economics of chicken farming as seen by the farmer. On the other hand, chickens kept in their thousands in a large tin shed may well be all too ready to attribute the worst motives to the farmer. It is the same secret intelligence, the same fact, but with two opposite interpretations. That is true of most factual information.

Context is therefore needed to infer meaning. And meaning is a construct of the human mind. It is liable to reflect our emotionally driven hopes and fears as much as it represents an objective truth. Intelligence analysts like to characterize themselves as 'objective', and great care is taken, as we see in Chapter 5, to identify the many possible types of cognitive bias that might skew their thinking. In the end, however, 'independent', 'neutral' and 'honest' might be better words to describe the skilled analysts who must avoid being influenced by what they know their customers desperately hope to hear.[4] The great skill of the defence counsel in a criminal trial is to weave an explanatory narrative around the otherwise damming evidence so that the jury comes to believe in the explanation offered of what happened and thus in the innocence of the accused. The observed *capability* to act cannot be read as a real *intention* to do so. The former is easier to assess, given good situational awareness; the latter is always hard to know since it involves being able to ascribe motives in order to explain what is going on. You may know from your employment contract the circumstances under which your boss may fire you, but that does not mean they (currently) have the intention to do so.

We know from countless psychological experiments that we can convince ourselves we are seeing patterns where none really exist. Especially if our minds are deeply focused somewhere else. So how can we arrive at the most objective interpretation of what our senses are telling us? Put to one side the difficulties we discussed in the last chapter of knowing which are sufficiently reliable pieces of information to justify our labelling them as facts. Even if we are sure of our facts we can still misunderstand their import.

Imagine yourself late at night, for example, sitting in an empty carriage on the last train from the airport. A burly unkempt man comes into the carriage and sits behind you and starts talking aggressively to himself, apparently threatening trouble. Those sense impressions are likely at first to trigger the thought that you do not want to be alone with this individual. The stranger is exhibiting behaviour associated with someone in mental distress. Concern arises that perhaps he will turn violent; you start to estimate the distance to the door to the next carriage and where the emergency alarm is located; then you notice the tiny earphone he is wearing. You relax. Your mental mapping has flipped over and now provides a non-threatening explanation of what you heard as the simpler phenomenon of a very cross and tired man off a long flight making a mobile call to the car hire company that failed to pick him up.

What made you for a moment apprehensive in such a situation was how you instinctively framed the question. Our brains interpret facts within an emotional frame of mind that adds colour, in this case that represented potential danger on the mental map we were making. That framing was initially almost certainly beyond conscious thought. It may have been triggered by memory of past situations or more likely simply imaginative representation of possibilities. If you had been watching a scare movie such as *Halloween* on your flight, then the effect would probably have been even more pronounced.

The term 'framing' is a useful metaphor, a rough descriptor of the mental process that unconsciously colours our inferential map of a situation. The marvellous brightly coloured paintings of Howard Hodgkin, for example, extend from the canvas on to and over the frame. The frame itself is an integral part of the picture and conditions our perception of what we see on the canvas itself. The framing effect comes from within, as our minds respond to what we are seeing, and indeed feeling and remembering. It is part of the job of TV news editors to choose the clips of film that will provide visual and aural clues to frame our understanding of the news. And of course, as movie directors know, the effect of images playing together with sound are all the more powerful when working in combination to help us create in our minds the powerful mental representation of the scene that director wanted. The scrape of the violins as the murderer stalks up the staircase, knife in hand, builds tension; whereas the swelling orchestra releases that tension when the happy couple dance into the sunset at the end. Modern political advertising has learned all these tricks to play on us to make their message one we respond to more emotionally than rationally.

Up to this point in history only a human being could add meaning. Tomorrow, however, it could be a machine that uses an artificial intelligence programme to infer meaning from data, and then to add appropriate framing devices to an artificially generated output. Computerized sentiment analysis of social media postings already exists that can gauge a crowd's propensity to violence. Careful use of artificial intelligence could shorten the time taken to alert analysts to a developing crisis.

However, there are dangers in letting machines infer an explanation of what is going on. Stock exchanges have already suffered the problems of 'flash crashes' when a random fall in a key stock price triggers via an artificial intelligence programme automated selling that is detected by other trading algorithms, which in turn start selling and set off a chain reaction of dumping shares. So automatic brakes have had to be constructed to prevent the market being driven down by such automation. A dangerous parallel would be if reliance is placed on such causal inference to trigger automatically changes in defence posture in response to detected cyberattacks. If both sides in an adversarial relationship have equipped themselves with such technology, then we might enter the world of *Dr Strangelove*. Even more so if there are more than two players in such an infernal game of automated inference. As AI increasingly seeps into our everyday lives, too, we must not allow ourselves to slip into allowing it to infer meaning on our behalf unchecked. Today the algorithm is selecting what online advertisements it thinks will best match our interests, irritating when wrong but not harmful. Which it would be if it were a credit rating algorithm secretly deciding that your browsing and online purchasing history indicate a risk appetite too high to allow you to hold a credit card or obtain affordable motorbike insurance.

Back to Bayesics: scientifically choosing an explanatory hypothesis

The intelligence analyst is applying in the second stage of SEES generally accepted scientific method to the task of explaining the everyday world. The outcome should be the explanatory hypothesis that best fits the observed data, with the least extraneous assumptions having to be made, and with alternative hypotheses having been tested against the data and found less satisfactory. The very best ideas in science, after sufficient replication in different experiments, are dignified with the appellation 'theories'. In intelligence work, as in everyday life, we normally remain at the level of an explanatory hypothesis, conscious that at any moment new evidence may appear that will force a re-evaluation. An example in the last chapter was the case of the Cuban missile crisis, when the USAF photographs of installations and vehicles seen in Cuba, coupled with the secret intelligence from the MI6/CIA agent Col. Penkovsky, led analysts to warn President Kennedy that he was now faced with the Soviet Union introducing medium-range nuclear missile systems on to the island.

In the last chapter I described the method of Bayesian inference as the scientific way of adjusting our degree of belief in a hypothesis in the light of new evidence. You have evidence and use it to work backwards to assess what the most likely situation was that could have led to it being created. Let me provide a personal example to show that such Bayesian reasoning can be applied to everyday matters.

I remember Tony Blair when Prime Minister saying that he would have guessed that my background was in Defence. When I asked why, he replied because my shoes were shined.

Most of Whitehall, he commented, had gone scruffy, but those used to working with the military had retained the habit of cleaning their shoes regularly.

We can use Bayesian reasoning to test that hypothesis, D, that I came from the MOD. Say 5 per cent of senior civil servants work in Defence, so the prior probability of D being true $p(D) = 1/20$ (5 per cent), which is the chance of picking a senior civil servant at random and finding he or she is from the MOD.

E is the evidence that my shoes are shined. Observation in the Ministry of Defence and around Whitehall might show that 7 out of 10 Defence senior civil servants wear shiny shoes but only 4 out of 10 in civil departments do so. So the overall probability of finding shiny shoes is the sum of that for Defence and that for civil departments

$$p(E) = (1/20)^*(7/10)+(1-1/20)^*(4/10) = 83/200$$

The posterior probability that I came from Defence is written as $p(D|E)$ (where, remember, the vertical bar is to be read as 'given'). From Bayes's theorem, as described in Chapter 1:

$$p(D|E) = p(D) . [p(E|D)/p(E)] = 1/20^*[7/10^*200/83] = 7/83$$
$$= \text{approx. } 1/12$$

Using Bayesian reasoning, the chances of the PM's hypothesis being true is almost double what would be expected from a random guess.

Bayesian inference is a powerful way of establishing explanations, the second stage of the SEES method. The example can be set out in a 2 by 2 table (say, applied to a sample of 2000 civil servants) showing the classifications of shined

shoes/not shined shoes and from Defence/not from Defence.
I leave it to the reader to check that the *posterior probability*
$P(D/E)$ found above using Bayes's theorem can be read from
the first column of the table as $70/830$ = approx. $1/12$. Without seeing the shined shoes, the *prior probability* that I come
from the MOD would be $100/2000$, or $1/20$.

	E: shined shoes	Not shined shoes	Totals
D: from MOD	70	30	100
Not from MOD	760	1140	1900
Totals	830	1170	2000

Now imagine a real 'big data' case with an array of hundreds or thousands of dimensions to cater for large numbers
of different types of evidence. Bayes's theorem still holds as
the method of inferring posterior probabilities (although the
maths gets complicated). That is how inferences are legitimately to be drawn from big data. The medical profession is
already experiencing the benefits of this approach.[5] The availability of personal data on internet use also provides many
new opportunities to derive valuable results from data analysis.
Cambridge Analytica boasted that it had 4000–5000 separate
data points on each voter in the US 2016 Presidential election,
guiding targeted political advertising, a disturbing application
of Bayesian inference that we will return to in Chapter 10.

In all sustained thinking, assumptions do have to be made –
the important thing is to be prepared in the light of new
evidence challenging the assumptions to rethink the approach.
A useful pragmatic test about making assumptions is to ask at
any given stage of serious thinking, if I make this assumption,
am I making myself worse off in terms of chances of success
if it turns out not to be sensible than if I had not made it? Put

another way, if my assumption turns out to be wrong then would I end up actually worse off in my search for the answer or am I just no better off?

For example, if you have a four-wheel combination bicycle lock and forget the number you could start at 0000, then 0001, 0002, all the way up, aiming for 9999, knowing that at some point the lock will open. But you might make the reasonable assumption that you would not have picked a number commencing with 0, so you start at 1000. Chances are that saves you work. But if your assumption is wrong you are no worse off.

As a general rule it is the explanatory hypothesis with the least evidence against it that is most likely to be the best one for us to adopt. The logic is that one strong contrary result can disconfirm a hypothesis. Apparently confirmatory evidence on the other hand can still be consistent with other hypotheses being true. In that way the analyst can avoid the trap (the inductive fallacy[6]) of thinking that being able to collect more and more evidence in favour of a proposition necessarily increases confidence in it. If we keep looking in Europe to discover the colour of swans, then we will certainly conclude by piling up as many reports as we like that they are all white. If eventually we seek evidence from Australia then the infamous 'black swan' appears and contradicts our generalization.[7] When there are more reports in favour of hypothesis A than its inverse, hypothesis B, it is not always sensible to prefer A to B if we suspect that the amount of evidence pointing to A rather than B has been affected by how we set about searching for it.

A well-studied lesson of the dangers of misinterpreting complex situations is the 'security dilemma' when rearmament steps taken by one nation with purely defensive intent trigger fears in a potential adversary, leading it to take its own defensive steps that then appear to validate the original fears. The classic example is a decision by country A to modernize by building a new class of battleships. That induces anxiety in country B that an adverse military balance is thereby being built up against it. That leads to decisions on the part of country B also to build up its forces. That rearmament intention in turn is perceived as threatening by country A, not only justifying the original decision to have a new class of battleships but prompting the ordering of yet more ships. The worst fears of country B about the intentions of country A are thus confirmed. And an arms race starts. As the Harvard scholar Ben Buchanan has pointed out, such mutual misassessments of motivation are even more likely to be seen today in cyberspace since the difference between an intrusion for espionage purposes and for sabotage need only be a few lines of code.[8] There is thus ample scope for interpreting detected intrusions as potentially hostile, on both sides. Acts justified as entirely defensive by one government are therefore liable to be labelled as offensive in motivation by another – and vice versa.

We can easily imagine an established couple, call them Alice and Bob, one of whom, Bob, is of a jealous nature. Alice one day catches Bob with her phone reading her texts. Alice feels this is an invasion of her privacy, and increases the privacy settings on her phone. Bob takes this as evidence that Alice must have something to hide and redoubles his efforts to read her text messages and social media posts, which in turn causes Alice to feel justified in her outrage at being mistrusted and spied on. She takes steps to be even more secretive, setting in train a cycle of mistrust likely, if not interrupted, to gravely damage their relationship.

Explaining your conclusions

Margaret Thatcher was grateful for the weekly updates she received from the JIC. She always wanted to be warned when previous assessments had changed. But she complained that the language the JIC employed was too often 'nuanced'. 'It would be helpful', she explained, 'if key judgments in the assessments could be highlighted by placing them in eye-catching sentences couched in plainly expressed language.'[9] In the case of the Falklands that I mentioned in Chapter 1, the JIC had been guilty of such nuance in their July 1981 assessment. They had explained that they judged that the Argentine government would prefer to achieve its objective (transfer of sovereignty) by peaceful means. Thereby the JIC led readers to infer that if Argentina believed the UK was negotiating in good faith on the future of the Islands, then it would follow a peaceful policy, adding that if Argentina saw no hope of a peaceful transfer of sovereignty then a full-scale invasion of FI could not be discounted. Those in London privy to the Falklands negotiations knew the UK wanted a peaceful solution too. Objectively, nevertheless, the current diplomatic efforts seemed unlikely to lead to a mutually acceptable solution. But for the JIC to say that would look like it was straying into political criticism of ministerial policy and away from its brief of assessing the intelligence. There was therefore no trigger for reconsideration of the controversial cuts to the Royal Navy announced the year before, including the plan to scrap the Falklands-based ice patrol ship HMS *Endurance*. Inadvertently, and without consciously realizing they had done so, the UK had taken steps that would have reinforced in the minds of the Junta the thought that the UK did not see the Islands as a vital strategic interest worth fighting for. The Junta might reasonably have concluded that if

Argentina took over the Islands by force the worst it would face would be strong diplomatic protest.

Explaining something that is not self-evident is a process that reduces a complex problem to simpler elements. When analysts write an intelligence assessment they have to judge which propositions they can rely on as known to their readers and thus do not need explaining or further justification. That Al Qaid'a under Bin Laden was responsible for the attacks on 9/11 is now such a building block. That the Russian military intelligence directorate, the GRU, was responsible for the attempted murder of the Skripals in Salisbury in 2018 is likewise a building block for discussions of Russian behaviour. That Saddam Hussein in Iraq was still pursuing an unlawful biological warfare programme in 2002 was treated as a building block – wrongly, and therein lies the danger. That was a proposition that had once been true but (unbeknown to the analysts) was no longer. The mental maps being used by the analysts to interpret the reports being received were out of date and were no longer an adequate guide to reality. As the philosopher Richard Rorty has written: 'We do not have any way to establish the truth of a belief or the rightness of an action except by reference to the justifications we offer for thinking what we think or doing what we do.'[10]

Here, however, lies another lesson in trying to explain very complex situations in terms of simpler propositions.[11] The temptation is to cut straight through complex arguments by presenting them in instantly recognizable terms that the reader or listener will respond to at an emotional level. We do this when we pigeonhole a colleague with a label like 'difficult' or 'easy to work with'. We all know what we are meant to infer when a politician makes reference in a television interview or debate to the Dunkirk spirit, the appeasement of fascism in the 1930s, Pearl Harbor and the failure to anticipate surprise attacks, or Suez and the overestimation of British power in the 1956 occupation of the Egyptian canal zone. 'Remember the 2003 invasion of Iraq' is now a similarly instantly recognizable meme for the alleged dangers of getting too close to the United States. Such crude narrative devices serve as a shorthand for a much more complex reality. They are liable to mislead more than enlighten. History does not repeat itself, even as tragedy.

The lesson in all of this is that an accurate explanation of what you see is crucial.

Testing explanations and choosing hypotheses

How do we know when we have arrived at a sufficiently convincing explanation? The US and British criminal justice systems rest on the testing in court of alternative explanations of the facts presented respectively by counsel for the prosecution and for the defence in an adversarial process. For the intelligence analyst the unconscious temptation will be to try too hard to explain how the known evidence fits their favoured explanation, and why contrary evidence should not be included in the report.

Where there is a choice of explanations apply Occam's razor (named after the fourteenth-century Franciscan friar William of Occam) and favour the explanation that does not rely on complex, improbable or numerous assumptions, all of which have to be satisfied for the hypothesis to stand up. By adding ever more baroque assumptions any set of facts can be made to fit a favoured theory. This is the territory where conspiracies lurk. In the words of the old medical training adage, when you hear rapid hoof-beats think first galloping horses not zebras escaping from a zoo.[12]

Relative likelihood

It is important when engaged in serious thinking about what is going on to have a sense of the relative likelihood of alternative hypotheses being true. We might say, for example, after examining the evidence that it is much more likely that the culprit behind a hacking attack is a criminal group rather than a hostile state intelligence agency. Probability is the language in which likelihoods are expressed. For example, suppose a six-sided die is being used in a gambling game. If I have a suspicion that the die is loaded to give more sixes, I can test the hypothesis that the die is fair by throwing the die many times. I know from first principles that an unbiased die tossed properly will fall randomly on any one of its six faces with a probability [1/6]. The result of each toss of the die should produce a random result independent of the previous toss. Thus I must expect some clustering of results by chance, with perhaps three or even four sixes being tossed in a row (the probability of four sixes in a row is small – [1/6]x[1/6]x[1/6]x[1/6] = 0.0008, less than 1 in a thousand. But it is not zero). I will therefore not be too surprised to find a run of sixes. But, evidently, if I throw the die 100 times and I return 50 sixes, then it is a reasonable conclusion that the die is biased. The more tosses of that particular die the more stable the proportion of sixes will be. Throw it 1,000 times, 10,000 times, and, if the result is consistent, our conclusion becomes more likely. A rational degree of belief in the hypothesis that the die is not fair comes from analysis of the data, seeing the difference between what results would be associated with the hypothesis (a fair die) and the alternative hypothesis (a die biased to show sixes).

The key question to ask in that case is: if the die was fair, how likely is it that we would have seen 50 sixes in 100 throws? That is the approach of Bayesian inference we saw earlier in the chapter. The greater the divergence the more it is rational to believe that the evidence points to it not being a fair die. We have conducted what intelligence officers call an analysis of competing hypotheses (ACH), one of the most important structured analytic techniques in use in Western intelligence assessment, pioneered by CIA analyst Richards J. Heuer.[13] The method is systematically to list all the possible explanations (alternative hypotheses) and to test each piece of evidence, each inference and each assumption made as to whether it is significant in choosing between them (this is known by an ugly term as the *discriminatability* of the intelligence report). We then prefer the explanation with the least evidence pointing against it.

Alas, in everyday life, most situations we come across cannot be tested under repeated trials. Nor can we know in advance, or work out from first principles, what ideal results to compare with our observed data (such as the characteristics of a fair die). We cannot know that a boss is exhibiting unfair prejudice against one of their team in the way we can establish that a die is biased. But if we have a hypothesis of bias we can rationally test it against the evidence of observed behaviour. We will have to apply judgement in assessing the motives of the people involved and in testing possible alternative explanations for their behaviour against the evidence, discriminating between these hypotheses as best we can. When we apply Bayesian inference to everyday situations in that way, we end up with a degree of belief in the hypothesis that we conclude best explains the observed data. That result is inevitably subjective, but is the best achievable from the available evidence. And, of course, we must always therefore be open to correction if fresh evidence is obtained.

Stage 2 of SEES: explaining

The first step in stage 2 of SEES is therefore to decide what possible explanations (hypotheses) to test against each other. Let me start with an intelligence example. Suppose secret intelligence reveals that the military authorities of a non-nuclear weapon State A are seeking covertly to import specialist high-speed fuses of a kind associated with the construction of nuclear weapons but that also have some research civilian uses. I cannot be certain that State A is pursuing a nuclear weapons programme in defiance of the international Non-Proliferation Treaty, although I might know that it has the capability to enrich uranium. The covert procurement attempts might be explicable by the caution on the part of State A that open attempts to purchase such fuses for civil use would be bound to be misunderstood. And the civil research institutions of State A might be using the military procurement route just for convenience since the military budget is larger. One hypothesis might be that the fuses are for a prohibited nuclear weapons programme. The obvious alternative would be that the fuses are for an innocent civil purpose. But there might be other hypotheses to test: perhaps the fuses were for some other military use. The important thing is that all the possible explanations should be caught by one or other of the hypotheses to be tested (in the jargon, exhausting the solution space). A further refinement might be to split the first hypothesis into two: a government-approved procurement for a nuclear weapons programme and one conducted by the military keeping the government in ignorance.

In that way we establish mutually exclusive hypotheses to test. Now we can turn to our evidence and see whether our evidence helps to discriminate between them. We start with identifying key assumptions that might be swaying our minds and ask ourselves how the weight of evidence might shift if we change the assumptions (the analysts might, for example, take for granted that any nuclear research would be in the hands of the military). We identify inferences that we have drawn and whether they are legitimate (the fact that the end-user was not revealed on the procurement documents may imply that there is something to hide, or it may be just that overseas government procurement is carried out in that country via an import–export intermediary. Finally, we examine each piece of intelligence (not just secret intelligence of course; there are likely to be open sources as well) to see in Bayesian fashion whether they would be more likely under each of the hypotheses, and can thus help us discriminate between them. In doing this we check at the same time how confident we are in each piece of information being reliable, as we discussed in the preceding chapter.

Some of the intelligence reports may be consistent with all our hypotheses and they must be put to one side, however fascinating they are to read. Frustratingly, that can happen with reports of hard-to-get intelligence where perhaps lives have been risked to acquire it. A table (known in the trade as a Heuer table, after the pioneer of the use of structured analytic techniques, Richards J. Heuer) can be drawn up with separate columns for each hypothesis and rows for each piece of evidence, whose consistency with each hypothesis can then be logged in the table.

The first few rows of such a table might look like this:

	Source type Credibility Relevance	**Hypothesis 1:** Is related to plan to conduct nuclear-weapon-related experiments	**Hypothesis 2:** Can be explained by research for civil purposes
Evidence 1: known capability to enrich uranium provides motive	An assumption Medium High	Consistent	Consistent
Evidence 2: procurement was via an import–export company	An inference High Medium	Consistent	Less consistent
Evidence 3: military security seen around warehouse	Imagery High Medium	Consistent	Less consistent
Evidence 4: covert channels were used to acquire high-speed fuses	Humint New source on trial High	Consistent	Much less consistent
Evidence 5: encrypted high-grade military comms to and from the warehouse	Sigint High High	Consistent	Much less consistent

A hypothetical example of part of a Heuer table

It may become apparent that one particular report provides the dominant evidence, in which case wise analysts will re-examine the sourcing of the report. A lesson from experience (including that of assessing Iraq's holdings of chemical and biological weapons in 2002) is that once we have chosen our favoured explanation we become unconsciously resistant to changing our mind. Conflicting information that arrives is then too easily dismissed as unreliable or ignored as an anomaly. The table method makes it easier to establish an audit trail of how analysts went about reaching their conclusions. A record of that sort can be invaluable if later evidence casts doubt on the result, perhaps raising suspicions that some of the intelligence reporting was deliberately fabricated as a deception. We will see in Chapter 5 how German, US and UK analysts were deliberately deceived by the reporting of an Iraqi defector into believing that in 2003 Saddam Hussein possessed mobile biological warfare facilities.

The analysis of competing hypotheses using Heuer tables is an example of one of the structured analytic techniques in use today in the US and UK intelligence communities. The method is applicable to any problem you might have where different explanations have to be tested against each other in a methodical way. Heuer himself cites Benjamin Franklin in 1772, when he was the US Ambassador to France, describing to Joseph Priestley (the discoverer of oxygen) his approach to making up his mind:

> . . . divide half a sheet of paper by a line into two columns; writing over the one Pro and over the other Con . . . put down over the different heads short hints of the different motives . . . for or against the measure. When I have thus got them all together in one view, I endeavour to estimate their relative weights; and where I find two, one on each side, that seem

equal I strike them out. Thus proceeding I find where the balance lies . . . and come to a determination accordingly.

In any real example there is likely to be evidence pointing both
ways so a weighing up at the end is needed. Following the logic
of scientific method it is the hypothesis that has least evidence
against it that is usually to be favoured, not the one with most in
favour. That avoids the bias that could come from unconsciously
choosing evidence to collect that is likely to support a favoured
hypothesis. I invite you to try this structured technique for yourself the next time you have a tricky decision to take.

A striking example of the importance of falsifying alternative theories rather than confirming the most favoured comes
from an unexpected quarter: the 2016 US Presidential election.
It was an election campaign beset with allegations of 'fake
news' (including the false stories created and spread by Russian
intelligence agents to try to discredit one candidate, Hillary
Clinton). One of the stories spread online featured a photograph of a young Donald Trump with the allegation that, in an
interview to *People* magazine in 1998, he said: 'If I were to run,
I would run as a Republican. They're the dumbest group of
voters in the country. They believe anything on Fox News. I
could lie and they'd still eat it up. I bet my numbers would be
terrific.' That sounds just like Trump, but the only flaw is that
he never said it to *People* magazine. A search of *People* magazine
disconfirms that hypothesis – he gave no such interview.[14] This
story is an example of a falsifiable assertion. The hypothesis
that he did say it can be checked and quickly shown to be
untrue (that may of course have been the scheming intent of
its authors, in order to lend support to the assertion that other
anti-Trump stories were equally false). Most statements about
beliefs and motivations are non-falsifiable and cannot be

disproved in such a clear way. Instead, judgement is needed in reaching a conclusion that involves weighing evidence for and against, as we have seen with the Heuer method.

Assumptions and sensitivity testing

In this second stage of SEES, it is essential to establish how sensitive your explanation is to your assumptions and premises. What would it have taken to change my mind? Often the choice of explanation that is regarded as most likely will itself depend upon a critical assumption, so the right course is to make that dependency clear and to see whether alternative assumptions might change the conclusion reached. Assumptions have to be made, but circumstances can change and what was reasonable to take as a given may not be with time.

Structured diagnostic techniques, such as comparing alternative hypotheses, have the great advantage that they force an analytic group to argue transparently through all the evidence, perhaps prompting double-checking of the reliability of some piece of intelligence on which the choice of hypothesis seems to rest, or exposing an underlying assumption that may no longer hold or that would not be sensible to make in the context of the problem being examined.

As we will see in the next chapter, turning an explanation into a predictive model that allows us to estimate how events will unfold is crucially dependent on honesty over the assumptions we make about human behaviour. Marriages are predicated on the assumption that both partners will maintain fidelity. Many is the business plan that has foundered because assumptions made in the past about consumer behaviour turned out to no longer be valid. Government policies can come unstuck, for example, when implicit assumptions, such as about whether the public will regard them as fair, turn out not to reflect reality. A striking example was the British Criminal Justice Act 1991 that made fines proportionate to the income of the offender, and collapsed on the outcry when two men fighting, equally to blame, were fined £640 and £64 respectively because they belonged to different income brackets.

Back in Serbia in 1995, General Mladić, to our surprise, simplified our assessment task of trying to understand and explain his motivations.

Pulling out a brown leather-backed notebook, every page filled with his own cramped handwriting, Mladić proceeded to read to us from it for over half an hour recounting the tribulations of the Serb people at the hands both of the Croats and, as he put it, the Turks. He gave us his version of the history of his people, including the devastating Serbian defeat by the Ottoman Empire in 1389 at the Battle of the Field of Blackbirds. That was a defeat he saw as resulting in 500 years of Serbian enslavement. He recounted the legend that the angel Elijah had appeared to the Serb commander, Lazar, on the eve of the battle saying that victory would win him an earthly kingdom, but martyrdom would win a place for the Serb people in heaven. Thus even defeat was a spiritual triumph, and justified the long Serbian mission to recover their homeland from their external oppressors.

According to Mladić's candid expression of his world view in that dining room in Serbia, he felt it was a continuing humiliation to have Muslims and Croats still occupying parts of the territory of Bosnia–Herzegovina, and an insult to have the West defending Bosnian Muslims in enclaves inside what he saw as his own country. In a dramatic climax to his narrative he ripped open his shirt and cried out, kill me now if you wish but

I will not be intimidated, swearing that no foreign boot would be allowed to desecrate the graves of his ancestors.

Mladić had effectively given us the explanation we were seeking and answered our key intelligence question on his motivation for continuing to fight. We returned to our capitals convinced that the ultimatum had been delivered and understood, but Mladić would not be deterred from further defiance of the UN. The West would have to execute a policy U-turn to stop him, by replacing the UN peacekeepers with NATO combat troops under a UN mandate that could be safely backed by the use of air power. And so it worked out, first with the Anglo-French rapid reaction force on Mount Igman protecting Sarajevo and then the deployment of NATO forces including 20,000 US troops, all supported by a major air campaign.

I should add my satisfaction that the final chapter in the story concluded on 22 November 2017, when the Hague war crimes tribunal, with judges from the Netherlands, South Africa and Germany, ruled that, as part of Mladić's drive to terrorize Muslims and Croats into leaving a self-declared Serb mini-state, his troops had systematically murdered several thousand Bosnian Muslim men and boys, and that groups of women, and girls as young as twelve years old, were routinely and brutally raped by his forces. The judges detailed how soldiers under Mladić's command killed, brutalized and starved unarmed Muslim and Croat prisoners. Mladić was convicted of war crimes and sentenced to life imprisonment.

Conclusions: *explaining why we are seeing what we do*

Facts need explaining to understand why the world and the people in it are behaving as they appear to be. In this chapter, we have looked at how to seek the best 'explanation' of what we have observed or discovered about what is going on. If we wish to interpret the world as correctly as we can we should:

- Recognize that the choice of facts is not neutral and may be biased towards a particular explanation.
- Remember that facts do not speak for themselves and are likely to have plausible alternative explanations. Context matters in choosing the most likely explanation. Correlations between facts do not imply a direct causal connection.
- Treat explanations as hypotheses each with a likelihood of being true.
- Specify carefully alternative explanatory hypotheses to cover all the possibilities, including the most straightforward in accordance with Occam's razor.
- Test hypotheses against each other, using evidence that helps discriminate between them, an application of Bayesian inference.
- Take care over how we may be unconsciously framing our examination of alternative hypotheses, risking emotional, cultural or historical bias.
- Accept the explanatory hypothesis with the least evidence against it as most likely to be the closest fit to reality.
- Generate new insights from sensitivity analysis of what it would take to change our mind.

3

Lesson 3: Estimations
Predictions need an explanatory model as well as sufficient data

In mid-August 1968, I was driving an elderly Land Rover with friends from university along the Hungarian side of the border with Czechoslovakia on the first stage of an expedition to eastern Turkey. To our surprise we found ourselves having to dodge in and out of the tank transporters of a Soviet armoured column crawling along the border. We did not realize – and nor did the Joint Intelligence Committee in London – that those tank crews already had orders to cross the border and invade Czechoslovakia as part of a twin strategy of intimidation and deception being employed by Yuri Andropov, then KGB chairman, to undermine the reform-minded government in Prague led by Alexander Dubček.[1]

US, UK and NATO intelligence analysts were aware of the Soviet military deployments, which could not be hidden from satellite observation and signals intelligence (I joined GCHQ a year later and learned how that had been done). The Western foreign policy community was also following the war of words between Moscow and Prague over Dubček's reform programme. They shared Czech hopes that, in Dubček's memorable campaign slogan, 'socialism with a human face' would replace the rigidities of Stalinist doctrine.

Dubček had run for the post of First Secretary of the Party on a platform of increased freedom of the press and of speech and movement; an economic emphasis on consumer goods; a reduction in the powers of the secret police; and even the possibility of multi-party elections. Dubček was in a hurry, with the wind of popular support behind him. But he was clearly and repeatedly ignoring warnings from Moscow that he was going too far too fast. In 1968, Prague was at risk of slipping from under Moscow's control.

In the JIC, senior intelligence and policy officials met with representatives of the '5-eyes' to consider whether Moscow would use military force as it had done in Hungary in 1956.[2] This is the stage of analysis that the layperson might consider the most important, trying to predict for the policymakers what will happen next. This is very satisfying when it is achieved, although intelligence professionals shun the word 'prediction' as an overstatement of what is normally possible.

Analysts had no difficulty explaining the massing of tanks just on the other side of the Czech border as putting pressure on the reformist Czech government. The JIC analysts must have felt they had had good situational awareness and a credible explanation of what was going on at a military level. But they failed to take the next step and forecast the invasion and violent crushing of the reform movement. They reasoned that the Soviet Union would hold back from such crude direct intervention given the international condemnation that would undoubtedly follow. That verb *reasoned* carries the explanation of why the analysts got it wrong: they were reasonable people trying to predict the actions of an unreasonable regime. When they put themselves in the shoes of the decisionmakers in Moscow, they still thought exclusively from their own perspective.

We now know from historical research much more than the analysts would have known at the time about the resolve of the Soviet leadership to crush the Czech reforms. Western intelligence analysts would probably have come to a different conclusion about the Soviet willingness to take huge risks if they had known the active measures being taken against the Czech reformers being masterminded by Yuri Andropov, Head of the KGB.

That the key inner adviser to President Brezhnev in Moscow was Andropov should have triggered alarm. Andropov had form. As Soviet Ambassador in Budapest in 1956, he had played a decisive role in convincing the Soviet leader, Nikita Khrushchev, that only the ruthless use of military force would end the Hungarian uprising. It was a movement that had started with student protests but had ended up with an armed revolt to install a new government committed to free elections and a withdrawal from the Warsaw Pact.

One of the main instruments being employed by Andropov was the use of 'illegals'. The West found that out much later in 1992 with the reporting of Vasili Mitrokhin, the Soviet KGB archivist and MI6 source. He revealed how specially selected and trained KGB officers had been sent in 1968 into Czechoslovakia, disguised as tourists, journalists, businessmen and students, equipped with false passports from West Germany, Austria, the UK, Switzerland and Mexico. Each illegal was given a monthly allowance of $300, travel expenses and enough money to rent a flat in the expectation that the Czech dissidents would more readily confide in Westerners. Their role was both to penetrate reformist circles such as the Union of Writers, radical journals, the universities and political groupings, but also to take 'active measures' to blacken the reputation of the dissidents. The Soviet Prime Minister loudly complained of Western provocations and sabotage (with the alleged uncovering of a cache of American weapons and with a faked document purporting to show a US plan for overthrowing the Prague regime). He used such arguments to justify Soviet interference in Czechoslovak affairs even though they were, in fact, the work of the KGB 'illegals'.

In August 1968, under the pretext of preventing an imperialist plot, the Soviet Union despatched armies from Russia and four other Warsaw Pact countries to invade Czechoslovakia, taking over the airport and public buildings and confining Czech soldiers to barracks. Dubček and his colleagues were flown to Moscow under KGB escort, where, under considerable intimidation, they accepted the reality of complying with the demands of their occupiers.

Today we have seen Moscow using all these tactics from the Soviet playbook to prevent Ukraine orientating itself towards the EU. Yet, despite their understanding of Soviet history, Western analysts failed to predict the Russian seizure of Crimea and their armed intervention in eastern Ukraine. Analysts knew of past Soviet use of methods involving intimidation, propaganda and dirty tricks including the use of the little grey men of the KGB infiltrated into Czechoslovakia in 1968. Yet the appearance of 'little green men' in Ukraine, as the Russian special forces were dubbed by the media, came as a surprise.

Modelling the path to the future

The task of understanding how things will unfold is like choosing the most likely route to be taken across a strange country by a traveller you have equipped with a map that sets down only some of the features of the landscape. You know that all maps simplify to some extent; the perfect map, as described satirically by Jonathan Swift in *Gulliver's Travels* is one that has a scale of 1 to 1 and thus is as big and detailed as the ground being mapped.[3] There are blank spots on the traveller's map: 'here be dragons', as the medieval cartographers labelled areas where they did not have enough information. The important lesson is that reality itself has no blank spots: the problems you encounter are not with reality but with how well you are able to map it.

An example of getting the modelling of future international developments right was the 1990 US National Intelligence Council estimate 'Yugoslavia Transformed' a decade after the death of its autocratic ruler, the former Partisan leader Marshal Tito.[4] The US analysts understood the dynamics of Tito's long rule. He had forged a federation from very different and historically warring peoples: Serbs, Croats, Slovenes and Bosnian Muslims. As so often happens with autocrats ruling divided countries (think about Iraq under Saddam, Libya under Gaddafi), Tito ruled by balancing the tribal loyalties. For every advantage awarded to one group there had to be counter-balancing concessions in other fields to the other groups. Meanwhile a tough internal security apparatus loyal to Tito and the concept of Yugoslavia identified potential flashpoints to be defused and dissidents to be exiled. After Tito's death the centre could not long hold. The Serb leadership increasingly played the Serb nationalist and religious card and looked for support to Moscow. The Croats turned to the sympathy of Catholic fellowship in Germany. The Bosnian Muslims put their faith in the international community and the United Nations for protection. The US 1990 estimate summarized the future of the former Yugoslavia in a series of unvarnished judgements that read well in the light of subsequent developments in the Balkans as described in the previous chapter:

- Yugoslavia will cease to function as a federal state within one year and will probably break up within two. Economic reform will not stave off the break-up . . .
- There will be a protracted armed uprising by the Albanians in Kosovo. A full-scale, interrepublic war is unlikely but serious intercommunal violence will accompany the breakup and will continue thereafter. The violence will be intractable and bitter.
- There is little that the US and its European allies can do to preserve Yugoslav unity. Yugoslavs will see such efforts as contradictory to advocacy of democracy and self-determination . . . the Germans will pay lip service to the idea of Yugoslav integrity, whilst quietly accepting the dissolution of the Yugoslav state.

In London, analysts shared the thrusts of the US intelligence assessment on Yugoslavia. But the government of John Major did not want to get involved in what promised to be internecine Balkan civil war, always the bloodiest kind of conflict. The Chiefs of Staff could see no British interest worth fighting for. I recall attending the Chiefs of Staff Committee and reporting on the deteriorating situation but having Bismarck's wisecrack thrown back at me, that the pacification of the turbulent Balkans was not worth the healthy bones of a single Pomeranian grenadier.

There can be many reasons for failure to predict developments correctly. One of the most common reasons is simply the human temptation to indulge in magical thinking, imagining that things will turn out as we want without any credible causal explanation of how that will come about. We do this to shield ourselves from the unwelcome truth that we may not be able to get what we want. The arguments over the handling of the UK Brexit process say it all.

The choice between being more right or less wrong

It is easy to criticize analysts when they fail to warn of some aggressive act. They know that they will be accused of an intelligence failure. As a rule of thumb, analysts will tend to risk a false positive by issuing a warning estimate rather than risk the accusation of failure after a negative report failed to warn. The costs of not having a timely warning if the event does happen are usually greater than the costs of an unnecessary warning when it does not. Cynics might also argue that analysts are realists and they know that if they issue a warning but the event does not take place there will be many exculpatory reasons that can be deployed for events not turning out that way. On the other hand, if policymakers are badly surprised by events after a failure to warn there will be no excuses accepted.

Analysts are faced in those circumstances with an example of the much studied false-positive/false-negative quality control problem.[5] This is the same dilemma faced by car manufacturers who inspect as the cars leave the factory and have to set the testing to a desired rate of defective vehicles passing the inspection (taken to be safe but actually not, a false positive), knowing that such vehicles are likely to break down and have to be recalled at great cost and the company reputation and sales will suffer; but knowing as well that if too many vehicles are wrongly rejected as unsafe (taken to be unsafe but actually not, a false negative) the car company will also incur large unnecessary costs in reworking them. This logic applies even more forcibly with medicines and foodstuffs. As consumers it is essential to expect foods labelled as nut-free to be just that, in order to avoid the potentially lethal risk to those allergic to nuts. The consequence, however, is that we have to recognize that the manufacturer will need a rigorous testing system achieving very low false-positive rejection rates, and that will put up the false-negative rejection rates, which is likely to add significant cost to the product. We can expect the cursor on most overall manufacturing industry inspection systems to be set towards avoiding more false positives at the expense of more false negatives. The software industry, however, is notorious for cost reasons for tolerating a high false-positive rate, preferring to issue endless patches and updates as the customers themselves find the flaws the hard way by actually using the software.

An obvious application in intelligence and security work is in deciding whether an individual has shown sufficient associations with violent extremism to be placed on a 'no-fly' list. Policymakers would want the system to err on the side of caution. That means accepting rather more false negatives, which will of course seriously inconvenience an individual falsely seen as dangerous because they will not be allowed to fly, as the price for having a very low level of false positives (falsely seen as safe when not, which could lead, in the worst case, to a terrorist destroying a passenger aircraft by smuggling a bomb on board). Another example is the design of algorithms for intelligence agencies to pull out information relating to terrorist suspects from digital communications data accessed in bulk. Set the cursor too far in the direction of false positives and too much material of no intelligence interest will be retrieved, wasting valuable analyst time and risking unnecessary invasion of privacy; set the cursor too far towards false negatives and the risk of not retrieving the material being sought and terrorists escaping notice rises. There is no optimal solution possible without weighing the relative penalties of a false positive as against a false negative. At one extreme, as we will see in the next chapter, is the so-called precautionary principle whereby the risk of harm to humans means there cannot be false positives. Application of such a principle comes at considerable cost.[6]

The false-positive/false-negative dilemma occurs with algorithms that have to separate data into categories. Such algorithms are trained on a large set of historic data where it is known which category each example falls into (such as genuinely suspect/not-suspect) and the AI programme then works out the most efficient indicators to use in categorizing the data. Before the algorithm is deployed into service, however, the accuracy of its output needs to be assessed against the known characteristics of the input. Simply setting the rule at a single number so that, say, 95 per cent of algorithmic decisions are expected to be correct in comparison with the known training data is likely to lead to trouble depending upon the ratio of false positives to false negatives in the result and the penalty associated with each. One way of assessing the accuracy of the algorithm in its task is to define its precision as the number of true positives as a proportion of positives that the algorithm thinks it has detected in the training data. Accuracy is often measured as the number of true positives and negatives as a proportion of the total number in the training set. A modern statistical technique that can be useful with big data sets is to chart the number of false positives and false negatives to be expected at each setting of the rule and to look at the area under the resulting curve (AUC) as a measure of overall success in the task.[7]

Reluctance to act on intelligence warnings

The policy world may need shaking into recognizing that they have to take warnings seriously. In April 1993 I accompanied the British Defence Secretary, Malcolm Rifkind, to the opening of the Holocaust Museum in Washington. The day started with a moving tribute at Arlington Cemetery to the liberators of the concentration camps. I remembered the sole occasion my father had spoken to me of the horror of entering one such just liberated camp in 1944 when he was serving as an officer in the Black Watch on the Eighth Army A Staff. It was a memory that he had preferred to suppress. Later that day Elie Wiesel, the Nobel Peace Prize winner, spoke passionately in front of President Bill Clinton, President Chaim Herzog of Israel and a large crowd of dignitaries about the need to keep the memory of those horrors alive. He issued an emotional appeal to remember the failure of the Allied powers to support the Warsaw Ghetto uprising and the Jewish resistance.[8] He quoted the motto chiselled in stone over the entrance to the Holocaust Museum: 'For the dead and the living we must bear witness'. Then, turning directly to face President Clinton and the First Lady, Hillary Clinton, he reminded them: 'We are also responsible for what we are doing with those memories . . . Mr President, I cannot not tell you something. I have been in the former Yugoslavia last Fall . . .

I cannot sleep since over what I have seen. As a Jew I am saying that we must do something to stop the bloodshed in that country! People fight each other and children die. Why? Something, anything, must be done.'

His message, genocide is happening again in Europe, and it is happening on your watch, Mr President, and the Allies are once again doing nothing, was heard in an embarrassed silence, followed by loud applause from the survivors of the camps who were present. Later that year the UN Security Council did finally mandate a humanitarian operation in Bosnia, the UN Protection Force (UNPROFOR), for which the UK was persuaded to provide a headquarters and an infantry battle group. As the opening of the previous chapter recounted, that small peacekeeping force in their blue helmets and white-painted vehicles sadly proved inadequate faced with the aggression of both Bosnian Serbs and Croats, and was helpless to stop the massacre of Bosnian Muslims at Srebrenica in the summer of 1995.

Providing leaders with warnings is not easy. The ancient Greek myth of Cassandra, one of the princesses of Troy and daughter of King Priam, relates that she was blessed by the god Apollo with the gift of foreseeing the future. But when she refused the advances of Apollo she was placed under a curse which meant that, despite her gift, no one would believe her. She tried in vain to warn the inhabitants of Troy to beware Greeks bearing gifts. The giant wooden horse, left by the Greeks as they pretended to lift the siege of the city, was nevertheless pulled inside the walls. Odysseus and his soldiers who were hidden inside climbed out at night and opened the city gates to the invading Greek Army. As Cassandra had cried out in the streets of Troy: 'Fools! ye know not your doom . . . Oh, ye believe not me, though ne'er so loud I cry!'[9] Not to have their warnings believed has been the fate of many intelligence analysts over the years and will be again. The phenomenon is known to the intelligence world as the Cassandra effect.

It might have been doubts about Cassandra's motives that led to her information being ignored. In 1982 there were warnings from the captain of the ice patrol ship HMS *Endurance* in the South Atlantic who was monitoring Argentine media that the point was coming close when the Junta would lose patience with diplomatic negotiations. But these warnings were discounted by a very human reaction of 'Well, he would say that, wouldn't he', given his ship was to be withdrawn from service under the cuts in capability imposed by the 1981 defence expenditure review. It is also quite possible that Cassandra might have made too many predictions in the past that led to nothing and created what is known as warning fatigue. We know this as crying wolf, from Aesop's fable. That might in turn imply the threshold for warning was set too low and should have been set higher than turning out the whole village on a single shout of 'wolf' (but remember the earlier discussion of false positives and false negatives and how raising the warning threshold increases the risk of a real threat being ignored). Sending signals which lead to repeated false alarms is an ancient tactic to inure the enemy to the real danger. Warnings also have to be sufficiently specific to allow sensible action to be taken. Simply warning that there is a risk of possible political unrest in the popular holiday destination of Ruritania does not help the tourist know whether or not to cancel their holiday on the Ruritanian coast.

Perhaps poor Cassandra was simply not thought a sufficiently credible source for reasons unconnected with the objective value of her intelligence reporting. Stalin was forewarned of the German surprise attack on the Soviet Union in 1941 by reports from well-placed Soviet intelligence sources, including the Cambridge spies, some of whom had access to Bletchley Park Enigma decrypts of the German High Command's signals. But he discounted the reporting as too good to be true and therefore assumed a deliberate attempt by the Allies to get him to regard Germany as an enemy and to discount the guarantees of peace in the 1939 Molotov–Ribbentrop non-aggression pact that Stalin had approved two years earlier.

A final lesson from the failure of the Trojans to act on Cassandra's warning might be that the cost of preventive action can be seen as too great. Legend has it that the Trojans were concerned with angering their gods if they had refused the Greek offering of the wooden horse. We may ignore troubling symptoms if we fear that a visit to the doctor will result in a diagnosis that prevents us being able to fly to a long-promised holiday in the sun.

Expressing predictions and forecasts as probabilities

It is sadly the case that only rarely can intelligence analysts be definitive in warning what will happen next. Most estimates have to be hedged with caveats and assumptions. Analysts speak therefore of their degree of belief in a forward-looking judgement. Such a degree of belief is expressed as a probability of being right. This is a different use of probability from that associated with gambling games like dice or roulette, where the frequency with which a number comes up provides data from which the probability of a particular outcome is estimated. When we throw a fair die we know that the probability that the next throw will come up with a six is 1/6. We know the odds we ought to accept on a bet that this is what will happen. That is the frequentist interpretation of probability. By analogy, we think of the odds that intelligence analysts would rationally accept on their estimate being right. That is the measure of their degree of belief in their judgement. It is of course a subjective interpretation of probability.[10]

Intelligence analysts prefer – like political pollsters – forecasts that associate with a range of possible outcomes an associated probability. For example, the US Director of National Intelligence, Dan Coats, predicted in a worldwide threat assessment given to the Senate Intelligence Committee that competitors such as Russia, China and Iran 'probably already are looking to the 2020 U.S. elections as an opportunity to advance their interests'.[11] 'Probably' here is likely to mean 55–70 per cent, which can be thought of as the gambling odds the analysts should accept for being right (in that case, just over 70 per cent probable equates to bookmakers offering odds of 2 to 1 on).

When a forecast outcome is heavily dependent on external events, that is usually expressed as an assumption so that readers of the assessment understand that dependency. The use of qualifying words such as 'unlikely', 'likely' and so on is standardized by professional intelligence analysts. The UK yardstick was devised by the Professional Head of the Intelligence Analysis profession (PHIA) in the Cabinet Office, and is in use across the British intelligence community, including with law enforcement. The example of the yardstick below is taken from the annual National Strategic Assessment (NSA) by the UK National Crime Agency.[12]

Probability and Uncertainty

Throughout the NSA, the 'probability yardstick' (as defined by the Professional Head of Intelligence Assessment (PHIA) has been used to ensure consistency across the different threats and themes when assessing probability. The following defines the probability ranges considered when such language is used:

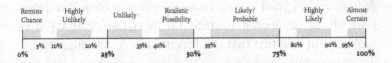

The US Intelligence Community also has published a table showing how to express a likelihood in ordinary language (line 1 of the table below) and in probabilistic language (line 2 of the table, with the corresponding confidence level in line 3).[13]

almost no chance	very unlikely	unlikely	roughly even chance	likely	very likely	almost certain
remote	highly improbable	improbable (improbably)	roughly even odds	probable (probably)	highly probable	nearly certain
01–05%	05–20%	20–45%	45–55%	55–80%	80–95%	95–99%

One difference between the approach taken by the UK and the US analysts is in the use of gaps between the ranges in the UK case. The intention is to avoid the potential problem with the US scale over what term you use if your judgement is 'around 20 per cent'. Two analysts can have a perfectly reasonable, but unnecessary, argument over whether something is 'very unlikely' or 'unlikely'. The gaps obviate the problem. The challenge is over what to do if the judgement falls within one of the gaps. If an analyst can legitimately say that something is 'a 75–80 per cent chance', then they are free to do so. The yardstick is a guide and a minimum standard, but analysts are free to be more specific or precise in their judgements, if they can. It is sensible to think in 5 or 10 per cent increments to discourage unjustified precision for which the evidence is unlikely to be available. I recommend this framework in any situation in which you have to make a prediction. It is very flexible, universally applicable, and extremely helpful in aiding your decisionmaking and in communicating it to others. You could start off by reminding yourself the next time you say it is 'unlikely' to rain that that still leaves a one in five chance of a downpour. You might well accept that level of risk and not bother with a coat. But if you were badly run down after a bout of flu even a 20 per cent chance of getting soaked and developing a fever would be a risk not worth running. That is an example of examining *the expected value* of the outcome, not just its likelihood, formed by multiplying together the probability of an event and a measure of the consequences for you of it happening.

The limits of prediction

The science fiction writer Isaac Asimov in his *Foundation and Empire* books imagined a future empirical science of psychohistory, where recurring patterns in civilizations on a cosmic scale could be modelled using sociology, history and mathematical statistics.[14] Broad sweeps of history could, Asimov fantasized, be forecast in the same way as statistical mechanics allows the behaviour of large numbers of molecules in a gas to be predicted, although the behaviour of individual molecules cannot (being subject to quantum effects). Asimov's fictional creator of psychohistory, Dr Hari Seldon, laid down key assumptions that the population whose behaviour was being modelled should be sufficiently large and that the population should remain in ignorance of the results of the application of psychohistorical analyses because, if it became so aware, there would be feedback changing its behaviour. Other assumptions include that there would be no fundamental change in human society and that human nature and reactions to stimuli would remain constant. Thus, Asimov reasoned, the occurrence of times of crisis at an intergalactic scale could be forecast, and guidance provided (by a holograph of Dr Seldon) by constructing time vaults that would be programmed to open when the crisis was predicted to arise and the need would be greatest.

Psychohistory will remain fantasy. Which is perhaps just as well. The main problem with such ideas is the impossibility of sufficiently specifying the initial conditions. Even with deterministic equations in a weather-forecasting model, after a week or so the divergence between what is forecast and what is observed becomes too large to allow the prediction to be useful. And often in complex systems the model is non-linear, so small changes can quickly become large ones. There are inherent limits to forecasting reality. Broad sweeps may be possible but not detailed predictions. There comes a point when the smallest disturbance (the iconic flapping of a butterfly's wings) sets in train a sequence of cascading changes that tip weather systems over, resulting in a hurricane on the other side of the world. The finer the scale being used to measure forecasts in international affairs, the more variables that need to be taken into account, the greater the number of imponderables and assumptions, and the less accurate the long-term forecast is liable to be.[15]

Even at the level of physical phenomenon not every activity is susceptible to precise modelling. Exactly when a radioactive atom will spontaneously decay cannot be predicted, although the number of such events in a given time can be known in terms of its probability of occurrence. The exact path a photon of light or an electron will take when passing through a narrow pair of slits can also only be predicted in advance in terms of probabilities (the famous double slit experiment that demonstrates one of the key principles of quantum physics).

Secrets, mysteries and complex interactions

There is a deeper way of looking at intelligence, and that is to distinguish between secrets and mysteries. Secrets can be found out if the seeker has the ingenuity, skill and the means to uncover them. Mysteries are of a different order. More and more secrets will not necessarily unlock the mystery of a dictator's state of mind. But intelligence officers trying to get inside the mind of a potential adversary have to do their best to make an assessment, since that will influence what the policymakers decide to do next. Inferences can certainly be drawn, based on knowledge of the individuals concerned and on reading of their motivations, together with general observation of human behaviour. But such a judgement will depend on who is making it. A neutral observer might come to a different view from one from a country at risk of being invaded.

Mysteries have a very different evidential status. They concern events that have not yet happened (and therefore may never happen). Yet it is solutions to such mysteries that the users of intelligence need. It was the case that from the moment early in 1982 when the Argentine Junta's Chief of Naval Staff and chief hawk over the issue, Admiral Anaya, issued secret orders to his staff to begin planning the Falkland Islands invasion then there were secrets to collect. But whether, when it came to the crunch, the Junta as a whole would approve the resulting plan and order implementation would remain a mystery until much later.

To make matters harder, there is often an additional difficulty due to the *complex interactions*[16] involved. We now know in the case of the Junta in 1982 that it completely misread what the UK reaction would be to an invasion of the Falkland Islands. And, just as seriously, the Junta did not take sufficient account of the longstanding US/UK defence relationship in assessing how the US would react. It may not have recognized the personal relationship that had developed between the UK's Defence Secretary, John Nott, and his US counterpart, Caspar Weinberger. Margaret Thatcher's iron response in sending a naval Task Force to recover the Islands met with Weinberger's strong approval, in part because it demonstrated to the Soviet Union that armed aggression would not be allowed to pay.

These distinctions are important in everyday life. There are many secrets that can in principle be found out if your investigations are well designed and sufficiently intrusive. In your own life, your partner may have kept texts on their phone from an ex that they have kept private from you. Strictly speaking, these are secrets that you could probably find a way of accessing covertly (I strongly advise you don't. Your curiosity is not a sufficient reason for violating their privacy rights. And once you have done so, your own behaviour towards your partner, and therefore your partner's towards you, is likely unconsciously to change). But whether you uncover the secrets or not, the mystery of why your partner kept them and whether they ever intend in the future to contact the ex remains unanswered, and not even your partner is likely to be certain of the answer. You would have the secret but not the answer to the mystery, and that answer is likely to depend upon your own behaviour over coming months that will exercise a powerful influence on how your partner feels about the relationship. Prediction in such circumstances of complex interactions is always going to be hard.

Missing out on the lessons of Chapter 2 and leaping from situational awareness to prediction – for example, by extrapolating trends or assuming conditions will remain the same – is a common error, known as the inductive fallacy. It is equivalent to weather forecasting by simply looking out of the window and extrapolating: most of the time tomorrow's weather follows naturally from today's, but not when there is a rapidly developing weather front. Ignoring the underlying dynamics of weather systems will mean you get the forecast right much of the time but inevitably not always. When it happens that you are wrong, as you are bound to be from time to time, you are liable to be disastrously wrong – for example, as a flash flood develops or an unexpected hurricane sweeps in. That holds as true for international affairs as it does for all life as well: if you rely on assumptions, when you get it wrong, you get it really wrong. Experts are as likely to fall into this trap as anyone else.[17]

I am fond of the Greek term *phronesis*, to describe the application of practical wisdom to the anticipation of risks. As defined by the art historian Edgar Wind, this term describes how good judgement can be applied to human conduct consisting in a sound practical instinct for the course of events, an almost indefinable hunch that anticipates the future by remembering the past and thus judges the present correctly.[18]

Conclusions: estimates and predictions

Estimates of how events may unfold, and predictions of what will happen next, are crucially dependent on having a reliable explanatory model, as well as sufficient data. Even if we are not consciously aware of doing this, when we think about the future we are mentally constructing a model of our current reality and reaching judgements about how our chosen explanatory model would behave over time and in response to different inputs or stimuli. It will help to have identified what are the most important factors that are likely to affect the outcome, and how sensitive that outcome might be to changes in circumstances. We are here posing questions of the 'what next and where next?' type. In answering them we should:

- Avoid the inductive fallacy of jumping straight from situational awareness to prediction and use an explanatory model of how you think the key variables interact.
- Be realistic about the limitations of any form of prediction, expressing results as estimates between a range of likely possibilities. Point predictions are hazardous.
- Express your degree of confidence in your judgements in probabilistic language, taking care over consistent use of terms such as 'likely'.
- Remember to consider those less likely but potentially damaging outcomes as well as the most probable.
- Be aware that wanting to see a reduction in the level of false positives implies increasing the level of false negatives to be expected.
- Do not confuse the capability of an individual or organization to act with an intent to act on their part.

- Be aware of your cultural differences and prejudices when explaining the motivations and intent of another.
- Distinguish between what you conclude based on information you have and what you think based on past experience, inference and intuition (secrets, mysteries and complexities).
- Beware your own biases misleading you when you are trying to understand the motives of others.
- Give warnings as active deliberative acts based on your belief about how events will unfold and with the intent of causing a change in behaviour or policy.

4

Lesson 4: Strategic notice
We do not have to be so surprised by surprise

Early in the blustery spring morning of 14 April 2010 an Icelandic volcano with a near unpronounceable name (Eyjafjallajökull) exploded, throwing a cloud of fine ash high into the sky. The debris was quickly swept south-east by the regular jet stream of wind across the Atlantic until the skies above Northern Europe were filled with ash. Deep under the Icelandic ice-sheet melt water from the heat of the magma had flowed into the site of the eruption, rapidly cooling the lava and causing the debris to be rich in corrosive glass particles. These are known to pose a potential hazard if ingested by aircraft jet engines. The next day alarmed air traffic authorities decided they had to play it safe since no one had prescribed in advance specific particle sizes and levels below which engines were considered not to be at risk and thus safe to fly. They closed airspace over Europe and grounded all civil aviation in the biggest shutdown since the Second World War.[1]

Yet there had been warning that such an extreme event might one day occur, an example of strategic notice that is the fourth component of the SEES model of intelligence analysis. The government authorities in Iceland had been asking airlines for years to determine the density and type of ash that is safe for jet engines to fly through. Had the tests been carried out, the 2010 disruption would have been much less. There would still have been no immediate forewarning of the volcano about to explode, but sensible preparations would have been in place for when it did.

The lesson is that we need sufficiently early notice of future developments that might pose potential danger to us (or might offer us opportunities) to be prepared to take precautionary measures just in case. *Strategic notice* enables us to anticipate. Governments had strategic notice of possible coronavirus pandemics – the COVID-19 outbreak should not have caught us unprepared.

There is an important difference between having strategic warning of the existence of a future risk, and a prediction of when such a risk might materialize. Scientists cannot tell us exactly when a specific volcano will erupt (or when a viral disease will mutate from animals to humans). But there can be warning signs. Based on historical data, some sense of scale of frequency of eruption can be given. In the Icelandic case it was to be expected that some such volcanic activity would occur within the next fifty years. But before the volcanic events of April 2010, aviation authorities and aircraft engine manufacturers had not recognized that they needed to prepare. Instead they had implicitly accepted the precautionary principle[2] that if any measurable volcanic ash appeared in the atmosphere they would issue an advisory notice that all planes should be grounded even at the cost of considerable disruption to passengers.

The airlines had known of the baseline precaution that would be taken of grounding planes in the event of volcanic ash appearing in the atmosphere, but they had not thought in advance how such a major global dislocation would be handled. After the April 2010 closure of European airspace, the effects rapidly cascaded around the world. Planes were diverted on safety grounds to countries for which the passengers did not have visas, and could not leave the airport to get to hotels. Coming at the end of the Easter holidays, school parties were unable to return for the start of the term. Nobody had considered if stranded passengers should have priority over new passengers for booking on flights when they restarted. For millions of people the result was misery, camping in airports until finally aviation was allowed to resume just over a week later. At the same time, test flights were rapidly organized by the aero engine manufacturers. These provided data on which calibrated judgements could be made of when it is safe enough to fly through ash clouds. By the end of a week of chaos and confusion, 10 million passengers had been affected overall, with the aviation industry facing losses of over £1bn.

The same thing happened in the 1982 Falklands crisis. The British government was given strategic warning by the JIC that Argentine patience might run out, in which case the Junta could take matters into its own hands. That warning could have prompted the stationing of naval forces as a credible deterrent, while a permanent solution could have been created by extending the runway to handle long-distance transports and the stationing of fast jets (as has now been done). That would have been expensive. But the expense pales in comparison with the loss of over 1000 lives, not to mention an estimated price tag of over £3bn that was involved in recovering the Islands for the Crown once lost.

'I just say it was the worst, I think, moment of my life' was how Margaret Thatcher later described the surprise loss of the Falklands: yet she and her senior Cabinet members and the officials supporting them had not understood beforehand the dangers they were running. It was painful for me as a member of the Ministry of Defence to have to recognize later that we had all been so preoccupied by other problems, including managing defence expenditure, that we failed to pay sufficient attention to the vulnerability of the Falklands. We implicitly assumed (magical thinking) that the need would never arise. It was a salutary lesson learned early in my career and one that stayed with me.

Living with surprise

The fourth stage of the SEES method involves acquiring strategic notice of the important longer-term developments that could affect you. If you do not have these at the back of your mind, the chances are that you will not have prepared either mentally or physically for the possibility of their occurring. Nor will you be sufficiently alert to spot their first signs. We will experience what is known to intelligence officers as *strategic surprise*.

The distinction between having strategic and tactical surprise is an old one in military history. It is often hard for a general to conceal the strategy being followed. But when it comes to choosing tactically when and where to attack, a commander can obtain the advantages of surprise by, for example, picking a point in the enemy's defences where at least initially he will have the advantage. In 1944 the Germans knew perfectly well that the Allies were preparing a major landing of US, British and Canadian troops on the continent of Europe. That intent was no surprise since the strategy of opening a second front in Europe was well known. But the tactics that would be adopted, the date of the invasion, and exactly where and how the landings would be mounted were secrets carefully kept from the German High Command. Come 6 June 1944, the

Allies landed in Normandy and enjoyed the immediate advantage of tactical surprise.

A tragic example of tactical surprise was the events of 7 July 2005, when terrorist suicide bombers with rucksack bombs struck at the London Underground network and surface transport during the morning rush hour. Fifty-two innocent passengers lost their lives and very many more suffered horrific injuries. The attacks came without intelligence warning and the shock across London and round the world was considerable. But they were not a *strategic surprise* to the authorities.

The likelihood of terrorist attacks in London in 2005 had been assessed by the Joint Terrorism Analysis Centre based in MI5 headquarters. Intelligence had indicated that supporters of Al Qaid'a living inside the UK had both the capability and intent to mount some form of domestic terror attack. The possibility that the London Underground system would be an attractive target to terrorist suicide bombers had been anticipated and plans drawn up and staff trained just in case. A full-scale live rehearsal of the response to a terrorist attack on the Underground, including emergency services and hospitals that would be receiving casualties, had been held in September 2003. Just as well, since many practical lessons were learned that helped the response two years later.[3] The same can be said for the experience of the pandemic exercise in 2016 for the COVID-19 outbreak in 2020. Exercises can never fully capture the real thing but if events come as a strategic surprise the damage done will be far greater.

The same is true for all of us. We have, for example, plenty of strategic notice that our possessions are at risk of theft, which is why we should think about insurance. If we do get our mobile phone stolen we will certainly feel it as an unwelcome tactical surprise, but if insured we can console ourselves that however inconvenient it is not as bad as if it had been a strategic surprise as well.

Forestalling surprise

Intelligence communities have the duty of trying to forestall unwelcome surprises by spotting international developments that would spell real trouble.[4] In 1973 Israeli intelligence was carefully monitoring Egypt for evidence that President Sadat might be preparing to invade. Signs of mobilization were nevertheless discounted by the Israelis. That was because the Israeli Director of Military Intelligence, Major General Eli Zeira, had convinced himself that he would have strategic notice of a coming war. He reasoned that without major new arms imports from Russia, and a military alliance with Syria, Egypt would be bound to lose. Since no such imports or alliance with Syria had been detected he was certain war was not coming. What he failed to spot was that President Sadat of Egypt also knew that and had no illusions about defeating Israel militarily. His plan was to launch a surprise attack to seize the Sinai Peninsula, call for a ceasefire and then to negotiate from strength in peace talks. It was a crucial report from Israel's top spy inside Egypt (the highly placed Israeli agent Ashwar Marwan was actually the millionaire son-in-law of Gamel Abdel Nasser, Egypt's second President), which arrived literally on the eve of Yom Kippur, that just gave Israel enough time to mobilize to resist the attack when it came. The near disaster for Israel provides a warning of the dangerous double power of magical thinking, not only imagining that the world will somehow of its own accord fit in with your desires but also interpreting all evidence to the contrary so as to confirm your belief that all is well.

An important conclusion is that events which take us unawares will force us to respond in a hurry. We did not expect it to happen today, but it has happened. If we have not prepared for the eventuality we will be caught out, red-faced, improvising rapidly to recover the situation. That includes 'slow burn' issues that creep up on us (like COVID-19) until we suddenly realize with horror that some tipping point has been reached and we are forced to respond. Climate change due to global warming is one such 'slow burn' issue. It has been evident to scientists for decades and has now reached a tipping point with the melting of polar ice and weather extremes. It is only very recently, however, that this worsening situation has become a matter for general public concern.

The creation of ISIS in Syria and Iraq is another example where intelligence officers slowly began to recognize that something significant and dangerous was afoot as the terrorists began to occupy and control areas of the two countries. The failure of strategic notice was not to see how a combination of jihadist participation in the civil war in Syria together with the strength of the remnants of the Sunni insurgency in Iraq could create a power vacuum. The early signals of major risks may be weak, and hard to perceive against the generally noisy background of reality. For example, we have only recently recognized the re-emergence of state threats through digital subversion and propaganda and the possibility of highly damaging cyberattacks against the critical infrastructure such as power and telecommunications.

The product of the likelihood of something happening (a probability) and a measure of its impact if it does arise gives us a measure of what is called *the expected value of the event*. We are all familiar with the principle from assessing the expected value of a bet: the combination of the chances of winning and pay-off (winnings minus our stake) if we do. At odds of 100 to 1 the chances are low but the payoff correspondingly large, and vice versa with an odds-on favourite. We also know that the expected value of a series of separate bets can be calculated by simply adding the individual net values together. Wins are sadly usually quickly cancelled out by losses. The effect is even more evident with games like roulette, in which, with a fair wheel, there is no skill involved in placing a bet. Over a period, the bookmakers and casino operators will always make their turn, which is why they continue to exist (but punters will still come back for more because of the non-monetary value to them of the thrill of the bet).

Very unlikely events with big consequences (events that in our experience we do not expect to happen to us or only rarely) do nevertheless sometimes pop up and surprise us.[5] Sometimes they are referred to as 'long-tailed' risks because of the way that they lie at the extreme end, or tail, of the distribution of risk likelihood rather than in the 'expected' middle range. An example might be the 2007 global financial crash.[6] Our intuition also can mislead us into thinking that the outcome of some event that concerns us is as likely to be above the average (median) as below since so many large-scale natural processes are governed by the so-called 'normal' bell-shaped symmetrical probability distribution. But there are important exceptions in which there is a sizeable long tail of bad outcomes.

That idea of expected value can be elaborated into what is known to engineers as the risk equation to provide a measure of overall loss or gain. We learned the value of this approach when I was the UK Security and Intelligence Coordinator in the Cabinet Office constructing the UK counter-terrorism strategy, CONTEST, after 9/11.[7] Our risk equation separated out the factors that contribute to the overall danger to the public so that actions could be designed to reduce each of them, as shown below.

The Strategic risk equation behind CONTEST, the UK counter-terrorism strategy

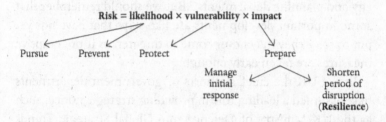

Risk = likelihood × vulnerability × impact

Pursue   Prevent   Protect   Prepare

Manage initial response

Shorten period of disruption (**Resilience**)

We can thus reduce the probability of terrorists attempting to attack us by detecting and pursuing terrorist networks and by preventing radicalization to reduce the flow of new recruits. We reduce society's vulnerability to particular types of attack by more protective security measures such as better airport screening. We reduce the cost to the public of an attack if the terrorists get through our defences by preparing the emergency services to face the initial impact when an attack takes place and by investing in infrastructure that can be repaired quickly. This logic is a major reason why CONTEST remains the UK's counter-terrorism strategy, despite being on its fifth Prime Minister and ninth Home Secretary. Military planners would recognize this lesson as applying 'layered defence',[8] just as the thief after an expensive bicycle might have first to climb over a high wall into the garden, dodge round the burglar alarms, break into the shed, then undo the bicycle lock. The chance of the thief succeeding undetected goes down with each layer of security that is added (and so does your overall risk).

The search for strategic notice of long-term developments is sometimes referred to as horizon scanning, as in looking for the tops of the masts of the enemy ships just appearing. Global banks, consultancies and corporations such as Shell have acquired a reputation for horizon scanning to help their strategy and planning departments.[9] But we should remember that some important developments are like ships that have not yet put to sea – they may never come to threaten us if pre-emptive measures are taken early enough.

In the UK the chief scientists of government departments have assumed a leading role in providing strategic notice, such as the UK Ministry of Defence 2016 Global Strategic Trends report looking ahead to 2045.[10] Another example is the 2016 report by the UK Chief Scientific Adviser on the potential revolution for government agencies, banks, insurance companies and other private sector organizations of blockchain technology.[11] The headline message is clear: watch out, a new disruptive technology is emerging that has the potential to transform the working of any organization that relies on keeping records. In the natural world we do have strategic notice of many serious issues that should make governments and companies sit up. One of the top risks flagged up by the UK government has long been a virus pandemic, alongside terrorism and cyberattacks.

It is worth bearing in mind when new technology appears which might pose risks to humans or the environment that most scientists prefer to hold back from offering advice until there is solid evidence on which to reach judgements. That understandable caution leads to the special category of 'epistemic' risk arising from a lack of knowledge or of agreed understanding, because experts are reluctant to commit as to whether the harm will ever crystallize or because they disagree among themselves as to its significance.

It is hard to predict when some theoretical scientific advance will result in brand-new technology that will impact heavily on our lives. Of the 2.5 million new scientific papers published each year[12] very few represent breakthroughs in thinking. Even when a theoretical breakthrough opens the possibility of a revolution in technology it may be years in gestation. Quantum computing provides a striking example where we have strategic notice of its potential, once such a machine is built, to factorize the very large numbers on which all the commercial encryption systems rely for secure internet communication and online payments. At the time of writing, however, no workable quantum computer at scale has been built that can operate to fulfil the promise of the theory: it could be decades ahead. But we know that the impact when and if it happens will be significant. Wise governments will therefore be investing (as the US and the UK are[13]) in developing new types of cryptography that will be more resistant to quantum computers when they arrive; and no doubt asking their intelligence agencies to report any signs that somewhere else the practical problems of implementation look like being cracked.

At a personal level, where we find some of our risks easily visualized (such as coming back to the car park to find the car gone) and the costs are low, we can quickly learn to manage the risk (this causes us to get into the habit of checking whether we locked the car). Other personal risks that are more abstract, although more dangerous, may be unconsciously filed as the kind that happen to other people (such as returning home to find the fire brigade outside as a result of a short circuit in old wiring). We look but do not see the danger, just as in everyday life we can hear but not listen.

The term 'risk' conventionally carries the meaning of something bad that *could* happen. But as the economist F. H. Knight concluded many years ago, without risk there is no profit.[14] A further lesson in using strategic notice is how it can allow advance notice of long-term opportunities that might present themselves. Perhaps the chosen route for the future high-speed rail link will go through the middle of the village (threat) or a station on the line will be built in a nearby town (opportunity).

Strategic notice has even become a fashionable theory governing the marketing of products in the internet age. Rather than the more traditional clustering of products around common types of goods and services, it is increasingly being found that it is the quirky niche products or services which might appear at first sight unlikely to have mass appeal that can go viral on social media and quickly generate large returns. Entrepreneurs expect most of such outlier efforts to fail, but those that succeed more than make up for them in profits earned. Who would have thought a few years ago that sportswear such as brightly coloured running shoes and jogging bottoms, then confined to the gym, would for many become staple outdoor wear.

Providing ourselves with strategic notice

Bangladesh Climate Geo-engineering Sparks Protests
April 4, 2033 – Dhaka

Bangladesh became the first country to try to slow climate change by releasing a metric ton of sulphate aerosol into the upper atmosphere from a modified Boeing 797 airplane in the first of six planned flights to reduce the warming effects of solar radiation. The unprecedented move provoked diplomatic warnings by 25 countries and violent public protests at several Bangladeshi Embassies, but government officials in Dhaka claimed its action was 'critical to self-defense' after a spate of devastating hurricanes, despite scientists' warnings of major unintended consequences, such as intensified acid rain and depletion of the ozone layer.

Note the date on that news report. That surprising glimpse of the future in 2033 was included in the 2017 report on Global Trends published by the US National Intelligence Council.[15] The intelligence officers drafting the report included such headlines to bring to life their strategic assessments of possible developments out to 2030 and beyond and the disruptive game-changers to be expected between now and then.

The then chair of the US National Intelligence Council, Professor Greg Treverton, explained in his foreword to the 2017 report that he examined global trends to identify their impact on power, governance and cooperation. In the near future, absent very different personal, political and business choices, he expects the current trajectory of trends and power dynamics to play out among rising international tensions. But what he expects to happen twenty years or more thereafter is explored through three stories or scenarios. The NIC report discusses the lessons these scenarios provide regarding potential opportunities and trade-offs in creating the future, rather than just responding to it.

It is possible to do long-term forecasting, starting with now and trying to work forwards into the far future, on the basis of mega-trends in technology, national wealth, population and so on. That quickly runs into the problem that there are too many possible intersecting options that humankind might or might not take to allow an overall estimate of where we will end up. That problem is getting worse with the interdependencies that globalization has brought. One of the fascinating aspects of the US NIC report quoted above is the use of 'backcasting' as well as forecasting, working backwards from a number of postulated long-term scenarios to identify the factors that might influence which of those futures we might end up near. It is important in all such work to challenge conventional wisdom (an approach known as red teaming). When preparing the report the US NIC team visited thirty-five countries, including the UK, and canvassed ideas from academics and former practitioners such as myself, as well as serving government and military planners.

Using risk management in practice

A number of things have to go right in order for strategic warning to be translated into effective action at both national and international level, inside the private sector and in the home. Forecasts of risk need to be communicated effectively to those who can make use of the information. They in turn must be able to mobilize some kind of response to reduce, mitigate or transfer the risk. And there must be the capacity to learn lessons from experience of this process.

Advised by the assessments of the Joint Intelligence Committee, and by the National Risk Assessment[16] from the Civil Contingencies Secretariat, the UK's National Security Council, chaired by the Prime Minister, promulgates the strategic threat priorities for government.[17] The 2015 Risk Assessment identified a major human pandemic as one of the most significant national security risks (in terms of likelihood and impact) facing the UK. A test of plans in 2016 exposed major gaps in capability. By the time COVID-19 struck in 2020 there was at least a national biological security strategy in place, although shortcomings still emerged along with shortages of essential protective equipment.

A comparable role must be played by the boards of companies, charitable organizations and government agencies in ensuring that major risks are identified and monitored and that plans for managing the risks are in place. A useful lesson I have learned is to divide the risks into three groups. The first group consists of the risks that are outside the influence of the business, such as a major disease outbreak. These are known as the exogenous risks. The second group of risks are those inherent in the nature of the business: banks suffer fraud, retailers suffer pilfering or 'shrinkage' of stock, trucking companies have accidents and so on. The final group of risks are those that the company took on itself, such as investment in a major IT upgrade on which the viability of the whole enterprise depends.

There is nothing most companies can do to eliminate the risks in the first group. But they can conduct periodic impact assessments, and exercise contingency plans. Even MI6 got caught out in September 2000 when a PIRA terrorist fired a small rocket at their Vauxhall Cross headquarters and the police then declared the building a crime scene and refused to allow staff back in until their investigations were complete, a more than trivial problem for an organization that has to operate 24/7.

For the second group of risks, those inherent in the nature of the business, discussion should be around the systems of control – for example, for cash flow, and whether there is sufficient pooling or transfer of risk through insurance or commercial alliance or partnership.

For the third category, the questions a company board must ask itself are much more pointed. Since the future of the organization depends on managing such changes successfully, directors need to ensure they personally have visibility of progress and that they allocate enough of their time to ensuring that key change managers have access to expertise, the delegated authority and the finance needed for success.

We can all follow such a three-part discussion of the risks we face, even at the level of the family. Do we have sufficient medical insurance from work to cover unforeseen traffic and other accidents or do we need extra cover? Is there adequate holiday insurance? Who has to meet the upfront cost of cancellations due to external disruption (such as COVID-19 in 2020 or the shutdown in 2018 of the busy Gatwick airport in the UK due to illegal drone flying over the runway)? Who has spare keys to the car or house in case of loss?

Conclusions: strategic notice

Having strategic notice of possible futures means we will not be so surprised by surprise. In this chapter we have looked at the perils of surprise, at not having strategic notice, and at what it means to say something is likely to happen. We examined the nature of surprise itself, sudden crises and slow-burn crises, how to think about the likelihood of events, and strategies for managing their risk. We looked at some of the ways in which long-term risks can be spotted and at the importance of communicating the results to achieve an alerted, but not alarmed, public. To learn to live with the expectation of surprise we should:

- Search for strategic notice of relevant developments in technology, international and economic affairs, the environment and potential threats.
- Think in terms of the expected value of events and developments (probability times impact), not just their likelihood.
- Think about a register of your major risks and use a risk equation to identify and link the factors that contribute to the value of overall outcomes.
- Use strategic notice to spot opportunities as well as identify dangers.
- Accept that you will usually suffer tactical surprise even when you have avoided strategic surprise.
- Beware magical thinking, believing that one event occurs, or does not occur, as a result of another without plausible causation and thus wishing away what strategic notice is telling you.
- Group risks into those you can do nothing about (but might want to prepare for and exercise contingency plans); those that go with the territory (where you can take sensible precautions); and those risks that accompany your major decisions (since your future depends on them you need to ensure they get the right priority and attention).

PART TWO

Three lessons in checking our reasoning

5

Lesson 5: It is our own demons that are most likely to mislead us

'Well, you can kiss my ass in Macy's window' was the brutal one-line dismissal by Ava, the CIA's Iraq Group Chief, of the over-reliance of US Biological Warfare (BW) expert analysts on a single human intelligence source on Saddam Hussein's BW programmes, codenamed Curveball. When she challenged the experts' faith in using information from that source, in her words, 'they looked at me like pigs looking at a wristwatch'.[1] Although not a weapons specialist, Ava, as an experienced intelligence officer, could sense that there might be a problem with the source. Her intervention was bound to be unpopular. Not least, pressure was mounting from the Bush administration to prepare for the invasion of Iraq and to justify this by revealing the extent of Saddam's holdings of illegal weapons of mass destruction. That included exposing his past use of BW weapons – deliberately engineered to spread lethal and incapacitating disease and among the most horrific known to man – and what were assessed to be his current capabilities.

Curveball seemed the answer to the BW experts' prayers. He was an Iraqi chemical engineer who had turned up in a German refugee camp claiming to have worked on Saddam's BW programmes and ready to spill the beans. To the old operational hands in the CIA and Britain's MI6 he seemed too good to be true. The German overseas intelligence service, the

BND, took charge of Curveball and between January 2000 and September 2001 shared almost 100 reports based on his debriefing with defence intelligence in the US and UK. Crucially, Curveball claimed that Iraq had built several mobile BW production units and that one of those units had begun production of lethal BW agents as early as 1997. A diagram of a truck adapted to be a mobile BW production unit based on Curveball's information was even included in the presentation by Colin Powell, Secretary of State, to the UN Security Council as part of the US justification for war.

The problem was, those mobile BW units did not exist. Curveball had invented them. The experts fell for his story.

After the war Curveball, real name Rafid Ahmed Alwan al-Janabi, was tracked down by journalists. He admitted that he had lied in his reporting, and said that he had watched in shock as it was used to justify the war. He told them he fabricated tales of mobile BW trucks and clandestine factories in an attempt to bring down the Saddam Hussein regime, from which he had fled. He added: 'Maybe I was right, maybe I was not right . . . they gave me this chance. I had the chance to fabricate something to topple the regime. I and my sons are proud of that . . . '[2]

Before the invasion of Iraq in 2003 CIA and MI6 humint (human intelligence) professionals had developed doubts about the credibility of Curveball, not least the CIA Iraq section chief, Ava, quoted above, and her counterparts in London. Although believing that much of Curveball's reporting was technically credible (he was after all a chemical engineer), they were not convinced that he was a wholly reliable source since not all his reporting checked out, and elements of his behaviour struck them as typical of individuals whom intelligence agencies would normally assess as fabricators.

One obstacle in checking out their suspicions was that the BND would not provide US or UK analysts with direct access to Curveball. The analysts did not know whether Curveball had been offered inducements, such as a German passport and assistance with resettlement. Nor how the questioning had been conducted. They wondered if the witness had been inadvertently led and had been able to infer what US analysts were most keen to know – and thus what information would most please them (always a problem with defectors). There were rumours about his drinking. Several inconsistencies were detected in Curveball's reporting which heightened doubts about his reliability. Disturbingly, the quality of intelligence from him seemed to get better over time. That might be his increasing confidence in the good faith of those questioning him, or it might be he was working out what to say that would produce the best reward.

Great efforts were made by the US and UK intelligence services to check out Curveball. Investigation into his background and university records revealed that he had indeed been trained in Iraq as a chemical engineer. He was known to have been involved on the fringes of Saddam's 1990 BW programme. On the one hand that made his reporting of what was currently going on entirely credible from a technical point of view; on the other hand, it put him in an ideal position to exaggerate or even make up details if he so chose.

In London, analysts pored over aerial photographs of Iraq trying to identify the locations for prohibited activity described by Curveball to see if his stories stacked up. One site seemed to be on the wrong side of the river from where he described it – perhaps a slip of memory. Or perhaps an ominous sign that he was fabricating. In 2001 Curveball's description of a facility that he claimed was involved in the mobile BW programme was contradicted by imagery of the site, which showed a wall blocking the view to what Curveball had claimed were the mobile trailers. Analysts explained away this discrepancy by speculating that the wall spotted by imagery might be a temporary structure put up by the Iraqis to deceive US satellite reconnaissance efforts. In another instance, Iraq was said to be filling BW warheads at a transportable facility near Baghdad. When imagery was unable to locate the transportable BW systems at the reported site, analysts assumed this was another example of Iraq hiding activities from US satellite over-passes. There is a very human tendency to search for or interpret information in a way that confirms one's preconceptions. It is comforting to think the information coming in bears out our prior beliefs. Psychologists call this *confirmation bias*. Confirmation bias is accentuated by the tendency for people to scrutinize fiercely information which contradicts their prior beliefs (sometimes known as *disconfirmation bias*) while accepting too readily without criticism information that is consistent with their preconceptions.

Placing too much weight on Curveball's reporting on biological weapons was not the only error that Western intelligence encountered in trying to assess the state of Iraq's capabilities. Analysts also misinterpreted the intelligence that was being reported on Saddam's chemical weapons programmes. The analysts misled themselves, not, in that case, through being subject to deliberate deception, but through a series of individual and collective cognitive errors. Burned by the experience of having been deceived by Saddam over the extent of his WMD capabilities, as uncovered by UN inspectors after the first Gulf War, analysts started with the strong presumption that he was playing the same game in 2002. They felt able to dismiss contrary indications that Iraq might not actively be pursuing its prohibited programmes by chalking these indicators up to Iraq's well-known denial and deception efforts. That outlook, that Saddam must be hiding prohibited materials not surrendered after the first Gulf War in 1991, was shared across all Western intelligence agencies.

Such was the strength of this pre-war 'group think' that when eventually UN inspectors returned to Iraq in 2003, the US and UK analysts were slow to admit openly to their bosses and to each other any secret thoughts they might have been harbouring that the reason the inspectors were not finding the predicted stocks of BW and CW weapons and material was because they no longer existed inside Iraq.

In hindsight, a key lesson was the failure to distinguish by the Bush and Blair governments between those parts of the intelligence assessments that were based on hard evidence (such as on Saddam's prohibited missile-testing capabilities) and those that rested on extrapolations and assumptions made by the analysts confident they already knew the answer. As Colin Powell lectured CIA analysts after the war, in future he wanted them to 'Tell me what you know. Tell me what you don't know. And tell me what you think', to which a highly experienced analyst added: 'And make clear which is which.'[3]

Another conclusion that is evident is that once suspicion has taken hold it breeds yet more suspicion. Saddam Hussein found this out in 2002 as he tried to persuade the West that he no longer retained the chemical and biological weapons capability that he had used against Iran and against his own people, and that he had gone to such lengths previously to conceal. His assurances to the West that work on those programmes had stopped, while failing to comply with the UN's demands for full accounting of his past capability, were not surprisingly disbelieved. As the CIA's Director, George Tenet, wrote in his memoirs: 'Before the war, we didn't understand that *he* was bluffing, and he did not understand that *we were not*.'[4]

The need to check our reasoning

The errors in the intelligence assessments over Iraq were not the result of conscious politicization of intelligence by the analysts to please their customers. They resulted from the great capacity of the mind for self-deception and magical thinking, believing we are seeing what deep down at an emotional level we want to see. It is then natural to find reasons to rationalize that belief.

One of the advantages of using the four-part SEES model, as discussed in the chapters of Part I, is that it makes it easier to spot at each level the cognitive biases that lead us to see what we want to see. We met this phenomenon in Chapter 1 with the example of how British Second World War deception efforts fooled the German High Command by feeding them information that they wanted to believe. We saw a different form of cognitive bias in Chapter 2 when policymakers anxious not to get involved militarily resisted seeing the developing Bosnian conflict as potential genocide. In Chapter 3 we identified the cognitive problem of mirror-imaging on the part of Western analysts failing to forecast how the communist regime in Moscow would react to the reform movement in Czechoslovakia in 1968. In Chapter 4 we had the example of the head of Israeli military intelligence convincing himself he had a way of providing strategic notice of Egyptian readiness to consider an attack on Israel, an error in imagination that was almost literally fatal for the state of Israel.

The vulnerability of analysts to cognitive biases was systematically examined in the 1970s and 1980s by Richards 'Dick' Heuer, a long-term CIA intelligence officer with forty-five years of experience to call on. In his major work, *The Psychology of Intelligence Analysis*, Heuer warned that prior knowledge of the prevalence of individual cognitive biases does not seem to stop people falling under their spell.[5] He argued that there have therefore to be systematic checks introduced to manage the risks they pose. After high-level inquiries into the evident intelligence failure to warn before the 1973 Yom Kippur war, the Israeli government set up a standing 'devil's advocate' group within military intelligence, staffed by the best analysts, with direct access when required to the Prime Minister and a remit to adopt a contrarian approach and to be expected to challenge the prevailing orthodoxy.[6] The motto of the group is 'Ipcha Mistabra', in Aramaic, translatable as 'The opposite is most likely' or 'On the contrary . . .'

The good news is that there is a great deal of experimental psychological research available, as well as much practical experience from government and business, about the many cognitive traps and illusions that can ensnare us whether at the level of the individual, of the work group or of the institution:

- *Individual.* Cognitive and emotional biases affect us as individuals. That is part of the human condition. These biases are usually not evident to us at the time, but a good supervisor or colleague will probably become aware of them if sensitized to what to look out for. Understandably, it may not be easy for us to acknowledge how our reasoning may have been influenced without our being consciously aware.
- *Group.* Groups can develop their own distinctive dynamics, the equivalent of a collective personality

that is more than just the sum of those of each of us in the group. Members of a group both consciously and unconsciously exercise a reciprocal influence on each other, such as a pressure for conformity or a desire for closure. The existence of such distinctive group behaviours has been established in many therapeutic settings by psychologists and psychoanalysts[7] – for example, in relation to hostile feelings towards the 'outgroup', i.e. those who are not members of the group.

- *Institutional.* Internal processes, rules, hierarchies and power structures can unconsciously influence the judgements and decisions reached by an analytic group, just as they can affect the institution's interaction with its stakeholders or the public. Dynamics at the level of the organization arise from the way that those within have internalized its culture, history and structure. There may be complicated psychic relationships between the different groups of people within the organization, such as between intelligence analysts and policymakers, or generalists and specialists, or civilians and uniformed services. There may also be important dynamics generated by the way the institution interacts with other organizations, such as the inevitable differences of perspective between law enforcement and intelligence agencies working on understanding the same threat. These influences are hard to pin down for those who are thoroughly accustomed to living within the organization's culture. Critics of the impact of institutional dynamics tend to be dismissed with 'that is just the way things are done round here'.

Under each of these three headings we can now identify the most significant cognitive biases to watch out for when engaged in significant reasoning.

Cognitive biases and influences on the individual

Psychologists have replicated in experiments under a range of different conditions the existence of specific cognitive biases in individual subjects carrying out perceptual and other mental tasks.[8] Some have entered into everyday speech, with labels such as cognitive dissonance, whereby the mind finds it hard to hold at the same time the favoured story and the contrary evidence that it might not be true. Such mental tension on the part of the intelligence analysts is liable to be transferred to the national security policymakers and operational commanders who can also fall victim to cognitive dissonance.[9] And we are all liable to have to wrestle with inconsistent beliefs, often suffering stress as a result.

In a study for the UK JIC in 1980 a seasoned intelligence professional, Doug Nicoll (who had worked during the Second World War on German Army and Air Force Enigma in Hut 6 at Bletchley Park and risen to be Deputy Director of its successor organization, GCHQ), concluded that even the most experienced analyst (and we can generalize this to all of us when we are faced with problems to solve) has cognitive blind spots, especially when faced with incomplete or ambiguous information. Nicoll identified six specific biases that he held responsible for why Western governments had too often been caught out when faced by foreign aggression.[10]

Mirror-imaging. This is the trap to be wary of on a first date: the presumption that your prospective partner is bound to feel the same way as you do about what makes for an exciting evening out. Nicoll identified the unconscious tendency to assume that factors which would weigh heavily in the United Kingdom would be equally serious constraints on countries ruled by one-party governments or under the control of a single leader. Analysts had, for example, too readily assumed that the weight of international opinion was a factor that would affect the formation of policy in autocracies to the same extent as it did in the democracies. Nicoll observed that public servants brought up in the post-war liberal democracies 'found it difficult to believe that the potential aggressor would indeed find the use of force politically acceptable'.[11] Margaret Thatcher at the time also did not disguise her belief that there was an inbuilt tendency for diplomats to over-emphasize the role of peaceful negotiation in solving international problems. She once cruelly said on television when discussing the Foreign Office: 'When I am out of politics, I'm going to run a business called "Rent-A-Spine".'[12]

Transferred judgement. This is the implicit assumption that others will think about and assess situations as you do. A mistake often made in showrooms, where you can too easily assume that the salesperson is thinking about the merits of the product on display in the same terms as you are and therefore has your interests at heart. Like mirror-imaging, this bias comes from an inability to put oneself inside the mind of the other. It can reflect unconscious cultural or racial stereotyping, as with the Vietnam War assessments by US logistics officers that it would not be possible for the North Vietnamese to bring sufficient supplies down the Ho Chi Minh jungle trail to sustain major offensives in the South, given US bombing. Earlier in Indo-China, French staff officers could not believe it would be possible for the Viet Minh to bring artillery to bear from the hills surrounding the isolated French base of Dien Bien Phu since that was not a feat they would have attempted. General Giáp calculated differently and in 1954 inflicted a humiliating defeat on the French forces, precipitating their withdrawal from Indo-China. After the war, Giáp concluded that French defeat had stemmed fundamentally from a failure by their commander, General Navarre, to understand the mind of his adversary: he had not realized that it was a people's war.[13] Perhaps the lesson we need to learn is two-fold: 'It is true we should avoid ethnocentrism, the idea that folks are all like us. But that doesn't mean we should indulge in condescending exoticism, the notion that *we* are strategic, modern and political whereas *they*, our benighted enemies, are visceral and primitive.'[14]

Perseveration. Nicoll saw that even with mounting evidence to the contrary analysts tended to stick with their original interpretation. In personal relationships this can be the questionable virtue of sticking by someone even when new evidence shows they are behaving as a heel. We remember their good qualities that first endeared them to us. The JIC in a developing crisis tended to make up its mind early and was resistant to changing it, downplaying any last-minute signals of the enemy's true intentions. Nicoll called this *perseveration*, from the psychological phenomenon whereby data (such as telephone numbers) if learned incorrectly the first time are more difficult subsequently to learn correctly. The medical profession also uses the term perseveration to describe an involuntary repetition of words or other acts long after the relevant stimulus has ceased. The bias affects policymakers too: even in the face of evidence that the policy is not working they will keep repeating the positive messages that led them to adopt it in the first place.

Perseveration can also be thought of as a special case of what psychologists would call *choice-supportive bias*. That is the tendency of the individual, after coming to a judgement from a choice of alternatives, to remember the positive features of their chosen hypothesis and to forget the negative indicators. We remember the best times with those who have been our friends over a long period of years. Without realizing it the analysts will end up skewing future assessments through having those features uppermost in their mind. That such an effect is shown in psychological experiments should be unsurprising. When a choice is made in good faith it is because the individual genuinely believed at the time that it was the right choice. As a result, it is the reasons that led to that choice that are more likely to stick in the memory and to come to the surface later since they help minimize any lingering feelings of doubt. As a general lesson it is unsurprising that most of us prefer to avoid the pain of regret at the choices we have made.

War as a deliberate act. Nicoll showed from his case studies that armed aggression is usually a deliberate act planned in advance and, he concluded, would very rarely be the result of response to some accidental crisis or by opportunistic chance. The JIC failure to forecast that Saddam Hussein in 1991 would invade Kuwait is an example. Saddam wanted to annul Iraq's substantial debts to Kuwait for financial support during the earlier Iran–Iraq War. Starting a war deliberately for such a reason did not seem credible to the Western analysts (mirror-imaging), especially given that there was Arab League mediation in progress and diplomatic optimism that a settlement could be reached. This would similarly be the case for our natural reluctance to believe that a friend might deliberately betray our confidences for their own advantage.

Limited information. Nicoll had plenty of experience over his long intelligence career of the difficulty of assessing what might happen next in circumstances where there was very little secret intelligence to illuminate the situation. The cases he examined were all ones where the JIC had been surprised by the outcome. These tended to involve countries and regions in which the priority for intelligence collection had been low precisely because aggression was not expected. This is a vicious circle we can all experience: failure to have strategic notice of trouble ahead means a lower priority for our attention, so the information we need to warn us is less likely to be spotted when it is needed and therefore the risk of unwelcome surprises is greater.

Deliberate deception. Several of Nicoll's case studies featured deliberate deception and he advised analysts always to look for attempts at deception by the potential aggressor, and sometimes by the victim trying to exaggerate their military strength to discourage an attack. These might be simple measures such as portraying troop movements as an exercise or very complex multi-dimensional deception programmes. A nation committing itself to military operations will almost certainly do everything in its power to preserve tactical surprise as to the time and place of operations through deception, even when as with D-Day in 1944 there could be no strategic surprise over the intention to open the second front in Europe.[15] The Soviet Union had already successfully used deception in battles such as Stalingrad, and its belief in the power of deception must have been reinforced by the success of the D-Day landings. The teaching of deception (*maskirovka*) became an important part of the syllabus of the Soviet military staff college (the Frunze military academy) and for training intelligence officers of the GRU and KGB. Detecting deception is so important in analysis (and today for all of us in spotting 'fake news' and deceptive propaganda) that Chapter 7 is devoted to the topic.

The Nicoll Report was discussed by the JIC at its meeting on 4 March 1982, and within a few weeks a copy of the report had been sent to the Prime Minister, with assurances from the JIC that the Committee considered itself alert to the lessons to be learned. As often is the case, history cruelly intervened. Just a few days later, the Argentine military Junta authorized the invasion of the Falkland Islands, and caught the UK by surprise. The UK had again fallen into the same traps as Nicoll had identified.

Doug Nicoll concluded with lessons in the need for care in the use of language in describing intelligence judgements (something much later that Lord Butler in his post-Iraq 2004 WMD inquiry found still wanting[16]). Nicoll emphasized the importance of policymakers understanding the meaning of phrases such as 'no evidence'. To take a contemporary example, an intelligence assessment today might state (as is very probably the case) that there is currently no evidence of terrorists within the UK having access to a surface-to-air missile with which a civilian airliner might be shot down. Such a statement does not mean that the intelligence community intends to convey a reassuring message that the risk of that happening over the next few years can be ignored (and so measures to detect such weapons being smuggled into the country are not needed) but only that at the moment there is no evidence of this having happened. A general lesson worth bearing in mind is that the answer you get depends upon the question you asked.

Group behaviours

Problems of bias also arise as a consequence of group dynamics. We have all heard of *group think* in which the desire for harmony or conformity within a group leads to judgements being nodded through without proper scrutiny. Most people want to feel they are valued members of a group and fear losing the respect and approbation of colleagues. When an individual group member has an insufficient sense of self-worth or of status within the group, then the individual may play to the group gallery and suppress private doubts. There are many examples of such feelings having inhibited dissenting voices. Resistance to an argument is often the result of a state of cognitive dissonance in which excuses are readily found for not accepting new relevant information that would conflict with a state of belief to which the group or individual is emotionally committed.[17] The harder it may have been to reach the original conclusion the more the individual group or individual analyst is likely to be invested in the result and thus to resist unconsciously the discomfort of having to hold in the mind a contrary view.

There is for most of us an inclination to be more likely to believe opinions if we know many other people do. This is called the *bandwagon effect*, the tendency that encourages the individual to conform to consensus. In group discussions it helps to have one or more contrarians, those who by inclination like swimming against the tide and thus help surface all the relevant arguments. That effect can, when necessary, be contrived by the leader of the group choosing an individual to be *the devil's advocate* with acknowledged licence to take contrary positions regardless of hierarchy. Or the whole group can indulge in *red teaming* to explore the problem from the adversary's point of view. A different group (Team B) could be asked independently to examine the material seen by the first group (Team A) and come to their own conclusions on the same evidence. There is a danger of politicization here. If the customer for some piece of analysis does not like the outcome, they may call for another analytic group to be set up and invited to examine the evidence independently. If, for example, the conclusions of the original analysis were seen as too cautious, then it is likely that the members of the new group will be chosen for their boldness.

The leader of an analytic group can make a huge difference to its work especially by setting reasonable expectations and insisting at the outset upon the standards of debate and argument to which members must conform, and ensuring that the group too becomes self-aware of its own thinking processes. Being open about the risk of bias within a group is the best antidote to cognitive failures. Poor group leaders are, however, liable to become the focus for negative feelings if the task of the group is not going well.

In the conduct of an analytic group, the leader has to insist that all possible explanations are explored. There is a known psychological tendency (called *the ambiguity effect*) to skip over possible hypotheses for which there is little or no direct reporting, and thus seem unjudgeable, and unknowingly to spend the time discussing hypotheses for which there is evidence. A rush to early judgement can be avoided by insisting upon working systematically through the evidence using structured analytic techniques, as already described in Chapter 2. But there will come a point in a prolonged debate in which the strong urge for the psychological relief of closure will come upon the group. In such circumstances taking time out to have a breather, to let interpersonal tensions relax and minds refocus, is usually a good idea, or even suggesting the group sleep on the issues and return the next morning to check whether they have had any second thoughts.

As the 2005 Robb–Silberman US Senate Inquiry into the intelligence misjudgements over Iraq concluded:

> We do not fault the Intelligence Community for formulating the hypothesis, based on Saddam Hussein's conduct, that Iraq had retained an unconventional weapons capability and was working to augment this capability. Nor do we fault the Intelligence Community for failing to uncover what few Iraqis knew; according to the Iraq Survey Group only a handful of Saddam Hussein's closest advisors were aware of some of his decisions to halt work on his nuclear program and to destroy his stocks of chemical and biological weapons. Even if an extraordinary intelligence effort had gained access to one of these confidants, doubts would have lingered.
>
> But with all that said, we conclude that the Intelligence Community could and should have come much closer to assessing the true state of Iraq's weapons programs than it did. It should have been less wrong – and, more importantly, it should have been more candid about what it did not know. In particular, it should have recognized the serious – and knowable – weaknesses in the evidence it accepted as providing hard confirmation that Iraq had retained WMD capabilities and programs . . .[18]

Another way of describing this general lesson about being less wrong is to highlight the need to take time out to double-check the thinking. But it is also likely that the more important the issue the more urgent will be the calls for information. It will take conscious and deliberate effort, and courage, of the group leader to insist upon going back over all the workings to check the reasoning and weight of evidence.

Institutional dynamics

Institutions have their own distinctive cultures, in which corporate behaviours considered correct get passed on from generation to generation. That can be a great strength in adversity but can also lead to a bias when it comes to interpreting the world. Institutions also exhibit personality traits and suffer from time to time the equivalent of nervous breakdowns or exhibit paranoia towards other organizations. National intelligence and law enforcement agencies around the world, for example, are notorious for feuding between themselves and refusing to share information on their cases. In the case of Curveball that opened this chapter, after questions about Curveball's credibility had begun to emerge, a CIA operational officer in February 2003 sent a message to Pentagon officials expressing concern that Curveball had not been vetted. The next day the Pentagon official who received that message forwarded it by electronic mail to a subordinate, requesting input to answer the CIA's query, saying that he was '*shocked*' by the CIA's suggestion that Curveball might be unreliable. The reply (which was inadvertently sent to the CIA) observed that 'CIA is up to their old tricks' and that the CIA did not 'have a clue' about the process by which Curveball's information was passed from the BND. That is an example of longstanding bureaucratic rivalry in action, resulting in the rationalizing away of awkward information.

There are inevitable cultural differences between domestic and external services, and between essentially human and technical services, and again between predominantly military and civilian organizations, and finally between those security organizations with law enforcement powers and functions and those that are primarily covert intelligence gatherers. Each of these distinctions – and the secrecy and danger that surround their work – can generate tensions, not least reflecting the sometimes very different personality types of the people they employ. These are the tribes that have to come together in analytic groups to draft all source intelligence assessments. Understanding the indirect influences that their institutions exert on their members is important knowledge for the leader of an analytic group.

Cognitive biases in everyday life

The individual, group and institutional biases that Nicoll identified for his case studies of intelligence failures can be seen as special cases of more general cognitive biases that we can see in business and everyday life. These biases are very common in political debate, as they are in intelligence analysis. The advent of social media with applications such as Twitter has, as we will discuss in Chapter 10, opened the way to deliberate exploitation of confirmation bias to sell political ideas and products alike.

A lesson that the founder of scientific intelligence in the Second World War, Professor R. V. Jones, highlighted (he called it Crow's law) was do not believe what you want to believe until you know what you need to know.[19] Those who subconsciously need the reassurance of confirmation would be already expecting intelligence to confirm their view (this common bias is known as the *observer-expectancy effect*).

Another example is what is called *inattentional blindness*. Looking is not the same as seeing. A related problem (known as the *focusing effect*) is that you can end up so focused on a task that you fail to spot what is going on around you. If you are not one of the 20 million who have already watched the YouTube video asking the viewer to count the fast passes between a team of basketball players I invite you to try it.[20] Given that tricky task of counting basketball passes, the first time most people see the video they fail to take note of the person dressed in a gorilla costume slowly walking across the court. A helicopter view of the basketball court would certainly reveal what a close focus on the passes being made by individual players will miss, that there is something beyond the immediate game going on.

In a comparable way close focus on what we already know can be at the expense of recognizing new information. This is a phenomenon known as *attentional bias*. Experimental evidence shows it affects particularly individuals who are in a state of anxiety in relation to material that is seen as threatening, or those suffering from depression likewise who may have their focus unconsciously drawn to examples of negativity. What you fear most will grab your attention.

Psychological experiments also show the tendency for an item that appears to be in some way exceptional to be more likely to stick in the memory. We are liable to register and retain in our memory news of plane crashes as dramatic events but not to take in the implications of the tens of millions of miles flown without an accident. We should not therefore be surprised that there is nervousness about flying. The tendency is known today as the *Von Restorff effect* after the pre-war German child psychologist who first demonstrated it systematically. It is easy to show by giving someone a varied list of names or items to remember. If some of these are readily distinguished from others then those will be the ones most likely to be recalled to memory.[21] The most striking intelligence material is liable to make more of an impact than its meaning may deserve. A case in point was the intelligence report received just before the war in Iraq which indicated that chemical munitions could be with military units and ready for firing within 20–45 minutes. This report was in itself unexceptional as a reference to the previous Iraqi battlefield capability, but after it was mentioned in the published British government dossier, the headline in the *Sun* newspaper was 'Brits 45 mins from doom' and in the *Star* 'Mad Saddam ready to attack: 45 minutes from a chemical war'.[22] It is those memorable reports that are likely to feature in discussion between intelligence chiefs and their ministerial masters, and between ministers and the media.

Managing the risk of cognitive bias

This chapter has been about the cognitive biases that can get in the way of our everyday thinking. We can all understand that they exist and why we might be susceptible to them. But managing the risk that they represent is much harder. That should not surprise us as most of the biases identified in this chapter operate at the unconscious level of the mind, and by definition are therefore not usually accessible to us. Having a developed academic understanding of them from reading textbooks is no guarantee that we will not still be susceptible to them. As the report of a 1977 CIA seminar on bias in intelligence analysis concluded: 'Personal biases are the most troublesome. They are frequently unique and hard to detect.'[23]

The best antidote to cognitive biases such as group think is for the group to discuss openly the danger such biases represent. A good group leader can encourage challenge from within the group, and pose the question: *Are we falling into group think here?* (Which will normally elicit laughter and lighten any tension there may be over reaching a conclusion.) A process of self-recognition of common cognitive biases can be developed whereby individuals develop first an intellectual understanding of these phenomena (and a historical feel for how they matter) and then through working with others, preferably with a trained facilitator, come to an understanding that they too might be subject to them and how they might recognize when that is happening. But resistance is to be expected when others suggest that we have fallen into one of these errors. What is most important in my experience in managing the risk to the SEES process is to have a 'safe space' where the dangers of bias can be discussed as a matter of professionalism without arousing a defensive feeling on the part of the participants that they are being expected to admit to personal weaknesses. We all suffer from cognitive biases.

Conclusions: mastering our internal demons of bias and prejudice

It is our own demons that are most likely to mislead our reasoning. In this chapter we examined vulnerability to our cognitive biases and prejudices and how they prevent us thinking straight. If we want to learn to think correctly we should:

- Accept that completely objective analysis is impossible since we are human, and have to interpret reality for ourselves. But we can try to be as independent, honest and neutral in our analytic judgements as we can.
- What you see or hear, or fail to see or hear, reflects your state of mind and degree of attention.

- Try to make explicit implicit biases and prejudices, identifying the assumptions we are making in our reasoning.
- Recognize that cognitive errors arise at the individual, group and institutional levels and that they may come together in the pressures on the individual from 'group think'.
- Do not believe what you want to believe until you know what you need to know. Remember that the answer you get is likely to depend upon the question you asked.
- Recognize the sign of displacement activity that goes with mental stress and how cognitive dissonance increases resistance to taking in new information.
- Beware transferred judgements and mirror-imaging in imputing motives to others.
- Keep an open mind and be prepared to change it on Bayesian principles when new evidence arrives.

6

Lesson 6: We are all susceptible to obsessive states of mind

James Jesus Angleton was fond of using T. S. Eliot's phrase 'the wilderness of mirrors' to describe the deceptive world he inhabited for twenty turbulent years as the chief of the CIA's counter-intelligence staff. At Yale, Angleton had edited a poetry review called *Furioso* that published works by T. S. Eliot. So it shouldn't surprise us that he found resonance in Eliot's poem *Gerontion* from which that phrase comes. The poem also speaks of 'Cunning passages and contrived corridors' and continues: 'What will the spider do, suspend its operations, will the weevil delay?' Angleton obsessed over what he imagined was the Soviet spy-chief, the spider spinning a web of deceit and sending communist weevils to bore into the fabric of the CIA.

Such was the imagined reach of the Soviet spider that Angleton came to believe that major international developments such as détente and the Sino-Soviet split were elaborate Soviet deception plots. Even more concerning, he held the USSR responsible for the assassination of President Kennedy, as well as alleging they had murdered the leader of the British Labour Party, Hugh Gaitskell, to enable Harold Wilson, who he believed was a KGB agent, to replace him. These plots, he concluded, must have involved high-level treachery on the part of senior officers in the CIA and MI5, stretching all the way up to the Head of MI5, whom he caused to be placed under surveillance as a suspected Soviet agent. Angleton argued that Soviet double agents were being sent to the West as weevils to rot the intelligence fruit, and to throw counter-intelligence officers like him off the true scent. In pursuit of them Angleton was responsible for ordering the lengthy unlawful detention and coercive interrogation of a genuinely valuable defector from the KGB, and blighting (and in some case wrecking) the careers of talented US and British intelligence officers.[1]

Tragically, the damage Angleton inflicted lived on after him. The revulsion felt by many senior operational CIA officers against the Angleton witch-hunts (his assumed Soviet deception masterplan became known by CIA sceptics as 'The Monster Plot') led to an understandable but misguided downgrading of the importance attached to counter-intelligence work. The result was that years later, when there really was a well-placed spy inside the CIA, Aldrich Ames, who sold vital secrets to the KGB for cash to fund his extravagant lifestyle, it took far longer to unmask him than it should have.

The Angleton case has much to teach us. It is an example of how even a highly talented individual can become emotionally unbalanced and as a result fall victim to paranoid thinking. Such an obsessive conspiratorial outlook can be thought of like the perspective of an ant trapped on a Möbius strip. A Möbius strip is where a length of paper is given a half-twist and the ends joined together to form a loop. There is then only one surface and one edge on the three-dimensional object you hold in your hand. However long the ant marches along the strip, however many times it climbs over the boundary, it cannot get to another side. It will always end up following its own footsteps. For as long as the ant remains on the surface there is no external perspective to lead it to recognize the twisted loop it is on. The lesson the ant on the Möbius strip needs to learn is that only evidence from outside can convince it that it is stuck on a conspiratorial one-sided loop.

The Möbius loop conspiracy mindset has much in common with that of cults and ideological fanatics. Today, society suffers from beliefs in many obsessive conspiracies encouraged by the exaggerating world of social media. We need to learn how to detect conspiracies, including those started by rumours deliberately manufactured and spread for malign purposes, and how to bring evidence to bear to diminish their power of attraction.

Angleton's career had started with great promise. He had quickly learned to be an effective counter-intelligence officer during the Second World War working with the US Office of Strategic Services (OSS) in London and then in Rome. His three years at school at Malvern College in England had given him a taste for classic English tailoring and conservative manners, and he fitted in easily with the public-school-educated MI6 officers he met in London – including, to his misfortune, the young Kim Philby. He was inducted into the deepest secrets of the British war effort, including the Double Cross system, which used captured and turned German agents in the UK to send back false information to the German High Command,[2] and the Bletchley Park decrypts of German intelligence traffic that showed how the falsehoods of British deception were being swallowed.

If Britain could so systematically manipulate German perceptions, Angleton must have asked himself, was the Soviet Union already using strategic deception to gull the West as to its true hostile intentions? He convinced himself the answer had to be yes, and that it had started back in the early days after the Russian Revolution. Moscow must also be using double agents, officers of the Soviet intelligence agencies pretending to be defectors, to spread disinformation and to send Western counter-intelligence officers chasing non-existent spies, while the real traitors continued to pass US secrets to Moscow undisturbed – a view that would understandably have been reinforced by Angleton's knowledge of the Soviet espionage effort in the US against the Manhattan Project to design and build the first atomic bomb.

After the war, as staff officer to the overseas operations director of the CIA, Angleton resumed his close friendship with Kim Philby, now MI6's highly thought-of representative in Washington, touted as a future Chief of the Secret Service. During their boozy weekly get-togethers, Angleton freely shared many of the CIA's operational secrets. Imagine his shock when he learned in 1951 that the FBI now (correctly) considered Philby – his wartime mentor, confidant and drinking buddy – to be a Soviet double agent.[3] That shock seems to have tipped Angleton over from an attitude of critical scepticism appropriate for a counter-intelligence officer into a delusional state of mind. Dedicated passion for the job became unhealthy obsession. Once the assumption of a deep-deception masterplan on the part of the Soviet spider had taken hold, it had to follow that most of what Western intelligence thought it knew of Soviet activity was actually, like the British Double Cross system, the result of deception. It was Philby's face that Angleton must have imagined on the Soviet spider continuing to weave Moscow's web of deception.[4]

The Angleton story illustrates vividly how a conspiratorial world view can come into being. In his case, the precipitating factor in his obsession was probably his strong feelings of betrayal by Philby, amplified by the conditions of great secrecy that surround spy hunting. Believing in the great Soviet masterplan would have eased the emotional pain of Philby's betrayal and assuaged his feelings of guilt over his own gullibility. Angleton's relentless single-minded pursuit of spies thereafter would have felt deeply reparative.

But the story goes deeper. It proves too how judgements become increasingly distorted once they enter a conspiratorial loop. In 1954 Angleton was made the Chief of the CIA Counter-Intelligence Staff, a post he then held for twenty years. He saw a major opportunity in the rare defection in 1961 of a KGB officer. Major Anatoliy Golitsyn of the KGB was not a huge catch in terms of counter-intelligence information. He had an inflated view of himself (he demanded to be taken to meet President Kennedy) and had a highly exaggerated view of KGB deception capabilities, dropping elusive hints about Soviet agents inside the CIA. For Angleton, however, Golitsyn was offering a window into the KGB spider's assumed masterplan. The two played off each other, with Angleton eagerly listening to Golitsyn's fantasies and Golitsyn exploiting the attention from Angleton to make himself appear to be a more important defector than he was.

Against all basic security rules Angleton allowed Golitsyn to study the CIA files of US officers who might fit the characteristics of a major spy within the CIA. Golitsyn helped Angleton identify several suspects, whose careers were halted without their knowing the reason why. Angleton believed Golitsyn when he warned that, such was his importance in Moscow's eyes as a traitor to the Soviet intelligence services, they would not only despatch assassins to kill him, but also send out double agents as defectors who would have instructions to persuade the US that Golitsyn and his views could not be trusted. When, henceforth, Soviet defectors offered their services they must therefore be treated as human KGB weevils to be uncovered, disbelieved and crushed, whatever the cost.

By unfortunate coincidence another KGB officer defected two years later. Lieutenant Colonel Yuriy Nosenko was almost everything that Golitsyn was not. Well connected in Moscow, a drinking companion of the General in charge of the KGB Internal Security Directorate, he had many genuine counter-intelligence secrets to reveal. He had served in the department monitoring American officials in Moscow and revealed how the KGB had succeeded in penetrating the US Moscow Embassy. His initial information also led to the uncovering of a major spy ring inside the US Army and the unmasking of a clerk in the Admiralty in London who had been blackmailed into working for the KGB (the Vassall affair).

What made the arrival of Nosenko even more timely was that he told his debriefers that he had seen a KGB file on Lee Harvey Oswald, arrested by the FBI for the assassination two months earlier of President Kennedy but then murdered three days later by a Texan strip club owner, Jack Ruby. Many in the US had suspected a Soviet hand in the Kennedy assassination, something Moscow had strongly denied. The Nosenko account was reassuring that Oswald, a former US marine, had indeed offered his services to the Soviet Union some years previously, but the KGB, having concluded that he was mentally unstable, had refused further contact with him.

Angleton convinced Nosenko's case officer that Nosenko was the double agent whom Golitsyn had predicted would be sent to muddy the waters. If Nosenko's story implied there had been no Soviet involvement in the Kennedy assassination, it was the proof that was required that there had been. Angleton therefore instructed the CIA to imprison Nosenko at one of their facilities in the US. They subjected him to coercive interrogation to get him to confess to being a double agent. This included two years in sensory isolation in a specially built concrete bunker, on a minimal diet without access to reading material.

But, despite being driven almost mad, Nosenko stuck to his story. That was because it wasn't a story. Nosenko was telling the truth.

Although Angleton never renounced his belief in the Soviet master conspiracy, other CIA officers became increasingly concerned over the weakness of the case against Nosenko.[5] Fresh inquiries provided new evidence confirming that he *was* a genuine defector. Apparent gaps in his story, inconsistencies Angleton had relied on, were due to slips of memory or mistranslations or simply prejudiced reporting. Nosenko was rehabilitated and compensated – and when the FBI were finally allowed access to him, he was still willing to provide new counter-intelligence leads that led to uncovering real Soviet spies in the US and Europe. Angleton was eased out into retirement with full honours, but with some embarrassment.

The Angleton obsession with Soviet subversion had a public face, too. In 1947, Hollywood and the US motion pictures industry fell under the blinkered gaze of the US House of Representatives Un-American Activities Committee, which feared communist sedition that threatened the form of government guaranteed by the US Constitution. Where better to look, thought the Committee, than the film industry with its liberal actors and screenwriters; refugees from Nazi Germany (many of whom were suspected of harbouring leftist leanings); and its reputation for decadent morals, including (in the Committee's eyes) 'unnatural', that is, homosexual, activities.

A moral panic over 'un-American' activities became, for a while, a form of inquisition. Nine days of hearings into alleged communist activities in the US film industry led to the blacklisting of actors, directors, producers and screenwriters who admitted to such sympathies, plus some who simply exercised their constitutional right to remain silent. Studios were intimidated by the general climate into refusing to employ those under suspicion, which in the end amounted to some 300 individuals. A few notable figures, such as Orson Welles and Charlie Chaplin, left the US to pursue careers elsewhere.

In parallel, the anti-communist activities of Senator Joe McCarthy and his Senate Permanent Sub-Committee on Investigations added another witch-hunt. Along with his lawyer, Roy Cohen (who acted for Donald Trump in the 1970s), McCarthy made accusations of widespread communist infiltration. McCarthyism has rightly entered the language to describe pejoratively the practice of investigating and accusing persons in positions of power or influence of disloyalty or subversion.[6]

The paranoia even crossed the Atlantic. Under the charismatic influence of Angleton, a small group of MI5 officers in London led by Peter Wright caught the obsession with continued long-term Soviet penetration.[7] Angleton sent the defector Golitsyn to London to brief them and help them uncover the Soviet weevils presumed also to be burrowing away within the British intelligence agencies.

Golitsyn made the extraordinary claim that he knew the former Labour Party leader Hugh Gaitskell, who had been a strong supporter of NATO and the US/UK relationship, to have been assassinated in 1963 by the KGB in order to pave the way for Gaitskell to be replaced as party leader by Harold Wilson. According to Golitsyn's way of thinking, this must have been because his successor, Harold Wilson, had already been recruited by the KGB. The only evidence claimed for this was that Wilson had had official contacts with the Soviet government during the war and had continued to be in contact with some of the senior wartime leaders he had dealt with in Moscow.

Unsurprisingly, when elected Prime Minister in 1964, Harold Wilson became aware of rumours that some in his own security service, MI5, believed he was a traitor and were conspiring to undermine him. In an increasingly fervid atmosphere in London, Peter Wright and a small group of counter-intelligence officers, under the influence of Angleton, now not only believed their Prime Minister was a Soviet agent but that their own MI5 bosses must be in on the conspiracy and covering it up.

This is an example of classic conspiracy loop thinking. The pro-NATO Gaitskell must have been murdered by the KGB so that he could be replaced by Wilson; who must be a KGB agent because of his wartime Russian contacts; the only reason Wilson had not been unmasked earlier must therefore be a cover-up at the highest level. Their search for the imagined traitors involved putting under intensive surveillance the Deputy Director of MI5 and then the Director General himself, Sir Roger Hollis.

After Hollis's death (of natural causes) the journalist Chapman Pincher, stoked by Peter Wright, continued to write about a massive Establishment/'deep-state' conspiracy he alleged had covered up treachery.[8] The Prime Minister, Margaret Thatcher, was eventually forced to make a statement to the

House of Commons in 1981 admitting that MI5's Director General, Roger Hollis, had indeed been investigated but stating categorically that the allegations were found to be false. We now know that he was cleared by high-level British government inquiries, confirmed by evidence from later KGB defectors. After the Cold War was over it was established that the Soviets had opened a file on Harold Wilson as a potential target for recruitment, given his legitimate wartime dealings with Soviet officials, and had given him a codename, Olding, but there has never been substance in Golitsyn's allegation that Wilson was recruited. Nor that Gaitskell was murdered.[9]

The Gaitskell conspiracy loop has yet another twist. Three years before his death, at the Labour Party conference in 1960, Hugh Gaitskell had opposed a motion on unilateral nuclear disarmament,[10] a motion supported by the communist leaders of some major trades unions. Gaitskell knew that the Labour attitude to the UK nuclear deterrent was the issue that would determine its suitability in the eyes of the electorate as a responsible future government. He was opposed ferociously by the pacifist wing of his party, which was led by the left-wing Tribune group. That group had been co-founded a decade earlier by the MP Tom Driberg, a former party chairman. Of those who had battled over the future of the UK's nuclear deterrent in the Scarborough conference hall, and in the smoky bars and pubs nearby, nobody knew that among them there was a paid covert agent of influence for the Soviet Union. Driberg was homosexual and had been blackmailed by the Czech intelligence service since the 1950s, as part of Soviet attempts to use agents of influence to manipulate left-leaning Western political circles.

There are, therefore, usually grains of truth upon which elaborate conspiracy theories are erected. But Driberg was an exceptionally rare Soviet success in penetrating the British left. For all the effort expended by the intelligence services of the Soviet Union and its Warsaw Pact allies, the number of agents of influence who could be recruited, or controlled by coercion or bribery, was tiny, especially when the policies they were required to support went against the grain of majority public opinion. But that was not how Angleton and his British followers had obsessively viewed the threat.

Conspiracy stories are hard to kill off. Part of their attraction is that they fulfil a need we all experience to have an explanation for disturbing events or changes in our lives which we fear and over which we feel we have not had control. For Peter Wright of MI5, that must have included the decline in the global position of the post-Empire UK, no doubt blamed on international communism, and the nation's continuing economic woes, blamed on domestic communists in the trade unions.

The nature of modern conspiracy thinking: the case of 9/11

From examples such as these we can draw out pointers to detecting obsessive thinking today. A conspiracy narrative is likely to conform to a number of stereotypes and contain common memes:[11]

- No evidence supports connecting the dots but the conspiracy theory.
- Near superhuman authority would be needed.
- The conspiracy is complex with many elements to go right.

- Large numbers of people who all need to keep the secret.
- The ambition of the conspiracy is grand (such as world domination).
- Fact and speculation are comingled.
- Small probable events are ratcheted up to larger improbable events.
- Sinister meanings are given to small events.

Most conspiracies would require extraordinary levels of authority to initiate and to get the necessary buy-in from the large number of people who would need to be involved to make it work and keep quiet about it. There will usually be an unreasonably large number of complex elements that have to go right to make a conspiracy happen. In real life, we know something usually goes wrong somewhere in such circumstances, but that never happens with conspiracies. The requirement for ever more elaborate reasoning to explain away contrary evidence is a sign that there is a conspiratorial loop involved.

One common meme is that the authorities are secretly allowing the public to be placed at risk for their own covert motives. A historical example is the oft-repeated allegation that Enigma decryption had revealed Coventry as the target of German bombing in 1942, but Churchill allowed the destruction of Coventry to take place rather than risk warning the city, an act that might have compromised the Enigma secret of Bletchley Park.[12] Not true, according to the researches in the archives by the official historian of intelligence during the Second World War, Cambridge University history professor Harry Hinsley, who showed that the decrypts did not mention which town was to be the target. Even when disproved, the meme continues to circulate, including on the stage with the play *One Night in November* by Alan Pollock highlighting the psychological dilemma that Churchill would have faced – had the story been true: an interesting example of the trend today to add fictional re-creation to historical events, in the interests of audience engagement, but at the expense of historical accuracy.

All of these features can be spotted in the conspiracy theories that circulate today about 9/11. There are claims that US intelligence and security authorities had advance knowledge of the attacks and chose to suppress it. When inquiries that have access to all the classified files and take extensive evidence, like the Congressional 9/11 Commission, conclude that that is untrue, the response of the believers in the conspiracy is that the 'deep state' is responsible for covering up the evidence and manipulated the files so that the Commission was misled. That no such evidence can be found (and that no whistleblowers have emerged to reveal their part in it) is for the believers simply further proof of how deep the conspiracy goes, the lesson of the conspiratorial loop.[13]

Other examples of 9/11 conspiracy thinking go further and blame Israel for masterminding the attacks, either with or without collusion on the part of the US 'deep state'. The motive is said variously to be to inflame US passions against the Muslim world, or to provoke US military intervention in the Middle East. There may well have been, as has been alleged by conspiracists, a number of Israeli intelligence officers in New York at the time of the attacks. But to see that as supporting circumstantial evidence for there being an Israeli hand in a plot to bring down the World Trade Center, and thus evidence for the plot itself, it would be necessary to make a totally unsubstantiated assumption there was a plot in the first place. It is only the conspiracy theory itself that connects those dots. There are bound to be coincidences with any controversial event – separate credible evidence of causation would be needed, and in the 9/11 case is completely lacking.

Another conspiracy angle comes from the group Architects and Engineers for 9/11 Truth asserting that the impact of the hijacked aircraft and fire from the fuel on board could not have brought down the towers, and that only controlled explosions could have done so.[14] The credible explanation by the National Institute for Science and Technology (NIST) is that the top part of the tower collapsed under the impact as a critical support column buckled, and such was the kinetic energy of that part of the tower falling under the force of gravity that the structure below the fire level could not absorb it, and thus the total collapse on itself resulted.

The conspiracy group have cited the distance to which debris was ejected as evidence of an explosion. Published civil engineering analysis, on the other hand, shows that as collapse took place such was the descent of so much weight under the force of gravity that the air pressure created at the base would have led to air being ejected at speeds of almost 500 mph, enough to explain the ejection of debris. Similarly, an assertion that only an explosion could have created concrete particles of such small size as were found in the debris is not borne out by calculation of the pressures formed by the collapse. But then to bolster their case the conspiracy group point out that a programme to modernize the lifts had taken place before 9/11 and that would have provided those who planted the explosives a way to get access to the core areas of the twin towers without creating suspicion. Would the absence of such a lifts programme have made the idea of a controlled-explosion plot impossible in the eyes of the conspiracy thinkers? No, other ways of smuggling in the explosives would have been advanced as part of the conspiracy. Citing the lifts programme adds nothing to the evidence for and against the plot itself (other than to cast more doubt on the credibility of those who used the argument). The visible record from TV and video in fact clearly shows the collapse of the tower with the roof elements sinking into the building to create interior collapse while the façade initially remained intact.

To maintain credibly an explanation of some event that involves a complex conspiracy there has to be factual evidence of the plot itself, not just asserting that it *could* have happened that way. That is a general principle applying to the many conspiracies that swirl around public events. One problem is that in today's world of social media once started such claims quickly spread and gain obsessional followers. Nor are most of us at work innocent of sometimes harbouring conspiratorial thoughts about rival departments trying to do down our efforts, or of worries that an unpopular boss is prejudiced against us and holding back our promotion or denying us the best opportunities. We can all let such thoughts, often motivated by fear of failure, lapse into obsession. And once in that state of mind we interpret every innocent sign as a pointer to an underlying conspiracy. My experience is certainly that even in the world of secret intelligence cockups outnumber conspiracies by a large margin.

When new evidence arrives

We would all like to think that we assess information rationally and use it to inform our understanding of what is going on around us. Typically, however, we hit unconscious resistance when some new piece of evidence, if accepted as valid, would have to trigger a major rethink of a strongly held opinion. Perhaps previous words spoken out of personal conviction will have to be eaten. There will be hard questions asked about the wisdom of past decisions that now no longer seem so well founded. And the harder it was to make such decisions in the first place, the more likely it is that unconsciously we will find ways of evading the implication that we had got them wrong.

Of course, we should learn not to attach blame to a rational change of mind on the arrival of new evidence. Nor should we feel guilty about decisions we took in good faith, in the light of all the evidence as it was then understood, when information arrives that could not reasonably have been known at the time. Nevertheless, rather than accept loss of face, both individuals and groups are liable to retreat into denial. One warning sign of that happening is engaging in displacement activity, frantically keeping busy on other things to avoid having to face the new facts. Other signs of denial are when we challenge the basis for the new evidence, probably accompanied with demands to defer all consideration until more evidence has been gathered.

You may have felt that sensation of vertigo that can come over you when you find out that what you thought was the case actually is not. Something else was going on that you had not understood before, but that now you can recognize. The future may be going to take a very different path from the one you had previously expected. The past that was explained according to one narrative of events now needs to be reconsidered in the light of new information. Intelligence officers know that feeling when, to use an overworked metaphor, dots that had been connected to form one pattern are now seen as making up a very different shape. John le Carré in his classic novel *Tinker Tailor Soldier Spy*, captures this moment when his ageing counter-intelligence officer George Smiley tumbles to the deception that the Soviet spymaster Karla has been wreaking on British intelligence.[15]

> Through the remainder of that same night . . . Unchanged, unshaven, George Smiley remained bowed at the major's table, reading, comparing, annotating, cross-referencing . . . Shaking the pieces . . . At this point, his mood could best be compared with that of a scientist who senses by instinct that he is on the brink of a discovery and is awaiting any minute the logical connection. Later . . . he called it 'shoving everything into a test-tube and seeing if it exploded' . . . And then he had it. No explosive revelation, no flash of light, no cry of 'Eureka' . . . merely that before him, in the records he had examined and the notes he had compiled, was the corroboration of a theory . . .

We can imagine George Smiley testing a number of hypotheses as to who might be the spy inside the organization. He knows that it is one of the officers nicknamed after the nursery rhyme 'Tinker, Tailor, Soldier, Beggerman and Poorman'. The key line of questioning when new evidence is discovered that appears relevant to such a search is to ask: if the hypothesis that it was, say, Tinker was in fact true, how likely is it that that evidence would exist? That is a question about the nature of evidence. It is an example of Bayesian inference, which we saw in Chapter 1. It might be that if Tinker is really the spy, then it is unlikely that piece of evidence could exist; for example, discovering by examining the files that it could not have been Tinker who passed information to the KGB since he would not have had access to it. In which case Tinker can go to the bottom of the list of suspects. Or it might be that none of the other suspects had access to the information but Tailor did, in which case the odds on the mole being Tailor rise sharply. If the evidence is consistent with all the hypotheses (all the suspects would have known that information), then it does not help Smiley choose between them. His degree of belief in the guilt of each of the suspects would remain unaltered.

The intelligence community is no stranger to Bayesian inference – the great computing pioneer Alan Turing at Bletchley Park during the Second World War independently rediscovered Bayesian methods to help him know when he was getting closer to solving the settings of the German Enigma cypher machine. We can use Bayesian reasoning to improve confidence in all kinds of judgements in the light of new evidence.

One advantage of the Bayesian approach to analysis is that it concentrates attention on the relevance of the evidence and not just its character. Each piece of evidence has to be assessed on its own merits as to whether it can be used to discriminate between the alternative hypotheses being examined. Only when that has been done is there a tallying up of how much of the evidence is inconsistent with each of the hypotheses. Such a structured way of thinking makes it much less likely that the state of mind of the analyst, including possibly fears about the consequence of arriving at a disturbing conclusion, will influence the weighing of the evidence. The method also helps guard against a form of bias that can come into play in such circumstances known to applied psychologists as *the sub-additivity effect*. That is the tendency to judge the likelihood of the whole being true as less than the likelihoods of the parts considered separately. All the evidence needs to be brought together to form a judgement.

Finally, having laid out the evidence the analyst can draw a conclusion. As a general rule, we have already seen that it is the hypothesis with the least evidence against it that is to be preferred. The classic scientific method (which in a modified form is what we are applying here) is to try to disconfirm theories by using them to make predictions and testing those against the evidence. If the evidence does not bear out the prediction, then the search is on for why that is. It could be problems with the experimental set-up, or that on closer examination the experiment is not really testing the theory that it was designed to, and finally having eliminated such possibilities concluding there appears to be something wrong with the theory itself and it needs to be modified or replaced. Evidence that appears to be supportive of a theory may come about even though the theory is false. Correct predictions tell us nothing about the underlying rightness of the theory.

Managing the risk of relying on incomplete information

Some risks we just have to live with. Some we can invest in managing. It is important to know what the odds of a risk arising are and how far we can reduce those odds. In the case of bets on mechanical devices such as dice or roulette wheels, if fair and unbiased, then the odds are fixed and we can derive them from the number of possible equally likely outcomes, six in the case of a die and thirty-eight for a roulette wheel (thirty-six black and red and one o and one oo). In roulette the best strategy if you want to keep playing for as long as possible to enjoy the game and the atmosphere, without straining your bank balance, is to bet on even odds that return your stake, such as betting on red/black and odds/evens, or on low/high numbers. In the long run you will still lose but more slowly than if you imitated James Bond and bet on individual numbers or zero.

In a smart casino in London you can assume that the roulette wheels are not biased through crooked croupiers or simply by wear and tear. There is an independent Gambling Commission that inspects against their technical standards before renewing a licence. But how does an inspector know if a roulette wheel is fair or not? Roulette wheels are straightforward, given some simple mathematics of probability, since it is possible to calculate the likelihood of obtaining the observed results from a fair wheel. A test of statistical significance can be applied to the difference between the theoretical fair wheel calculation and the observed results. If the spins are delivering genuinely random results then it is possible (although very unlikely) that in a series of spins the number zero will come up say five times in a row. But there is no real limit to the number of spins the inspector can demand as evidence to feed the calculation if they have concerns. In that way, in practice the fairness of the wheel can be given a reliable test.

The interesting cases come when the events being bet on are not repeatable: if there are six horses in a race, then they are all not equally likely to win. Some will run better if the going is muddy, others not. Each will have its own history, and, of course, the choice of jockey matters. The punter needs to work out how far new information, such as a late change of jockey, should affect the odds they would accept.

Risk judgements permeate all security work. The security service analyst may have to alter their prior degree of belief in a judgement they had previously reached about an individual of interest in the light of a report of his recent sighting in the company of known violent extremists. Such a revised, or posterior, probability may then trigger renewed surveillance or even disruptive action, including arrest. Such revision of belief in the light of new evidence is the essence of the inverse probability problem that Bayesian methods address: starting with the prior probability of the hypothesis (the individual of interest is not believed to be currently engaged directly in terrorist activity), how far should that degree of belief be changed given new intelligence reporting to arrive at the posterior probability?

Nevertheless, as the lessons of the next chapter reveal, among the information we receive is material that is untrue, deliberately or innocently painting a false view of the world. We need to be on our guard against manipulation, deception and fakes.

Remembering to check our working

At school we will all have been told by teachers when learning maths, from simple arithmetic to more complex problems, always to check our working. It does not come naturally. For most of us, myself included, to have reached an answer, any answer, is the spur to move on to addressing the next problem. It was only after many years of studying mathematics that I really accepted that what I had rather resented as unnecessary time spent on checking is in fact an integral part of the process of reaching a reliable answer from a calculation, or a respectable proof of a mathematical result. And that without showing your working it is hard to check you got it right, and impossible if it is someone else doing the checking. That is why intelligence analysts cannot simply write down their key judgements. They have to be able to demonstrate the chain of reasoning, and the evidence they brought to bear, that led them to those conclusions. In the seven years I spent serving as a member of the UK Joint Intelligence Committee there were very many times when the drafters of the assessment before the JIC were forced to explain how they had arrived at their judgements; and in the process often identified the weaker steps in the argument, leading the JIC to amend the draft so that the readers of the assessment could take that into account.

We also have to learn that checking has to be an active, creative process. It is not the same as redoing the problem by simply following the same steps again in the same order as in the calculation or proof. If there is an error in your reasoning, such a method of retracing your footsteps is likely to lead you unconsciously into making the same misstep again.

One valuable way of checking is to approach the problem afresh, having obtained what you think is a solution, to see – on the assumption that it is correct – whether you can work backwards to establish whether the answer is consistent with the terms of the original problem. To take the simplest example, in long division (never my forte in primary school) the best check is to multiply the answer just arrived at by the divisor and see if the answer is the same as the dividend you started with. If not, there is an error in the original calculation.

Following that train of thought, once you have reached a conclusion and before you find you are required to justify it, would you be able to work back and identify each step in the reasoning as demonstrably valid under the conditions of the problem? This is when employers struggle at Employment Tribunals having to justify their reasons for firing someone who then claims they were the victim of unlawful discrimination. Even the British Prime Minister found that his decision in 2019 to prorogue (shut down) Parliament for a lengthy period as the Brexit deadline approached was open to review by the Supreme Court. In that case he was unable to provide the Court with convincing evidence of why he had made that decision, which helped the Court conclude that the decision was illegal. In short, quality control of reasoning will involve an active process of stress testing that is sufficiently distinct from the original thinking to throw up any errors, preferably before the conclusion has been turned into a decision.

An analytic team might therefore begin with a quality check on the underlying intelligence and information on which they hope to base their assessment. Ideally, analysts would have a retrieval-and-search capability on a sources database with type and date, and additional notations indicating strengths or weaknesses in those sources, so that they can carry out periodic reviews to check that their assessments are still up to date.

For a review or checking exercise to be fully effective, analysts will need as much background information on the sources of their intelligence as is feasible and is compatible with security. Knowing the circumstances in which reporting was obtained is often critical to weighing its validity when used in the assessment. In the run-up to the Iraq war MI6 issued to senior readers what appeared to be an important report confirming that Iraq was producing chemical and biological weapons, but for security reasons as this was a new source on trial MI6 did not show it to the experts in Defence Intelligence, leading Lord Butler to ' . . . conclude that arrangements should always be sought to ensure that the need for protection of sources should not prevent the exposure of reports on technical matters to the most expert available analysis'.[16] The report was later withdrawn.

Conclusions: obsessive and conspiratorial states of mind

Even otherwise rational people can fall into obsessive and conspiratorial states of mind. To avoid such lapses we should:

- Watch for signs of conspiracy, including:
  No evidence supports connecting available evidence but the conspiracy theory itself.
  Near superhuman authority would be needed for it.
  The conspiracy is complex with many elements to go right.
  Large numbers of people who all need to keep the secret.
  The ambition of the conspiracy is grand (such as world domination).
  Fact and speculation are comingled.
  Small probable events are ratcheted up to larger improbable events.
  Sinister meanings are given to small events.
- Provide an external perspective to spot when someone is stuck in a conspiratorial closed loop (Möbius strip).
- Test whether new evidence is being explained away within the logic of a closed loop.
- Bring new evidence to bear by Bayesian thinking to diminish the power of attraction of an obsession or belief in a conspiracy, and by checking your reasoning, preferably working backwards.

- Remember obsessions can be catching because they offer emotionally satisfying explanations of states of suffering, fear and anxiety.
- Argue against excessive secrecy by the authorities, which breeds conspiracy thinking about the 'deep state' concealing evidence of harm to the public.
- Be aware that conspiracy stories, like rumours, are more easily spread with digital media and are harder to kill off. Help prevent them becoming public witch-hunts.

7

Lesson 7. Seeing is not always believing: beware manipulation, deception and faking

The Old Admiralty Building in London's Whitehall is hidden behind a stone screen erected in 1760 after a mob of sailors surrounded the building demanding their overdue back-pay. Entering, you pass the room where Nelson's body lay overnight after the Battle of Trafalgar, on its way up the River Thames to burial in St Paul's Cathedral. Above that room and along a narrow corridor is another piece of history, Room 40, where British naval intelligence had set up shop at the outset of war in 1914. In 1917, the cryptographers in Room 40 possessed three deep secrets: they could read the high-grade German diplomatic cypher, they were tapping the US transatlantic cable, and they knew how to use their secret intelligence to influence US public opinion.[1]

The British had manipulated the battle-space by cutting German undersea cables to the USA. This forced Germany to use the US cable, which landed in Cornwall and was being secretly tapped by the Admiralty. This was extremely useful for intelligence gathering, but in January 1917 the head of naval intelligence, Rear Admiral 'Blinker' Hall, had the insight that the contents of one such intercepted telegram could also be 'weaponized', that is, deliberately released to harm the enemy. In this case, the desired goal was nothing less than the entry of the United States into the war on the side of Britain, France and their allies. The problem Hall faced was how to allow an embarrassing German telegram gleaned from the cable intercept to be made public without giving away the secrets of its source. The Germans must not learn that their cyphers were being read and the United States should be shielded from the knowledge that US cables were being routinely tapped by the British.

What happened in January 1917 was that Arthur Zimmermann, State Secretary for Foreign Affairs in Berlin, had proposed to Mexico a military alliance in the event of the United States entering the war against Germany. The idea was that if the Mexican government declared war on the United States it would tie down American forces and slow the export of American arms to the UK. The proposal was in a highly secret telegram to be sent via the US transatlantic cable to the German Embassy in Washington and thence to Mexico City. The Germans assumed that their cypher was secure. But in Room 40 Nigel de Grey, a remarkable cryptographer, started to decipher it. By the next day, the first few startling sentences were decoded, outlining the deal Germany was offering Mexico in return for its support in the war:

> We intend to begin on the first of February unrestricted submarine warfare. We shall endeavor in spite of this to keep the United States of America neutral. In the event of this not succeeding, we make Mexico a proposal of alliance on the following basis: make war together, make peace together, generous financial support and an understanding on our part that Mexico is to re-conquer the lost territory in Texas, New Mexico, and Arizona.

Hall and de Grey had grasped immediately the potential anti-German impact on US public opinion of the German offer to Mexico of recovering territories that had been annexed by the US or captured in the 1845–8 war with Mexico. Under no circumstances would the American public agree to give them back to Mexico. The very suggestion would turn them against Germany.

At this point, the story becomes a perfect case study for learning lessons of how to conduct covert information activity. Hall had a clear objective for his operation. He believed his target would be receptive to the message. But he had three challenges to overcome if he was to reveal to President Wilson the existence of the telegram in the expectation that it would become public: the Germans must not realize that their current high-grade cypher could be broken; the US must not realize that the British were tapping their transatlantic cables; yet the US President would have to be told enough to be convinced that the telegram was genuine.

Hall and his team waited three weeks before informing anyone outside Room 40, during which time they completed the decryption and prepared their plan. For the benefit of the Germans, the British could publicly claim when the news broke that their agents had stolen the telegram's deciphered text from their Embassy in Mexico (a cover story that the US agreed to back once they had been convinced of the authenticity of the message).

To deceive the US, they could claim that the telegram had been sent over three routes, by radio and by two transatlantic cables operated by neutral governments for the use of their diplomatic services, thus complicating any eventual search by the Americans (and the Germans) for the source. Hall suspected that the German Embassy in Washington would have to send the note from Washington on to Mexico by American commercial telegraph for which they would use an older, weaker cypher. There would be a copy of that enciphered text in the Mexico telegraph office. Hall arranged for a Mexican employee to be bribed so as to secure a copy. They could then show the US the decrypted version of that copy. This meant revealing to the US their ability to read the weaker cypher but protected the deep secret of the readability of the current German diplomatic cypher.

Finally, to convince the US authorities of the authenticity of the intercept, it could be suggested to them that they retrieve the text for themselves by comparing the enciphered text provided by the British from the Mexico end with the copy of that cypher text that would have been deposited in the records of the American commercial telegraph in Washington, and applying the weaker German cypher that the British would provide.

On 1 February 1917 Germany announced resumption of unrestricted submarine warfare, an act that led the United States to break off diplomatic relations with Germany. Hall must have felt the conditions for his operation were ripe, and, on 5 February, he revealed the cable to the Foreign Office and told his contact in the US London Embassy, who arranged for the US Ambassador to call on the Foreign Secretary. He was given the enciphered text, and the plain text in English and German. The Ambassador reported the story, with due outrage over the German proposal, to President Wilson, including the details to be verified from the telegraph company. Wilson released the text publicly on 28 February. The understandable scepticism of pro-German sympathizers in the US, who naturally suspected a British plot, were stilled by Zimmermann himself, who, on being asked about the telegram at a press conference on 3 March, told an American journalist, 'I cannot deny it. It is true.'

The German Foreign Ministry refused to consider their cyphers might be insecure, and instead embarked on a witch-hunt for a traitor in the Embassy in Mexico. On 6 April 1917, the US Congress declared war on Germany. Intelligence had been successfully weaponized. The weapon had had its desired effect. And the intelligence sources had remained intact.

Malinformation

The Zimmermann telegram was genuine but was intended to remain secret. Such deliberate use of true information obtained covertly that was never intended to become public now has its own term of art. This is malinformation.[2] 'Weaponizing' such genuine but embarrassing or compromising material by revealing it publicly so as to influence a selected audience is an increasingly common tactic of covert operations, not to mention a form of political dynamiting. Recent examples include the Russian hacking of the emails of the Chairman of the Democratic National Committee and their release via Wikileaks during the 2016 US Presidential campaign. A similar operation against the En Marche party of President Emmanuel Macron occurred during the 2017 French Presidential election.

Sites run by organizations such as Wikileaks (set up in 2006 by Julian Assange) act as portals for those who want to leak classified or sensitive information anonymously. Wikileaks came to prominence in 2010 and 2011 by making available the trove of classified information on US operations in Iraq and Afghanistan that had been passed to Wikileaks by Chelsea (previously Bradley) Manning, who was working with the US Army in Iraq as an intelligence analyst. Some 750,000 classified documents were handed over to Wikileaks, including over 250,000 State Department cables. The motive of Chelsea Manning appears in her account at her trial to have been a wish to see wider public debate of US overseas policies and interventions in the interests of world peace.[3]

Wikileaks was also involved in helping the US NSA contractor Edward Snowden evade the US authorities after he fled to Hong Kong – he ended up in Moscow, where he remains. Snowden had stolen a large cache of very highly classified US and UK intelligence documents, which formed the basis of a series of accusations in the media starting in 2013 regarding surveillance activity by the NSA and GCHQ involving bulk access to communications data and other digital intelligence activity.[4] Most recently, in 2019, there was a leak of confidential telegrams from the British Ambassador in Washington reporting candidly on the well-known flaws in the Trump administration. This prompted an angry tweet by the President and the resignation of the British Ambassador. These, among many other cases, where apparently genuine classified documents are stolen or leaked and then widely publicized on the Internet in order to achieve some wider political purpose, represent modern malinformation activity. Today, it is far easier than in Hall's day to mount a malinformation campaign due to digital storage of emails and other documents.

Of course, there have been many old-fashioned leaks of classified information in the past and I expect more in the future. One of the Snowden allegations that received headlines was that the NSA and GCHQ were tapping into the global network of undersea cables. That should not have come as such a shock. As we saw earlier in this chapter, it was the interception of a transatlantic cable in 1917 that revealed the Zimmermann telegram, a story that has been known to historians for very many years.

Usually the motives for the release or leaking of true information that was never intended to be made public are deliberate, but sometimes they are inadvertent. This happened in the high drama of the debate in the House of Commons the day after the Argentine invasion of the Falkland Islands. The former Labour minister Ted Rowlands fiercely criticized the government for being caught by surprise. To give weight to his criticism that the government had been asleep at the wheel, he blurted out that when he was a junior minister in the Foreign Office in 1977 he had derived great value from reading sigint decrypts of Argentine traffic: 'As well as reading the mind of the enemy, we have been reading its telegrams for many years.' A horrified Margaret Thatcher later commented that the Rowlands blunder, although the information had been true, had been 'totally and utterly devastating in the amount that it gave away to those against whom intelligence was directed . . . The moment you say too much the sources dry up.'[5]

Misinformation

There is always information in circulation that turns out not to be true, or to be only a misleading part of the truth. We all make innocent mistakes, and that includes academics, journalists and politicians in their writings and speeches. When the error is pointed out, we ought to want to correct the record. Such innocently misleading material is known by the term misinformation to distinguish it from disinformation, the deliberate use of false information to deceive.

Reputable media outlets have columns or web pages where corrections can be issued when misinformation is recognized. The better class of politician will also inform Congress or Parliament when they have inadvertently misinformed their colleagues and thus the public, and they will place the corrected information on the record as soon as they are able. That is a legal requirement for companies that discover errors in the accounts. It is a moral requirement for those who wish to be considered trustworthy. In my time in the British public service there were few greater offences for officials to commit than to have provided ministers with information that inadvertently misled Parliament. I recall at least one promising career being abruptly stalled when the individual was found by the Permanent Head of the Department to have been negligent in checking the figures given in an answer to a parliamentary question on a politically sensitive topic.

Sometimes, however, it is not possible to tell the full story in circumstances when an underlying truth has nevertheless to be conveyed. In 1982, despite the blunder by Ted Rowlands referred to in the previous section, GCHQ had nevertheless (just) managed to keep up with changes in the Argentine naval cyphers. GCHQ had thus been able to decipher an intercepted Argentine order on 1 May for the first armed attack by the Argentine Navy on the British Task Force after it had arrived in the South Atlantic. This attack was to be a major two-pronged operation by the Argentine Navy to take place the following day. The intercepted orders revealed that one wing of the attack was being led by the sole Argentine aircraft carrier and the other by the cruiser *Belgrano*.

It was clear as a result of reading these orders that events were moving irretrievably from the diplomatic sphere to open warfare. The RN nuclear-powered submarine HMS

Conqueror had managed to detect by sonar the tanker sent to refuel the *Belgrano* group, and now reported that it was tracking the cruiser itself. Fearing the risk of losing contact and knowing the problem of intermittent communications, the Task Force commander sought urgent approval from the War Cabinet to engage while opportunity presented itself and thus disrupt the Argentine attack. Permission was rapidly given. The *Belgrano* was duly sunk by torpedoes fired by HMS *Conqueror*.

Back in London the Defence Secretary, John Nott, felt strongly that he had to inform Parliament as quickly as possible of the fact of the attack, although next to nothing was known in London of the tactical circumstances of the engagement. A form of words was hastily put together in the Ministry of Defence. As his Principal Private Secretary, I was still amending the draft sitting in the official car beside the Secretary of State speeding to the House of Commons minutes before the statement was due, very mindful of the need both to provide genuine justification of the attack in the light of the Argentine hostile intent and to safeguard the signals intelligence source, not least after Ted Rowland's earlier gaffe.

The final statement as delivered tried to square that circle and spoke of the general threat to the British Task Force posed by Argentine units, including the *Belgrano* group, that the *Belgrano* was close to the Total Exclusion Zone around the Islands, and stated that it 'was closing on elements of our Task Force, which was only hours away', a form of words that was intended to convey truthfully the hostile intent revealed in the secret Argentine signal but without revealing that the British had access to the content of the Argentine orders. Churchill after D-Day had been guilty of a comparable misleading of the House of Commons by referring to 'the first of a series of landings' to bolster the deception of Operation Fortitude, described in Chapter 5.[6]

It later transpired that, unknown to London at the time, the Argentine Navy had postponed its attack and, when hit, the *Belgrano* had already changed course and was heading southwest, away from the Task Force. Although that in no way invalidated the legality of the decision to sink the cruiser, the subsequent years were spent battling fruitless conspiracy theories that the British motivation had not been defence of the Task Force but had really been to scupper further peace talks, or that the War Cabinet had changed the rules of engagement under a misapprehension. The record was finally set straight in the Official History of the Campaign by Professor Sir Lawrence Freedman, published in 2005, in which he was allowed to quote from the clear text of the (by then declassified) Argentine naval signals as demonstrating the original Argentine intent to attack the Task Force.

The misinformation episode illustrates the lesson discussed in the last chapter, that once a conspiratorial interpretation takes hold it is next to impossible to get it out of circulation. Regardless of subsequent corrections, misinformation continues to circulate.

Disinformation

The category of information operation that democratic societies, and all of us within them, have most to fear is disinformation (also known by the term black propaganda) – that is, information which is known to be false before it is circulated. The most dangerous covert information operations today are those that deploy material which is carefully crafted to be believable by the public, and comes on trusted channels, but is false. This is the terrain today of the massive Russian subversion operations described in Chapter 10. The key to deception is to have the false message conveyed to the target through as many channels as possible. A single report may not be believed, but if there is corroboration, then the report rapidly achieves reliable status. And once that is achieved, subsequent reports through the same channel will be believed. The corollary is that to detect deception as many different channels should be examined as possible. It requires great skill to make the messages consistent on each channel and avoid errors. One inconsistency may be enough to reveal the deception. A lesson that we need to heed comes from the way that digital channels, including social media, provide the ideal way of spreading disinformation.

There is nothing novel about 'fake news' stories being circulated for political effect. With four days to go before the 1924 British General Election the headlines of that morning's *Daily Mail* newspaper splashed the story of a 'Civil War Plot by Socialists: Moscow Order to our Reds', alleging that if re-elected the Labour Party would help 'paralyse the Army and the Navy'. The newspaper claimed to have seen a letter from Grigory Zinoviev, the President of the Communist International, addressed to the UK representative of the Comintern, to the effect that the Labour Party wanted treaties with the Soviet Union to be pursued so that it could then 'assist in the revolutionizing of the international and British proletariat . . . make it possible for us to extend and develop the ideas of Leninism in England and the Colonies'. The Labour Prime Minister, Ramsay MacDonald, might well have lost the October 1924 election in any case, but the Zinoviev story made his defeat certain.

The Zinoviev letter was later shown to be a clever forgery produced by White Russians who were opposed to MacDonald's policy of recognizing the Soviet government and that had been acquired by the British Secret Intelligence Service in Riga and passed to London. The *Daily Mail* story had been, in today's jargon, 'fake news'. As with all the more effective information operations, it was a story that in the public mind might have been true (and for many *Daily Mail* readers should have been true). Although Zinoviev did not write the letter, it was *the sort of thing* he might have penned since the views in it were ones he had previously expressed, as the White Russian forgers well knew. The story therefore resonated in the public mind and crystallized existing public doubts about the policies that would have been followed by a new Labour government.

The Zinoviev fake letter is also yet another example of the lesson that 'fake-news' stories can be hard to disprove.[7] Although there is legitimate doubt about whether this really swung the election, and whether British intelligence officers did knowingly collude in publicizing the fake letter, there is no doubt that to this day many Labour Party supporters feel that they were denied power in 1924 by a 'deep-state' plot by British intelligence.

Spreading slanders about political opponents is also as old as politics. One of the most recent examples from the US is the 'birthergate' story spread on social media that Barack Obama's Presidency was illegitimate since he was not a natural-born citizen of the United States. This controversy was exploited by Donald Trump in the 2016 Presidential campaign, adding his voice to the 'birthers' demanding that Obama produce his birth certificate, thus further circulating the allegation. When the birth certificate was finally produced, Donald Trump himself was then able to claim credit for resolving the matter, although 'birthers' still believe that the birth certificate was forged anyway.

Deliberate use of deception and disinformation as state policy in peacetime

In wars for survival – as we saw with the Zimmermann tele-gram in the First World War, and with the British double agent system of the Second World War – deception is to be expected as a *ruse de guerre*. In peacetime we may think it best for the democracies not to lie to their publics, and in a world of glo-balized information that usually means shunning the peacetime deception of others. The intelligence agencies of the Soviet Union learned early on, however, the power of intelligence in peacetime to create political weapons against both their own population and the West. They defined secret intelligence work 'as a secret form of political struggle which makes use of clandestine means and methods for acquiring secret informa-tion of interest and for carrying out active measures to exert influence on the adversary and weaken his political, economic, scientific and technical and military positions'. In the hands of the authoritarian Soviet government such active measures included spreading disinformation about the 'main adversar-ies', the United States and the United Kingdom.

A vivid example was the deliberate creation and circulation by the KGB of the story that the AIDS epidemic of the 1990s had its origins in biological warfare experiments conducted by the US military. Given past US work (openly avowed) on bio-logical agents before the introduction of the Biological Warfare Convention and continuing effort on defence against such agents, the story had an initial plausibility for those who wanted to think ill of the USA, especially when coupled with information that has come to light on CIA covert programmes in the 1970s, including plots to poison the Cuban leader, Fidel Castro. The Soviet motives in spreading this story in Africa and elsewhere in the developing world were probably two-fold. The Soviet agencies would see advantage in inflaming anti-American feeling and distrust of the US military. There may well also have been a motive of creating the ability to point to the US should the (now well-documented) Soviet biological-warfare programmes of the period have come to light and attracted international condemnation.[8]

Russia as the successor state to the Soviet Union has developed digital active information measures. False stories are spread on social media by its intelligence agencies, its diplomatic service and its state-controlled media. The old AIDS lie has become the claim that COVID-19 originated in a US bio-weapons lab. Russian propaganda justifies the illegal annexation of Crimea, the violation of the territorial integrity of Ukraine, the downing of flight MH17, and there is constant pressure from cyberattacks on Ukrainian systems, the attempted coup in Montenegro, as well as interference in Western elections. All accompanied with the drumbeat of hostile propaganda. The lesson that we need to heed comes from the scale and speed with which digital disinformation operations can be mounted today to spread such 'fake-news' stories, as we shall see in Chapter 10.

The risks of deploying intelligence in public

As the intelligence officers in Room 40 recognized in 1917, there is always risk in using in public information derived from secret intelligence to expose a plot or bolster an argument. That is a lesson which would be heartily endorsed by the intelligence analysts whose assessments were used for public justification of the US and UK government decisions to invade Iraq in 2003.

A decade after the Zimmermann telegram the British government had again run into the problem of deploying secret intelligence in public, with significant consequences for intelligence operations. In 1927 Scotland Yard and MI5 carried out a surprise raid on the offices of the All-Russian Cooperative Society (ARCOS) in London.[9] ARCOS was a trade mission but was known from messages intercepted and decrypted between it and Moscow also to be a front for Soviet subversion operations. The raid followed a tip-off received from a well-placed agent that ARCOS had copied a classified Army Signals Manual which it had been passed by a communist sympathizer. The ARCOS office was shared with the Soviet Trade Delegation, which benefited from diplomatic immunity. Recovering the Army document was used as the justification for obtaining a search warrant on the grounds of activities by the Soviet legation incompatible with diplomatic convention.

To the huge embarrassment of the UK government, no usable evidence was found. The raid provoked a fierce complaint from the Soviet authorities about the unprecedented invasion of their diplomatic premises. The public row then led to a debate in the House of Commons. With the government forced on to the defensive, the Prime Minister, Stanley Baldwin, felt he had to justify the raid by quoting in his statement to Parliament from four telegrams from the London Russian legation back to Moscow 'that had come into the hands of His Majesty's Government'. The awkward truth was that they had been intercepted and decrypted by GC&CS, the forerunner of today's GCHQ. Baldwin was of course promptly challenged on how he had obtained the information and Parliament descended into a day's heated debate about secret intelligence and Soviet subversion in the course of which even more was unwisely revealed of the British government's knowledge of communications that Moscow until then would have regarded as secure. The inevitable outcome was that the Soviet authorities realized that their cables were being read by the British cryptographers and henceforth only sent such messages using unbreakable one-time pad systems. The Head of GC&CS, Alastair Denniston (who came to notice as a brilliant young cryptographer in Room 40 in the Admiralty during the First World War and who rose to be Director of Bletchley Park on the outbreak of war in 1939), wrote that Baldwin had 'found it necessary to compromise our work beyond question'. Almost no high-grade Soviet diplomatic traffic was read by the UK from then on.

Such stories enter the folk memory of those engaged in signals intelligence. When I joined GCHQ as a young recruit in 1969 the old hands constantly impressed on all of us newcomers to signals intelligence just how fragile are successes in decryption. Even general publicity about the existence of agencies such as NSA or GCHQ (or during the early Cold War even any public mention of the successes of Bletchley Park during the Second World War) could spark off a train of doubt by the signals authorities of some overseas military force of interest and lead to a decision to change cyphers, just in case. A vivid example we were given was the publication of the book *The American Black Chamber*, by the leading American cryptographer of his day, H. O. Yardley, after he lost his job when his organization was abolished (in a fit of ethical foreign policy by the US Secretary of State, Henry L. Stimson, who wrote later in his memoirs: 'Gentlemen do not read each other's mail'). The book revealed past US communications intelligence successes, including examples of Japanese cryptosystems and their solutions. The Japanese, realizing that their codes had been insecure, and in particular that their cyphers had been exploited against them at the Washington Naval Conference in 1922, immediately changed their codes and cyphers, creating a major headache for the US on the approach to the Second World War.

The logic still applies today. Media reporting on communications monitoring by NSA and GCHQ as alleged by Edward Snowden in 2013 led to the rapid application of strong end-to-end cryptography to the apps used on mobile devices. Ordinary users demanded to be shielded from intelligence gathering of the content of their messages when using WhatsApp, Telegram, Viber and many others. But inadvertently this benefited terrorists and others with criminal intent. Communications data, rather than content of messages, has therefore become the prime data source from which intelligence can be derived on suspects of 'who called whom, when, where and how'. Very recently internet users have become conscious that the intelligence and security agencies are not the only ones, or indeed the most voracious, collectors of personal data. The popular media has started to pick up on what the tech media have always known about the way that political advertising and messaging are targeted. The use of this ad tech directed at voters identified by their personal data, first in the UK Brexit referendum and then in the 2016 US Presidential election, has changed politics for ever.

When is it justified for governments to deceive their own publics?

Sitting behind his leather-topped desk in his eighteenth-century wood-panelled office, sunlight streaming in from the tall windows overlooking Horse Guards Parade, Sir John Hunt,

Secretary to the British Cabinet, read through the minute he had dictated earlier that day and initialled it. The instruction in it was to close down the covert cross-government programme of counter-subversion activities that he had been overseeing.[10]

But now it was 1974. A Labour government had just been elected under Harold Wilson and was in the process of taking office. Tough and determined as he was, Hunt did not want his first months establishing a relationship with the Prime Minister, Harold Wilson, overshadowed by any risk of scandal over the counter-subversion work he had been overseeing. The Cabinet Secretary would have been all too aware that the incoming Prime Minister had been, as we saw in the previous chapter, the subject of unofficial inquiries by a clique of MI5 officers in response to the CIA's Angleton into whether Wilson was a KGB agent of influence. Hunt would not have doubted Wilson's loyalty to his country but he certainly would have feared the reaction of left-wingers in Wilson's Cabinet if word got out about the covert measures the British government had been taking during the early Cold War to keep left-leaning sympathizers (including some distinguished academics) out of positions of influence.

In the previous chapter I compared the paranoid view of Soviet deception of James Angleton, CIA counter-terrorism chief, to that of an ant trapped on the single surface of a Möbius strip, formed by giving a strip of paper a half-twist and joining the ends together to form a twisted loop. Even if the ant crawls over the edge it still finds itself trapped on the same surface. We have seen how Angleton was trapped inside his belief in a conspiratorial Soviet masterplan. If, on the other hand, the ends of a strip of paper are simply joined together to form a closed loop or band without a twist then there are two surfaces formed, an inside of the loop and an outside. On the outside is the open world as would be seen by an ant on the surface. On the inside we can think of the secret world the ant may suspect exists underneath. By looking over the edges of the strip it may be possible to get glimpses of what is happening on the inside track. Perhaps the ant might misunderstand what is going on down there but that there is an inside track is undeniable. 'Just because you're paranoid doesn't mean they're not after you' is the wise warning from Joseph Heller's novel *Catch 22*. There was secret activity to manage the real threat of communist subversion in the trades unions and among left-wing intellectuals.

What might be called today the 'deep state' of the intelligence and security apparatus of the UK had over the previous quarter-century been mobilized through a Group on Subversion in Public Life, chaired by the Cabinet Secretary with the heads of the British intelligence agencies and the permanent secretaries of the key government departments. The strategy was based on the experience of the post-war Labour government that British liberals and trade unionists could be nudged towards the soft left and Keynesian market socialism, and away from ideas of state communism. Although there was no legal ban on British citizens joining the Communist Party, if they did so they were openly disbarred from joining the armed forces, police or senior civil service. And an unofficial security network overseen by the Group ensured that communist academics did not get professorships at major universities, including Oxford and Cambridge. The avowedly Marxist historian Eric Hobsbawm spent his career at Birkbeck College in London – he knew he had been discriminated against and to the end of his long life pressed me among others to get to see his MI5 file, but to no avail. The Oxford historian Christopher Hill was turned down (given his open communist sympathy) for a professorship at Keele University, although he got his own back by being elected the Master of Balliol College, Oxford. We know all this today from the public records that have been released, but it was not disclosed at the time.

In private life we would, I hope, regard it as deeply unethical to attempt to manipulate those close to us to believe untruths about ourselves, or even peddle varnished semi-truths to conceal our failings. Such behaviour would need a very strong justification indeed. The use of hidden means to manipulate public perceptions in a democracy in peacetime should likewise require the most carefully argued rationale. Such a case was made out at the time for Britain in the depth of the Cold War to expose the true nature of Soviet life under Stalin's successors. Britain already faced the reality of communist influence in the trades unions and had reasons to fear infiltration by Soviet agents of influence. The new 1974 Labour Cabinet contained strongly anti-communist figures such as the Foreign Secretary, Jim Callaghan, and Defence Secretary, Denis Healey. They knew MI5 needed to continue its traditional defensive task of tracking down suspected Soviet agents. But the Cabinet also contained figures from the left of the party who had always been wary of what they saw as the innate right-wing tendencies of the British security and intelligence establishment. The Cabinet Secretary judged it wise to cease the covert measures being taken to nudge domestic opinion. But by 1976 a rising threat of industrial subversion in the UK led the Prime Minister to task the Cabinet Secretary with chairing a reactivated Official Home Security Committee of the Cabinet to advise ministers on counter-measures, a remit that was notably not confined to industrial subversion but included the public service, education and the media.[11]

During the height of the Cold War, therefore, there were fears at the highest levels in the UK on the part of both Conservative and Labour governments of the extent to which the Soviet Union was directing a campaign of subversive activity through penetration of organized labour, academia, the media and liberal intellectual circles. There were suspicions in left-wing circles that the government was engaged in a politically motivated domestic campaign of surveillance and disruption. Both views had some justification, but we now know neither lived up to their conspiratorial billing.

The temptation is always to over- or underestimate the dangers of alleged subversive developments. As you read a news story online that disturbs you, instinct may either cause you to dismiss it as obviously slanted and to be totally ignored or conversely to seize upon it as obviously true and to be retweeted as widely as possible. In either case, as we discussed in Chapter 5, it is likely that the story either jars with deep-held convictions or validates long-held prejudices. Critical examination of the evidence and quality of argument is the best defence.

Conclusions: manipulation, deception and faking

There is a long history behind information manipulation for military and political purposes. Motivation matters in considering the ethical acceptability of information operations. Deception is a legitimate military tactic and can be justified on the grounds that successful deception helps achieve the military objective more swiftly and therefore at lower human cost. Nations in war and times of national peril must be expected therefore to resort to information operations. In peacetime, deception of the domestic public should be avoided, and if really necessary the record put right at the earliest safe opportunity (that is the logic behind the 1966 doctrine that bears Harold Wilson's name restricting any government-authorized interception of the communications of Members of Parliament[12]). What has, however, changed is the means of production and delivery of information. Today digital information can easily be manipulated, targeted and disseminated. It is not only governments that take advantage of this change. Political movements, commercial interests, our colleagues and friends, and ourselves can all mislead.

If we want to safeguard ourselves from information manipulation, deception and faking we should:

- Try to distinguish when we are faced with:
  Malinformation: true information but never intended to be public.
  Misinformation: false information but innocently so.
  Disinformation: false information and known to be so before circulation.
- Regard ourselves as being under an obligation to correct misinformation errors as quickly as reasonably possible.
- Be very wary of genuine information that has been 'weaponized' by being leaked, especially online, and recognize that it may have been made more potent by omissions and alterations before release.
- Be aware that those seeking to deceive us know that the most effective 'fake news' will be false information that we are likely to think could be (and should be) true.
- Avoid the temptation to over- or underestimate the import of what you read on the web.

- Protect reputations by avoiding spreading what looks like disinformation or 'fake news' (and certainly not by adding to it). Retweet therefore with discretion.
- Remember that, even when disproved, fake stories still hang around like a bad smell.

Three lessons in making intelligent use of intelligence

8

Lesson 8: Imagine yourself in the shoes of the person on the other side

'I think we can do business together' was Margaret Thatcher's comment to the media about Mikhail Gorbachev before her meeting with him in London in the summer of 1984 on his first visit to a Western capital. He was being tipped as the Politburo member most likely to take over as Soviet leader from the ailing Soviet General Secretary Chernenko. This invitation to London with his wife, Raisa (a telegenic figure totally unlike the spouses of previous Soviet leaders), was not just a result of Margaret Thatcher's political intuition about the value of getting ahead of the changes taking place in the Soviet Union. It rested on the secret insights provided by a remarkable intelligence success, whose fruits were also being shared with President Reagan and a few key members of his administration. The case illustrates the strategic impact that well-timed secret intelligence can have on international relationships and negotiations.

The great intelligence secret was that MI6, thanks to invaluable assistance from the Danish Intelligence Service, had recruited a well-placed agent, Oleg Gordievsky, inside the heart of the KGB. Gordievsky was now the Acting Head of the KGB Residency inside the Soviet Embassy in London.[1] During his three years in Denmark, he had provided SIS with a series of remarkable intelligence and counter-intelligence coups exposing Soviet spies as well as giving invaluable insights into the last days of the old Soviet Union under the ageing and ill Brezhnev and his successor, Andropov (whom we met in Chapter 3, as the ruthless head of the KGB intent upon crushing the Prague Spring of Alexander Dubček).

When Gordievsky returned reluctantly to a desk job in the KGB Centre after his tour in Copenhagen, SIS prudently agreed with him that they would not run him there. Given the intense level of surveillance to be expected and the operational difficulties of intelligence activity in Moscow, MI6 judged it was simply too risky. The penalty of any slip would be torture and death, as it had been for Colonel Oleg Penkovsky of the GRU in 1962, when he was uncovered through surveillance of his contacts with MI6 and the CIA in Moscow. Instead the strategic calculation was of the long-term value he could represent as an agent in place within the KGB, to be reaped when he was posted overseas again.

In 1982 Gordievsky resurfaced on being appointed to the KGB Residency in the Soviet Embassy in London, to the secret rejoicing of the small number of those in the know. I was rightly not one of that small group given the policy post I held, although working in the Ministry of Defence I later benefited from being on the distribution of his reporting without of course knowing his identity or role in the Embassy in London. Thanks to some subtle manipulation orchestrated by British intelligence in order to clear the way for him by discrediting his rivals, he was quickly promoted to the key post of head of political intelligence work in the KGB Residency (head of the PR Line in KGB-speak).

A stream of invaluable secret intelligence reporting to MI6 followed Gordievsky's posting to London. So important was it that Margaret Thatcher herself was indoctrinated into the case in December 1982. 'Probably no British Prime Minister has ever followed the case of a British agent with as much personal attention as Mrs Thatcher devoted to Gordievsky,' wrote her biographer.[2] Carefully selected reports based on Gordievsky's intelligence, with elaborate arrangements to disguise the source, were passed to the CIA and to the White House. The CIA's assessment was that 'Gordievsky's intelligence was an epiphany for President Reagan' in revealing the inner workings of the Soviet leadership.

Posted to London and contact resumed, it was Gordievsky who was able to reveal to MI6 that Gorbachev was the KGB's preference for future leader well before he came to power. He described Gorbachev as a very different type of leader, who recognized the need for economic change if the Soviet Union was to survive. Unlike his predecessors Gorbachev saw the desirability of easing Cold War tensions and thereby reducing the burden of armaments expenditure. In part, his modernizing strategy failed because Gordievsky's advice, passed to President Reagan, was that Russian attempts to keep up with American defence technology (including Reagan's Star Wars programme) would eventually crack the Soviet system. As it did.

In preparation for that important first meeting between Gorbachev and the Prime Minister, Margaret Thatcher, briefs were prepared on both sides in the usual way on issues that should be raised, together with defensive lines to take on matters raised by the other side. The extraordinary thing about this meeting was that the briefs on *both* sides contained substantive material from Gordievsky. Thatcher had the benefit of the insights provided by Gordievsky's covert role as an SIS agent reporting on Gorbachev; and Gorbachev's brief relied on Gordievsky's advice as his head of KGB political reporting in the Residency in London. So Gordievsky was suggesting to Gorbachev lines to take on issues he knew, from MI6 and the Foreign Office, were of importance to the UK. Thatcher had not only advance warning from Gordievsky of what the issues to be raised by Moscow were, but also had his advice as a Soviet insider on the best manner of replying to ensure her responses struck home with the future leader of the Soviet Union. Gordievsky knew the plan was succeeding when he saw the daily KGB briefing for Gorbachev during his eight-day visit coming back 'with passages underlined to show gratitude or satisfaction'. 'Both sides were being briefed by us,' said an MI6 analyst involved at the time. 'We were doing something new – really trying to use the information, not distort it, to manage relations and open up new possibilities. We were a handful of people working amazing hours on the cusp of history.'[3]

The visit to the UK was a huge success for Gorbachev and burnished his international credentials. On the back of it, in January 1985, the KGB promoted Gordievsky again, this time to be Acting Head of the Residency. That made him the most senior Soviet spy in London, giving both him, and thus his MI6 handlers, unparalleled access to the secrets of the KGB.

Gordievsky's unique intelligence access proved to be even more important in US–Soviet relations. His reporting helped educate President Reagan and key members of his administration about the frightening level of paranoia felt by the old Soviet leaders about US nuclear capabilities and their fears of a US and NATO first strike. A genuine Soviet fear of the US deciding to launch first strikes against Soviet strategic forces had seemed the realm of airport novel fantasy. Having been the Defence Counsellor in the UK delegation to NATO from 1985 to 1988, and having participated in numerous nuclear release exercises in response to scenarios postulating Soviet aggression, I knew at first hand how hard it had been even with the artificiality of exercises to get unanimous decisions from the NATO nations, let alone to imagine a collective decision to start a war with the Soviet Union.

Gordievsky revealed how the Politburo in Moscow not only believed the Marxist doctrine that a final showdown between capitalism and communism was inevitable but that the 'principal adversary' (the United States) was actively preparing for that day. The KGB Centre had sent instructions out to its residencies in NATO capitals for an intelligence-gathering exercise codenamed Project Ryan to report indicators of Western preparations, such as stockpiling blood and the number of lights burning at night in ministries of defence.[4] According to Gordievsky, the KGB officers in NATO capitals knew perfectly well this was the stuff of paranoid nightmares on the part of their leadership, but cynically fulfilled their quotas in the interests of retaining their highly prized Western postings. Today Russian state media under President Putin, himself a former KGB officer from this era, still pumps out propaganda accusing NATO of preparing to attack Russia – as improbable a scenario today as it was back in the 1980s, as I know from my years spent in NATO.[5]

In 1983 that Soviet paranoia almost led to global crisis. US naval and air forces were closely shadowing Soviet forces and engaging in intelligence gathering on Soviet exercises, all designed to demonstrate President Reagan's early resolution in the face of what was seen as growing Soviet military power.[6] The regular NATO exercise to practise nuclear release procedures, Exercise Able Archer, was monitored by Soviet intelligence, and a Soviet military commander became concerned it might be the precursor of attack and placed some Soviet forces on a heightened state of alert, precautionary moves previously only seen in real crises. Those forces included Soviet air forces in East Germany and Poland, and some nuclear units. These measures that were detected in turn by US intelligence, who interpreted them as potentially offensive. That ran the risk of provoking the US to raise automatically its own nuclear alert states in response. Sensibly, the US did not. Had the US done so then that step would most likely in turn have been interpreted by the Soviet High Command as confirming their worst fears of an impending first strike, thus triggering further Soviet precautionary steps. Those in turn would be detected by the US and set off an unintended and dangerous escalatory cycle of action and reaction.

It was Gordievsky who provided the reason for these Soviet moves by explaining the paranoid origin of Project Ryan in the fear of a US first strike. The helpful outcome of the Able Archer scare, given Gordievsky's intelligence-based explanation, was that Washington subsequently took greater care to avoid changes in US military posture that might be interpreted as part of an escalatory pattern. As the CIA internal summary of the Able Archer alert concluded: ' . . . only Gordievsky's timely warnings to Washington via MI6 kept things from going too far'.

In circumstances where one party feels threatened it can therefore be reassuring to have inside-track knowledge of what is really going on. That helps avoid the sort of nasty surprises that can lead to conflict. All countries make spying against them an offence in domestic law. But there is no prohibition on conducting secret intelligence activity in international law, in large part because nations take very different views about what constitutes an offence against national security interests (as academic researchers, innocent tourists taking photographs of beauty spots near defence establishments and plane spotters noting down tail serial numbers have discovered to their cost), but also because implicitly they understand that it is in their mutual interest. In arms control agreements in particular, intelligence is seen as essential to maintain confidence that the other side is not cheating. 'Trust, but verify' is a Russian proverb that expresses this thought, one which President Reagan became fond of during the years he spent seeking arms control agreements with the Soviet Union.

The same learning applies to commercial joint ventures and contracts where transparency between the parties from the outset avoids later misunderstandings that could lead to destructive mutual distrust. Not every new couple thankfully sees the need for a legal prenuptial agreement but all can benefit from being open from the start about the contribution each will make to the household financially and from continuing to demonstrate that these responsibilities are being met. That theme of delivery of what was promised building trustworthiness is developed further in the next chapter. It is an important contributor to the maintenance of long-lasting partnerships in all walks of life

In the 1970s US and UK intelligence warned the NATO allies that the Soviet Union was developing a new class of intermediate-range nuclear missile, the SS-20, that could hit targets across Western Europe when fired from well within the Soviet Union. The SS-20 would have independently targetable multiple warheads, and a mobile launcher that could be concealed from satellite reconnaissance. Public concern in NATO nations grew about this major increase in Soviet nuclear offensive capability facing the European members of NATO, one not covered by existing US–Soviet strategic arms control.

By the late 1970s, driven by Germany's concern that the missile effectively undermined NATO strategy, NATO controversially invited the US to deploy its own medium-range missiles and cruise missiles in Europe. At the same time, on a parallel track, the US invited the Soviet Union to negotiate a total ban on weapons of this class (hence the popular description of the NATO policy of 1979 as a 'double track' decision, although the justification for the NATO deployments strictly did not depend upon 'countering' the SS-20 with matching capabilities). Two years of negotiation in Geneva to ban these weapons led nowhere. By 1983 the German Bundestag felt obliged to agree to the deployment of the new US missiles and the UK began to prepare bases for US cruise missiles. Moscow pulled out of the talks in response. Three years later the negotiations finally resumed. The difference this time was that the negotiations were under the new Soviet General Secretary, Mikhail Gorbachev. And, as we have just seen, MI6's former key source, Oleg Gordievsky, was now, from a position of safety in the UK, able to provide detailed analysis of Soviet moves.

As Thatcher had written to Reagan about Gorbachev: 'I certainly found him a man one could do business with. I actually rather liked him – there is no doubt that he is completely loyal to the Soviet system, but he is prepared to listen and have a genuine dialogue and make up his own mind.'[7] Gordievsky himself was flown to Washington in secret to brief President Reagan again in person before he met Gorbachev in Reykjavik in 1986. That summit and the openness of the discussions between the leaders stimulated the search for nuclear arms control, of which the 1987 INF Treaty was a concrete result, signed in Washington by President Reagan and General Secretary Gorbachev on 8 December 1987. The INF Treaty prohibited both parties from possessing, producing or flight-testing ground-launched intermediate-range ballistic and cruise missiles and the destruction of existing weapons in that class. It had taken seven years of hard negotiation and several attempts to reach this point. But finally it was achieved with intelligence help from Oleg Gordievsky. The British government viewed the agreement with genuine relief. It avoided the need for the highly controversial deployment of US nuclear-armed cruise missiles to Molesworth and Greenham Common in the UK. Greenham Common in particular had a highly publicized peace camp established at the perimeter of the base by women protestors, an expression of solidarity that had become an important way-point in the development of the feminist movement in the UK.

The sad end of the INF Treaty in 2019 also came as a result of secret intelligence. Technical reporting on missile tests revealed to the US and NATO in 2008 that Russia was developing another new class of short-range missile, the SSC-8, with a potential range greater than 500 kilometres, the limit permitted under the INF Treaty. The US had complained, but Russia in response had asserted that the missile only had a maximum range of 480 kilometres. There the matter had rested until the Trump administration arrived, bringing with it a long-held scepticism about the wisdom of arms control agreements with an autocratic state like Russia. To the surprise of European NATO leaders, President Trump announced to reporters after a campaign rally in Nevada: 'Russia has violated the agreement. They've been violating it for many years . . . We're the ones that have stayed in the agreement and we've honored the agreement. But Russia has not, unfortunately, honored the agreement. So we're going to terminate the agreement. We're gonna pull out.' By December 2018 NATO Foreign Ministers had been briefed on the latest intelligence on the actual deployment of the SSC-8 and had endorsed the US position regarding non-compliance. The INF Treaty therefore has sadly died.

The Gordievsky case itself nearly had a tragic ending. Not long after Gordievsky was appointed as the Acting Head of the London Residency in 1984, KGB counter-intelligence officers became suspicious of him after a Soviet spy inside the CIA, Aldrich Ames, had told them SIS was running an important double agent. Gordievsky was summoned back to Moscow for consultations. As he recounts in his own memoir, most disturbingly his wife and family were also brought back to Moscow, a standard ploy by the KGB so that they could be used as hostages if necessary. He was interrogated under a truth drug and his apartment bugged. Gordievsky survived this ordeal with his story intact but he knew suspicions about him had not been put to rest. Fearing the net was closing in, SIS extricated Gordievsky secretly from inside Russia and brought him via Finland and Norway to the UK in a complex and risky operation (the first of its kind). After his escape the Soviet authorities found Gordievsky guilty in absentia and sentenced him to death, the inescapable Soviet penalty for treason. He nevertheless continued from his new place of safety in the UK to provide valuable insights into the changes taking place in Moscow as the Soviet empire imploded and the Berlin Wall came down. He met President Reagan himself in July 1993. Reagan noted in his diary at the end of the entry for that day:[8] 'Forgot – this morning had a meeting with Col Oleg Antonovich Gordiyeveski [sic] – the Soviet KGB officer who defected to Eng. His wife and two little girls were left behind. We've been trying to get them out to join him.' They finally joined him in the UK six years later, following personal appeals to Gorbachev by Margaret Thatcher.

Negotiating safely guided by backchannels

We have seen the importance of strategic intelligence assessment in modulating the dealings that Reagan and Thatcher had with the Soviet leadership under Mikhail Gorbachev. Such an extraordinary covert access to the secrets of another state is highly unusual. Secret intelligence rarely therefore has such an impact on international relations. But backchannels can play an important role to keep open communications in circumstances in which neither party wants to acknowledge publicly that they were in contact. In commercial life it is often the external financial advisers to a company who are asked to get together with their opposite numbers to take soundings in the strictest confidence on whether a merger, demerger or acquisition might produce mutual benefits. In personal life when, sadly, couples begin to break up, it is often the friends of both parties who can play the essential role of discreet backchannels between potentially warring parties.

One notable example was the use of such a backchannel by President Kennedy to help defuse the 1961 Berlin crisis. Bobby Kennedy, then Attorney General, had been in the habit of regularly meeting, in Washington, the GRU agent Colonel Georgi Bolshakov, who was posing as the press attaché in the Soviet Embassy, in order to maintain a private direct means of communication between his brother and Khrushchev. When a crisis blew up in Berlin in 1961 that looked like escalating into hostilities over the Berlin Wall, the President passed a personal request to Khrushchev to withdraw his tanks aggressively positioned just behind the wall (with, we can assume, private assurances that there would be matching de-escalation on the Allied side). Face was saved on both sides when de-escalation happened.[9] Recalling Chapter 7, backchannels need to be chosen with care. The same Bolshakov deceptively assured Attorney General Bobby Kennedy at the time of the Cuban missile crisis that the Soviet Union did not have missiles in Cuba.

The Northern Ireland campaign provides a different example of a backchannel in operation, in the most sensitive of circumstances, when a democratic government wants to be in contact with a terrorist organization.[10] In 1972, the level of violent attacks by the Provisional IRA (PIRA) against police officers, soldiers and prison officers in Northern Ireland had risen to disturbing levels, coupled with rioting and inter-community disorder fomented by so-called Loyalist paramilitary groups. London felt the situation had slipped out of local control and instituted direct rule from London. That created an urgent demand for impartial strategic intelligence to be acquired directly for London, and not just through local police channels. One of the measures taken by the British authorities was therefore to set up the equivalent of an MI6/MI5 intelligence station in Belfast. A senior MI6 officer, Frank Steele, was sent out along with a small number of British officials who could act as political advisers. They set up camp in Laneside, a large house in an affluent suburb on Belfast Lough which served as both office and residence. Given the level of violence on the streets, the growing terrorist campaign from the Provisional IRA and the so-called Loyalist paramilitary groups, the personal risk to British officials was very high. The mission was kept a deep secret. Steele's brief was to develop covert contacts with, and to seek ways of influencing, the IRA in order to persuade them to halt their terrorist campaign.

In 1972 the PIRA did call a short ceasefire, and just before the ceasefire was due to end, with the acquiescence of the Prime Minister, Edward Heath, a secret meeting was brokered by Laneside to allow the Opposition leader, Harold Wilson, and shadow Northern Ireland Secretary, Merlyn Rees, to meet PIRA leaders in Dublin. Hours of discussion about extending the ceasefire led nowhere and they were still talking when midnight came and with it the resumption of active terrorism by the PIRA. Undaunted, Frank Steele himself met PIRA leaders in a country house near Donegal and agreed arrangements for key terrorist leaders to be flown to London to meet with Willie Whitelaw, by then Secretary of State for Northern Ireland. On 7 July 1972 Steele accompanied six PIRA leaders, including Sean MacStiofain, Gerry Adams from the PIRA Belfast Brigade and Martin McGuinness from the Derry Brigade, on to an RAF aircraft to be flown secretly to England. The meeting took place in the smart surroundings of the Cheyne Walk apartment of Paul Channon, one of Whitelaw's ministers. It went badly from the outset and Whitelaw later described agreeing to it as the worst political mistake of his career. MacStiofain banged the table and demanded that the British side set a date for withdrawal. Whitelaw, who had been led to expect discussions about a longer ceasefire, remained polite but necessarily immovable. The lesson was learned: both sides had been insufficiently prepared about the expectations of the other.

When Steele's tour of duty came to an end he was replaced by another highly experienced MI6 officer, Michael Oatley, who described himself as being in 'a situation where intelligence would not simply be a matter of reporting on situations, but of influencing them'. MI6 officers are used to operating at the outer limits of their brief. British Prime Ministers had a stated policy of not negotiating with terrorists. When Roy Mason was Northern Ireland Secretary he went as far as to expressly forbid contacts by British officials, direct or indirect, with PIRA while the violence continued. Yet, despite the political risks and on their own authority, Laneside kept open covert channels of communication with the PIRA leadership with arrangements known only to a handful of senior British officials (the channel was known as the 'pipe', after the metaphor of a bamboo pipe down which puffs of air could be sent so that both sides knew there was someone there even if there were no substantive exchanges). As Oatley described it: 'I didn't think I was running any serious risk politically for the Government in letting the IRA know that there was still a point of contact if they should ever need it and it would operate wherever I happened to be in the world.'

Oatley found a trusted and secure (and brave) intermediary, Brendan Duddy, who could be at one end of the 'pipe' and carry messages when needed to and from the PIRA leadership in hiding in the Republic. Duddy ran a pie and chips shop in Derry; he had employed the young Martin McGuinness delivering pies, and knew he was a rising star in the PIRA. Duddy was an ardent Republican who was convinced of the case for a united Ireland, yet he deeply disapproved of the indiscriminate violence of the PIRA campaign and so was willing to take risks to keep the prospect of peace alive. Duddy's PIRA codename was the 'mountain climber'. He died in 2017.

Some of the darkest days in Northern Ireland were in 1980, when convicted Republican prisoners at the Maze Prison went on hunger strike demanding political-prisoner status, including the right to wear their own clothes. With one of them close to death, the 'mountain climber' used the 'pipe' to suggest to Oatley (who by then had left Northern Ireland on another MI6 posting) that some compromise could be possible. Oatley then re-engaged and crafted a revision of the prison regulations, with the Permanent Secretary, the senior official in the Northern Ireland Office and through him ministers and the Prime

Minister herself, Margaret Thatcher, that his contacts suggested might also be acceptable to the hunger strikers and the PIRA hierarchy. The hunger strike was called off in anticipation of the deal. Sadly, the level of ambiguity in the understanding, necessary to get both sides on board, proved too great for the prison authorities to cope with and PIRA disillusion set in, with Margaret Thatcher claiming victory and the PIRA responding that they had been misled. A second hunger strike started, this time literally to the death. Ten of the prisoners had died before the strike was called off. The government then quietly made the key concessions on clothing, free association and loss of remission for the protesters. The episode illustrates the value of backchannels, but also their limitations in brokering deals. The 'pipe' was nevertheless kept open and covert contacts maintained.

A decade later, in February 1993, a message was sent through the 'pipe' to Oatley's successor in Belfast which was passed back to the Prime Minister, John Major. It read: 'The conflict is over but we need your advice on how to bring it to an end. We wish to have an unannounced ceasefire in order to hold a dialogue leading to peace. We cannot announce such a move as it will lead to confusion for the volunteers because the press will interpret it as surrender. We cannot meet the Secretary of State's public renunciation of violence, but it would be given privately as long as we were sure we were not being tricked.' The response from London was quick and positive. There were nevertheless to be many ups and downs in the subsequent manoeuvring on both sides before a peace process became firmly established under Major's successor, Tony Blair, and the PIRA could not resist a final bombing campaign to try to put extra pressure on London. When the text of the message leaked later to the press, however, it provoked a strong denial from Martin McGuinness that that was the message as sent. It may well be that the intelligence officers in Belfast suggested the wording or may have reworded parts of it in transmitting it to London to make clearer what they had assessed was McGuinness's intent and make it appear more palatable. If so, they gave the search for peace a boost when it was most needed.[11]

In complex negotiations both sides will be equally concerned to establish that they are not being duped or misled in some way. Wise negotiators recognize that. We can only speculate whether Margaret Thatcher, and her successors John Major and Tony Blair, would have authorized the delicate backchannel contacts with the Provisional IRA had it not been for high-level secret intelligence confirming that some leaders of the Republican movement, including its military wing, had concluded that they should cooperate in trying to bring an end to the armed conflict. Their decisions led, after several false starts, to the peace process, even as terrorist violence continued, and eventually to the signing of the Good Friday Agreement.

The nature of successful negotiation

The examples just given show that having private access to some of the other side's thinking can help when it really matters (including confirmation that what is being said is genuinely meant). Often it is obvious what the other side wants, and why, with plenty of detail and context that can be derived from open sources. But it would be a great mistake to draw the conclusion that somehow just establishing what is in the negotiating brief of the other side will ensure success. Some negotiations nevertheless fail. And even where a deal is agreed, in many cases it then collapses after a short time when it is put into effect. Why?

A good deal has to provide needed benefit for both parties to a negotiation. Without that aspiration why would any party enter negotiation, and without assurance of that benefit why would anyone sign up to the deal? There is a modern branch of economics – so-called mechanism design – that builds on mathematical game theory to try to design rules for bargaining situations such that even when neither of the parties has privileged access to the other side's brief, and both are acting selfishly to maximize their own interest or may be trying to deceive the other, nevertheless the outcome will be the best collectively. The 2007 Nobel economics prize was shared by the developers of this approach, Leonid Hurwicz, Eric Maskin and Roger Myerson.

Both parties in a negotiation will have 'bottom lines' that they do not want to cross as concessions are being horse-traded. Typically, in the final stages of a poor negotiation, the stronger party will try to push the other into just one more small concession after another, hoping to make the loss of ground seem a marginal concession given the larger prize to be gained from a deal. Such salami slicing may indeed induce the weaker party to go below their bottom line. But, even if agreed, such deals are unlikely to stick for long. The aggrieved party that felt it was pushed too far will try to make up lost ground. The fine print of the negotiated deal or contract may well be scoured for weaknesses that can be exploited. This is the opposite of a strategic outcome, as described in the next chapter.

One approach to negotiation that helps to avoid the risk of being salami-sliced at the end is to have established in some detail at the outset what the preferred alternative to the negotiation is. Rather than thinking in terms of the 'bottom line', the advice is to establish the BATNA: the best alternative to a negotiated agreement.[12] That is the negotiating strategy which I was taught at the UK Civil Service College. Before the negotiation starts, the parties should work out privately what for them would be the best alternative if the negotiation does not succeed. This BATNA is then worked up into a credible plan of action that you know you can execute if it becomes necessary. If the negotiations run into difficulties, the parties enjoy the confidence given by having their own alternative route ready. The approach rests on the observation that it is always better psychologically to be prepared to advance to a known position than to retreat into the unknown.

Knowing when to walk safely away from a negotiation that is in difficulties is certainly going to be easier when the alternative way ahead has previously been established. The negotiating partner will sense that you have a well-developed BATNA and that discourages attempts to chisel last-minute concessions. When moving house and negotiating to sell your flat so that you can buy the new one you have already made an offer on it is wise to have prepared your BATNA, perhaps having already spoken to the bank about a bridging loan. If the potential buyer then tries to get you to drop the price at the very last moment, guessing you are pressed for time to get the sale, you have your alternative plan ready and can respond firmly to such a try-on. Chances are your sale will still go through at or very close to the previous price. It may be that in the summer of 2019 the Prime Minister, Boris Johnson, thought that he had a powerful Brexit BATNA in his insistence that the UK had worked up contingency plans and was ready and willing to leave the EU without a deal on 31 October if negotiations failed to deliver what he wanted. The evident risks of chaos and economic damage with a 'no deal' Brexit, notwithstanding the contingency planning, nevertheless persuaded Parliament that it was not 'the best alternative to a negotiated deal' and Parliament then passed a law mandating an extension of the deadline (to which the EU agreed) rather than crashing out in 2019 without a deal.

Short-term advantage does not ensure a long-term outcome

For that and many other reasons it is unwise to rush into a negotiation, despite the wish to get it over with so that uncertainty about the future can be lifted. It may well have been a profound error for the British government to send its Article 50 withdrawal letter to the European Union so quickly after the very unexpected (and narrow) win in the 2016 Referendum by the Brexiteers. There had not been time to think through what would represent outcomes consistent with the range of views of those who had voted to leave the EU, nor what might be done to reconcile the many who had voted to remain. In grinding and protracted negotiations the British side reiterated that the alternative to their preferred outcome was simply to crash out of the EU without a deal. This is the polar opposite of a BATNA.

The UK Brexit process has also been a failure to match negotiating strategy to the objective. The ministers initially in charge talked a very tough game in public to reassure their domestic supporters, but do not seem to have made much attempt to explain why they did this to their EU counterparts and thus to build trust with them. Quite the reverse, making evident their expectation that the EU would try to punish the UK for the referendum result. Unsurprisingly, the result was high levels of mutual suspicion. Nor did the British ministers show any understanding of the legitimate interests (from an EU point of view) in preserving the EU legal and constitutional order. What the UK side demanded by way of 'having your cake and eating it' in preserving many valued benefits of EU membership after having left was bound to be resisted.[13] UK ministers saw such cases as continuing membership of Europol or the Galileo satellite system as being in the interests of both sides, and thus it seemed obvious that some solution would be found. In UK eyes this was applying simple pragmatism. They grossly underestimated that, for EU member states, this would be seen as rule breaking that threatened their fundamental interests in the EU as an institution. Failure to appreciate these cultural differences of outlook inevitably led to impasse, followed by UK concessions.

Preparing sensibly for a negotiation takes time and objective analysis to understand the other side. That is the opposite of the magical thinking which holds that all that is needed in negotiation is sufficient willpower and obstinacy. We can think of preparation for a sound negotiation working through the four-step SEES intelligence analysis process described in Chapters 1–4. The intelligence needed for this process in everyday life can be gleaned from open sources. This should start with identifying possible future benefits and if possible wider opportunities to both sides, not just your own, drawing on your situational awareness of what both you and the negotiating partner faces. At the same time possible risks have to be identified and strategies worked out to minimize the chances of ending up there. It is important to have the understanding of why both sides have come to the negotiating table and therefore what they will need to take away from the negotiation to count as success. Such thinking makes it easier to model how they are likely to react to different moves in the negotiation.

Lessons in the ethics of negotiation

Serious negotiations are concerned with securing more lasting outcomes on the basis that both parties will gain, not that one will suffer loss at the hands of the other. There is a principle followed by British intelligence officers not to use blackmail to force agents to work for them. The blackmailed agent is likely to minimize the intelligence they hand over or try to get their revenge by distorting their reports in order to deceive. Similarly, it is not a good idea to pressure the other side in a negotiation to the point where after the deal is forced through the loser will try to get their own back. In commercial life it may mean reducing the effort put into the minimum stipulated in the contract, or even a little less if it is thought that will not be noticed, or trying to recoup more by claiming for extra work not originally contracted for, a favourite of the construction industry.

In devising a negotiating strategy much depends therefore upon how important it is to have a lasting and productive relationship with the partner. In *The Art of the Deal*, written over thirty years ago, Donald Trump famously set down an aggressive win-at-all-costs approach to the art of negotiation. The partner in a Trump negotiation is an adversary to be vanquished. His co-author, Tony Schwartz, has described this obsession with winning (and when thwarted still claiming success by redefining what the negotiation was about) as grounded in fear of failure.[14] He warns that in the process of behaving this way we will lose the capacity for empathy, rationality, proportionality and attention to the longer-term consequences of our actions. In such negotiations there is the temptation to try to unbalance the opponent by unexpected moves, including making excessive compliments followed by unsettling threats.

Apparently maximalist demands are slapped on the table, to force the unnerved opponent to move from their preferred outcome range. Suddenly reversing concessions already made can have the same effect. Such destructive negotiating tactics may well provide negotiating 'wins', where it is a short-term gain that is sought at the expense of the other party. This is perhaps workable in a few areas such as attempting to finance property deals because if, later, the forced-through deal unwinds, then it can always be sold on. That cannot be done if it is the national interest that has to be jettisoned. The result of adopting this approach to any negotiation is that you are liable to be winning a battle at the expense of losing the war. Real negotiation looks to the longest term.

Besides, ethical risks accompany guilty knowledge. This is information that has come into your hands that you are not supposed to have. Motive matters if your intention is then to make use of it. The leading nineteenth-century advocate of utilitarian philosophy, John Stuart Mill, warned: 'the only purpose for which power can rightfully be exercised over any member of a civilized community, against his will, is to prevent harm to others'.[15] A nation under threat is unlikely to hesitate long before acting, citing the greater good. That will include gathering intelligence and using the power to act in secret. It is hard not to see Gordievsky's intelligence, described earlier in this chapter, as contributing to good outcomes. On the other hand, it may be a desire selfishly to better your own circumstances at the expense of someone else.

Let me give a business example of an ethical dilemma over exploiting for advantage information you are not supposed to have. Suppose you are preparing to pitch your bid in an overseas commercial competition for a contract. The evening before, you eat in a smart downtown restaurant. Finally seated at a table, you feel something under your foot and realize it is a folder of papers left by a previous diner. Glancing through the documents to see who might have left them you realize with a shock that you are examining a copy of the presentation of your main rival in the competition.

Guiltily you look around to see if anyone is watching. Should you continue to study the pitch and then put the papers back where you found them? Should you just ignore what you have learned? Or do you rush back to your hotel and rewrite your own presentation? The thought may even occur to you that this might be a trap, leading to accusations of industrial espionage and thus being eliminated from the competition. The better angel of your nature will say you cannot benefit from information that you are not supposed to have. But if the roles were reversed, the devil on your shoulder whispers, competitors would not hesitate to benefit. But that is what makes us different, you conclude. That is our brand of trusted integrity. If we do not live our corporate values, then why should we convince others to trust us?[16] So, the next day, you explain what happened to the commercial director of the potential client and that you cannot hide the fact that you have read the opposing bid. The director tells you that in accordance with best practice he is cancelling the competition, which will be rerun. In the best case he will add, your action exemplifies what he hoped to find in a company they could rely on as a long-term partner with access to the secrets of the corporation. Your reputation goes up.

Jack Straw, then Home Secretary, once explained to me when I was his Permanent Secretary the ethical rule he personally applied. Simply put, when in doubt, do the right thing. It may not end up as you would hope, often it will not, but you have a defence you can mount of honestly having tried to do the right thing. If you resort to subterfuges and wriggling around the truth and it still goes wrong, you are exposed and have no ethical justification to fall back on. Your lack of integrity will become all too apparent. One of the ways of knowing that a course of action is 'the right thing' to do is that it usually appears harder than the alternatives. We may, for example, fear immediate criticism or reprimand. Another is that it may involve telling more of the truth than we feel immediately comfortable with. We have all learned this from the pain of having to own up to misdeeds as young children, and when relief comes from experiencing eventual forgiveness. We will all, I hope, have learned as adults from watching young children come to recognize through experience the virtue of honesty as 'doing the right thing'.

Conclusions: imagining yourself in the shoes of the person on the other side

In this chapter we have looked at the process of negotiation in which (usually) two parties settle disagreements about how far each can simultaneously satisfy their objectives to generate a joint outcome acceptable to both sides. Having well-thought-through analysis about the objectives and motivation of the other party is key (and vice versa) and likely to be more important than knowing their negotiating hand at any one time. In such circumstances the lessons are:

- Do not rush into a negotiation feeling under pressure to get it over with.
- Prepare carefully, including setting a BATNA you believe in (the best alternative to a negotiated agreement – a more reliable guide than a 'bottom line').

- Use the SEES model to establish what you need to know about the short- and long-term objectives of the other party, as seen by them.
- Work out in particular what the other party needs to secure an agreement – it may include matters that are much less important to you.
- Search for outcomes that will meet the interests of both parties and that both will count as success.
- Having guilty knowledge does not always help get the best outcome: when in doubt do the right thing.
- Do not try to intimidate the other party by gamesmanship: a deal they are forced to accept is unlikely to last.
- Be prepared to accept the maxim that nothing is agreed until everything is, but do not withdraw points already provisionally settled just to try to unbalance the other side.

9
Lesson 9: Trustworthiness creates lasting partnerships

The value of strategic partnerships

Lieutenant General Ken Minihan, Director of the NSA, was reverentially holding a rare first edition of Isaac Newton's *Principia* when I reminded him of one of my favourite sayings of Winston Churchill: 'The further back you look, the further ahead you can see.' I was showing him round the library of Chevening House in Kent, the outstandingly beautiful Grade 1 listed official residence allocated to the British Foreign Secretary. As Director of GCHQ I had been privileged to borrow the house for a few days to host one of the regular joint meetings of the Boards of GCHQ and the National Security Agency. Chevening's 800 years of history provided an impressive backdrop to our discussions about how to develop the NSA/GCHQ partnership into the coming digital age. And what better way to start discussions of the impact of developments in number theory on cryptography than browsing the mathematics library assembled by an eighteenth-century owner of the house, Charles Stanhope, mathematician and inventor of an early mechanical calculator. The treasures of the library included first editions of Napier's original logarithm table and the pioneering works of Leibniz and Gauss, not to mention the discoveries of the brilliant John Wallis, Savilian Professor of

Geometry at Oxford University, whose portrait hung in the GCHQ Director's office in Cheltenham to celebrate his secret role as the nation's Chief Cryptographer for forty-six years from 1643 to 1689.

Intelligence agencies have learned more than most the lesson that strong partnerships add value. And they know the time it takes to build the necessary reputation for trustworthiness in handling other people's confidences. Even the largest of nations will struggle to provide satisfactorily on its own for the intelligence requirements of its decisionmakers in a world of global threats if relying only on its own resources. Intelligence officers in the twenty-first century have to learn to think about which organizations and which nations they are going to have to work with in order to achieve their objectives. In each case they will have to be aware of the ethical outlook of their partners and the legal regime under which they operate, and whether these are compatible with the need to maintain confidence that in the relationship they will still act with proportionality and necessity.

Comparable claims can be made for the need for trustworthy relationships between democratic governments and their publics, not least over trusting that advanced digital access to the personal data of citizens will not be misused in future by governments to monitor and control behaviour. Human rights legislation provides a framework for the democracies within which trust can be built, but individual balancing acts are still needed; for example, between our right to privacy and our right to security, and between our right to exercise freedom of speech and our right to be protected from hate speech of all kinds. There must be trust that those balances will be reached after the sort of rational and mature analysis that this book has advocated.

Today's global business and commercial world is digital. Dominant influence is exercised by a small number of very powerful Internet-based mega-corporations. Democratic governments need their active cooperation and technical prowess to develop ways of keeping the Internet an open, free and safe space. Such cooperation can only proceed on the basis of trust on all sides that the relationships will not be abused for private or political gain.

Similarly, engendering lasting cooperation from others in your own life will ultimately boil down to your ability to be trusted.

The strongest relationships are those that rest on voluntary agreement (rather than just satisfying bare legal requirements, as would most likely be the case if there has not been recognition of long-term mutual interests). Joint initiatives that are voluntarily entered into can combine the most powerful attributes of different organizations, generating results that would have been impossible to produce alone in any reasonable timetable. In the commercial world we see long-term relationships with key suppliers increase quality and stability of production. Having trusted partners overseas to handle marketing and sales in the regions with which the partners are most familiar not only cuts costs but reduces the inevitable risks associated with operating inside what may be very different cultures.[1]

There is an example in the secret intelligence world that has much to teach us all about how to go about building partnerships in conditions that might at first sight suggest that levels of trust would be too low to make this possible. That is the so-called '5-eyes' signals intelligence partnership between the US, UK, Canada, Australia and New Zealand with at its heart the relationship between the United States and the United Kingdom.[2] For over seventy years the security of each of those nations has benefited during peace and war, and continues to benefit, from that cooperation.

In different posts during my career I have seen in particular the mutual value of the exceptional US–UK relationship, working together in signals and other intelligence, in defence technology, on nuclear deterrence as NATO nuclear partners, and after 9/11 in counter-terrorism and constructing modern homeland security. I know from personal experience that there are principles of sound cooperation that are essential for sustaining such relationships. A culture of cooperation as the default position has consciously to be fostered and handed on from generation to generation. In my time as Director GCHQ I worked closely with Lt General Ken Minihan Director NSA. We shared our ideas for how our organizations could best tackle the operational challenges of meeting the different intelligence requirements of the post-Cold War era, and how to ride the huge wave of digital technology we could see advancing towards us as the commercial world adopted and developed the Internet and the World Wide Web. We became and remain friends (I was introduced to his signature drink, Jeremiah Weed Kentucky bourbon, and in return I encouraged appreciation of the finer Islay, Skye and Orkney single malts from my Scottish heritage).

The characteristics that make the US–UK intelligence relationship work

Personal working relationships as well as sound processes matter in building lasting partnerships. When the US Army arrived on the Western Front in 1918, there was a brilliant young cryptographer, William F. Friedman, on General Pershing's intelligence staff.[3] Senior officers in the British High Command, with remarkable foresight, took Friedman under their wing. Friedman learned not just about their early Army signals intelligence efforts on the Western Front but also about the pioneering work on diplomatic as well as naval cyphers achieved by the cryptographers of Room 40 in the Admiralty (as we saw in Chapter 7 with the Zimmermann telegram). Friedman got to respect and trust the leading figures in British signals intelligence, including the young Alastair Denniston in Room 40.[4] William Friedman had by the Second World War become the leading figure in US cryptography. In 1941 he was tasked with re-creating the relationship with his old UK friends, by then established at Bletchley Park under the Directorship of none other than Alastair Denniston.

Such personal friendship as well as professional respect between US and UK cryptographers helped the development of the strategic intelligence partnership that was so vital later in the war, even when there were significant policy differences between the British Chiefs of Staff and the US Joint Chiefs. I was pleased to discover that on his 1941 visit Friedman was taken to my old Cambridge college, Corpus Christi (founded in 1352), by one of its Fellows who had become a senior analyst at Bletchley Park, Professor E. R. Vincent, prompting Friedman to write in his diary: 'Here stand in quiet dignity and great strength buildings devoted to learning and democratic institutions and the dignity of man.'[5]

Churchill as Prime Minister would not have forgotten that Vincent was one of the group who founded in 1919 the UK cryptographic organization that became Bletchley Park, bringing together the Admiralty Room 40 responsible for the Zimmermann telegram and the Army military intelligence department which William Friedman had worked with on the

Central Front. I cannot resist citing the letter to Churchill in 1941 from the leading Bletchley Park cryptanalysts, including the computing pioneer Alan Turing:

> *Dear Prime Minister,*
>
> *Some weeks ago you paid us the honour of a visit, and we believe that you regard our work as important. We think, however, that you ought to know . . . the finding of the [Enigma] naval keys is being delayed by at least 12 hours every day . . . owing to the shortage of trained staff and the fatigue of our present decoding staff . . . all we need to put matters right is about 20 trained typists . . . if we are to do our job as well as it could, and should, be done then it is absolutely vital that our wants, small as they are, should be promptly attended to.*
>
> *We are, Sir, your obedient servants*
>
> *A M Turing, W G Welchman, CHO'D Alexander, P S Milner-Barry*

Stuart Milner-Barry, one of the original signatories, was dispatched to hand-carry the letter to London since the cryptanalysts feared if sent through usual channels it would never reach the great man. Stuart bluffed his way past the armed sentry at No. 10 and found a Private Secretary he could intimidate with the secrecy of the matter, and thus it reached Churchill. I had the good fortune shortly before joining GCHQ to meet Stuart Milner-Barry, by then knighted and working in HM Treasury and still active in British chess. He had left the secret world at the end of the war since, in his words of caution to me, nothing could in peacetime recapture the intensity of that kind of work in wartime. I joined nevertheless. The letter he had carried turned out to be vital for the war effort: the copy in the National Archives shows that Churchill minuted on it: 'Action this day. Make sure they have everything they want on extreme priority and report to me that this has been done' (which it was within a month).

For the rest of the war Churchill remained the greatest supporter of Bletchley Park, and its decrypts were hand-carried to him personally every day. The story of the cryptographers' plea in 1941 for extra typists brings to mind the medieval German proverb (much later applied to the loss of King Richard III at the Battle of Bosworth Field): 'For the want of a nail, the shoe was lost, for the want of the shoe, the horse was lost, for the want of the horse the King was lost, and with him the kingdom.' Another historical resonance I cherish was that it was one of the signatories of the letter, Hugh Alexander, an international chessmaster himself, who gave me a very stiff interview for entry to GCHQ in 1969 in his role then as its Chief Cryptanalyst. We argued I recall over the epistemological differences between the results from econometric models and from the models of mathematical economics as ways of understanding the world. He won.

After the end of the war, and as the threat from the Soviet Union became apparent, the US Joint Chiefs and the UK Chiefs of Staff met and resolved to continue this highly exceptional level of joint intelligence enterprise, as noted by the British Chief of Naval Staff:[6] 'Much discussion about 100 per cent cooperation with the USA about Sigint. Decided that less than 100 per cent was not worth having.' A sharing agreement between the US and UK signals intelligence establishments was duly signed on 5 March 1946 which provided for sharing of collection, analysis of signals traffic, cryptanalysis and much else. Detailed appendices to the original agreements set down the mutually agreed tight security arrangements, essential to maintain trust and allow raw intercept to be shared directly between the partners. That in turn meant greater mutual advantage since each party could contribute collection where they were best able (with the UK's global reach an important contributing factor) as well as sharing out the tasks of processing, translation and reporting, extending the capability of each party to cover global issues.

The bilateral US–UK arrangement was extended after the war to encompass wartime allies from the former British Dominions: Canada (1948), and Australia and New Zealand (1956), to become what is now known as the 5-eyes partnership of today, further increasing its global value.[7]

The wide scope envisaged by the founders at the end of the war remains the same today for the 5-eyes, although the terminology now in use is not that of radio but of the Internet (for example, traffic analysis would be called communications data analysis and much of the collection is via bulk accesses to the Internet). Generations of cryptographers and technologists have grown up together in the strategic relationship, they have shared in successes and failures alike, there are many cross-postings and secondments, their families become friends, and they are prepared to trust each other with the most sensitive information and work together on joint projects at the leading edge of technology. Such deep cooperation also made it possible to have meaningful peer review of intelligence assessments, including having US representatives contribute to many discussions of the UK Joint Intelligence Committee.[8]

A good example of joint working was the Venona project, successfully deciphering KGB one-time pad communications.[9] That led to the uncovering of the Russian spies Donald Maclean (a diplomat who was Head of Chancery in the British Embassy in Washington) and Klaus Fuchs (a leading British nuclear physicist in the US atomic and hydrogen bomb projects). The exposure of these spies was due to brilliant US/UK cryptanalytic cooperation but alas paradoxically led to temporary reductions in cooperation in atomic research and in human intelligence work because of the fears of James Angleton, among others, as we saw in Chapter 6, that there could be further British traitors not yet exposed.

The principles that underlie successful strategic partnerships

The example of the transatlantic intelligence relationship provides sound guidelines for any partnership. I would start with recognition of mutual trustworthiness as the most valuable attribute of any successful partnership.[10] Deep cooperation inevitably means that many of the secrets of each partner get to be known to the other. This is as true in personal relationships as in the government and commercial world. The opportunities to take selfish short-term advantage will be there but there has to be confidence these temptations will be resisted. Being recognized as trustworthy comes from a long history of respect for the sensitivities of the other, demonstrating that commitments entered into and restrictions imposed will be honoured. Trustworthiness therefore comes from consistent, predictable, reliable behaviour over a long period of time demonstrating honesty, competence and reliability.

It did not surprise me that in his memoirs a former Director of the NSA, Mike Hayden, recounts that after 9/11, facing the possibility of another terrorist attack on the US that might disable much of NSA intelligence processing, the contingency plan was for GCHQ to take over the work of the US sigint servers until NSA was back online.[11] GCHQ could be trusted with that heavy responsibility based on its past record of being a reliable strategic partner.

To make such close cooperation work over a long period there must be shared values to fall back on. For the US and UK agencies their enduring beliefs – for example, in defending the freedom of the democracies – has sustained their relationship through difficult periods when national political interests and ambitions differed. I remember an example from my own time as the Deputy Under Secretary of State for defence policy in the Ministry of Defence in 1994. The Royal Navy and US Navy were attempting to enforce at sea in the Adriatic the UNSC arms embargo on Bosnia. Key Congressional leaders believed instead in 'Lift and Strike': lifting the arms embargo and using US air power to strike the Bosnian Serbs, despite the danger to the UK-led UN international peacekeeping force UNPRO-FOR, with its soldiers exposed to retaliation as they rode around in white-painted vehicles wearing blue helmets trying to escort the delivery of humanitarian aid. Following Congressional resolutions, President Clinton in November 1994 directed that the US would not enforce the UN Resolution and would cut off intelligence sharing on the subject.[12] The US Navy's Aegis cruiser understandably pulled out of intelligence-gathering work to support the embargo but I am not aware that the overall joint NSA/GCHQ intelligence effort was impeded. Those who believed in the underlying values of the relationship made it work. Day-to-day transatlantic intelligence cooperation continued and built the basis for the successful intervention of NATO in Bosnia and Kosovo.

Sustained will is needed to put shared objectives first, regardless of ups and downs in the details of the relationship at any given moment or indeed the level of personal chemistry between leaders. For cooperating organizations in government or the private sector the message must be clear from the top that the long-term value of the strategic partnership is too important to be sacrificed to short-term pressures. It is no co-incidence that in the signals intelligence relationship both the UK and the US select some of their best leaders to be the senior liaison officers in each other's organizations who can be expected after their posting to rise to the C-Suite of top management. Who is selected from each partner if a new relationship is being set up will really matter.

Sharing sensitive technology will have specific consequences, in government as in commercial partnerships. The side sharing a secret trusts the other not to abuse the opportunity it may offer, but the act implicitly builds trust in the other direction, that the recipient implicitly feels trust in the giver. This is true of all sharing in life. The implication was obvious at the time the US would make good use after the war of the secrets of the world's first programmable computer, codenamed Colossus. This pioneering device was built for Bletchley by Tommy Flowers of the Post Office Engineering Department from telephone plug boards, switching gear, over 1000 radio valves and paper tape for input. The US was also able, with its greater resources, to mass-produce the proto-computers, the 'bombes' designed at Bletchley Park by the mathematician Alan Turing for cryptanalysis of the Enigma machine cipher, and thus become the dominant partner.

We can see in the cases just described that the aim of any true partnership is to arrive at a position of mutual advantage where all parties to the relationship benefit, and thus we can genuinely say that gains are shared. The shares do not necessarily have to be equally divided – there will be ups and downs – but there have to be returns commensurate with the effort put in over the long term. Nor are gains simply about short-term monetary value. But over a period of years there has to be evident benefit to the parties if it is to be sustained. It helps that the process is usually cumulative in adding value. As trust builds up, so relationships deepen and the value to be derived from them increases. With that greater mutual confidence, the parties can plan new ventures and mutual investment together. Higher risk can be accepted in those circumstances, with the corresponding potential for higher gain.

When two people come together on a date they will both initially be searching for points of mutual interest and connections which they can explore in the hope that they will help build a relationship. In the same way, when two organizations with different structures and processes come together, they are bound to bump against each other, trying to establish good points of contact. Those who lead the process must have, or quickly acquire, a feel for the ethos of the organizations concerned. Understanding any clashing psycho-dynamic tensions that may arise from the nature of the work that goes on within the cooperating organizations is very necessary, as we saw in Chapter 5. In the case of intelligence agencies that work has very unusual and stressful characteristics deriving from the very nature of secret intelligence, information that others do not want you to have and will try actively to prevent you acquiring. Success in obtaining secret intelligence, and the specific sources and methods by which it is acquired, must be concealed from outside gaze. It is a working environment where reticence, if not outright concealment, is second nature. The shared risks and need for mutual support for those within create strong interpersonal bonds, but at times create barriers in communicating with those perceived to be on the outside. In such an environment the partnership narrative must be compelling, be practical and achievable, but must also be seen to be honest, consistent with the ethos and mission of the organizations. In our personal lives most of us have reticences and well-defended boundaries we prefer to keep within. But establishing a constructive relationship with another person means being prepared to open up to the gaze of the other, sharing confidences and building mutual trust.

The ability of partners to challenge each other and point out areas for improvement, without a retreat into defensiveness, provides an important safety valve as well as opportunities for mutual growth. I experienced an interesting example of nations voluntarily accepting challenges from partner nations when working in the 1980s in NATO. I was the UK Defence Counsellor and represented the UK on NATO's Defence Review Committee. The major NATO commanders proposed goals for the development of each nation's armed forces after intensive consultation with the nation concerned and in the light of threat assessments by the NATO intelligence staffs, with the intention that national plans reflect the needs of NATO collective defence. Of course, most of the goals were modernization objectives the nations would have wanted to set themselves eventually, but the process nudged nations to align their priorities with those of the Alliance. Unlike the EU with its majority voting system, NATO issues are decided by unanimity so that a national veto is preserved, at least in theory. But over time the process of peer review by the Committee, and some good-natured naming and shaming, helped ensure gaps in capability were filled by the nations best able to do so, and overall that the minimum requirements for credible collective defence were met – a good example of the working of a strategic multi-partner partnership.

Transparency between partners also builds trust. Shortly after the United States entered the Second World War in 1942 following the Japanese attack on Pearl Harbor, a trusted messenger delivered to President Roosevelt a secret and personal letter from the British Prime Minister, Winston Churchill:[13]

My dear Mr. President,

One night when we talked late, you spoke of the importance of our cipher people getting into close contact with yours . . . some time ago, however our experts appeared to have discovered the system . . . used by your Diplomatic Corps. From the moment when we became allies, I gave instructions that this work should cease. However, the danger of our enemies having achieved a measure of success cannot, I am advised, be dismissed . . . I shall be grateful if you will handle this matter entirely yourself, and if possible burn this letter when you have read it . . .

With every good wish and my kindest regards, believe me,

Your sincere friend, Winston Churchill

The letter reveals that British cryptographers 'had discovered the system' – and thus must be assumed to have been reading US diplomatic cyphers. Since the US was entering the war on the Allied side those cyphers would, in future, also carry British secrets. The Germans might succeed as the British had done in exploiting the weaknesses in US cyphers. A US scholar of intelligence wrote of the US/UK relationship that 'Never before had sovereign states revealed their vital intelligence methods and results even to their closest allies.'[14] Despite Churchill's request at the end of the letter that it be burned after reading, the White House did keep a copy, which is how scholars have come to know of it.

What makes partnerships hard?

The evidence is that forming lasting partnerships turns out to be hard whether in personal relationships, in business or in intelligence. The UK Office for National Statistics estimated that in 2012 (the latest year for which figures are available) 42 per cent of marriages in England and Wales would end in divorce. Studies report that over 70 per cent of business relationships fail over time and less than 10 per cent deliver to or above original expectations.[15] There are many attempts that founder on misreading the motives of the other partners, as we saw in Chapter 2. Strategic partnerships in the commercial world, for example, require a mature acceptance on both sides that deep access to the partner organization will not be exploited for selfish purposes and there will be respect for intellectual property and commercial sensitivities.

Affording what it takes to make a successful partnership is often hard. It is to be expected that at first, in forming such partnerships, the costs may seem more tangible than the, necessarily more speculative, gains that are hoped for in the future. And there will be nay-sayers who fear the loss of their freedom of action and autonomy if tied into a relationship with another organization. When it comes to give and take, it may look like you will do most of the giving and the other party the taking. Of course, very much the same calculations will be going on inside the intended partner. It is essential early on to start building safe spaces where these fears can be exposed, some of which will be real and need managing on both sides.

If the partnership strategy occupies its own niche, distinct from the major motivations that drive the work of the cooperating organizations, then it is unlikely that the arrangement will last. A new couple in which each is determined to continue what had been their separate lives, without compromise with the interests of the other, is unlikely to last. The US and UK sigint partners are joined at the hip (of course, a source of criticism for those who disapprove of the closeness of the relationship). Their cooperation is at the heart of their enterprise, influencing many different components such as security arrangements, accessing data streams, cryptography, applying advanced algorithms, and generating intelligence insights on targets of common interest.

If the approach to the relationship is, on the other hand, heavily transactional, then each proposal for work on a cooperative project will tend to be judged only by the short-term benefits gained from the last one. Immediate benefits will be the principal measure of success. If a track record of good projects builds up, then such relationships can nevertheless still generate considerable mutual benefit even if at first falling short of strategic partnership. Earlier we referred to hugely beneficial operations such as the joint CIA/MI6 running of the GRU's Colonel Oleg Penkovsky in the 1960s, and the MI6/Danish Intelligence Service cooperation that led to the Gordievsky case. Over time such cases can develop a habit of cooperation that becomes genuinely strategic and thus even more valuable.

The business world illustrates different ways of managing the risks of remaining too short term and transactional. There are coordinational models in which underlying structures remain largely unaltered, but processes ensure adequate coordination within the partnership. Taking a step further, integration models can be used whereby a joint team is created for operations carried out in partnership, and finally and most effectively there are leadership models where senior staff with considerable authority are designated to lead the partnership.

As with any partnership, it has to be accepted that there are bound to be some sensitive or tricky areas that one of the parties to an agreement wishes to manage outside the agreement. In the case of the US/UK intelligence relationship that could be for legal reasons (such as the purely national responsibility for warranted intercept of domestic communications) or because of political sensitivity (such as is the case for the US with its intelligence relationship with Israel). It is wise therefore to have agreed caveats applying to a strategic partnership covering what it should not be used for. Restrictions, for example, prohibit the use of material acquired under the US/UK signals intelligence agreement for the commercial advantage of national companies (a point reinforced by President Obama in his revised Directive to the NSA after critical reporting in Europe arising from misunderstood Snowden material).[16]

Differences in the legal framework applying to each partner can create obstacles. There must be a shared understanding that the domestic legal framework in each partner country will regulate activity by that country. For example, in the signals intelligence relationship each agency must always be understood by its partners as having to obey its own domestic law. So no partner can ask another partner to engage in activity that it would not be able to conduct legally itself, assuming it had the necessary access. When, for example, GCHQ in the course of its work into serious and organized crime groups comes across US nationals, it cannot share the names of the individuals with US partners until they have themselves obtained the necessary court authorization as they would have had to do were they the ones collecting the intelligence. And the same applies when it is the US that has intelligence about a UK citizen; for example, on individuals suspected of having terrorist links. Some of the documents stolen by Edward Snowden from the NSA carry the caveat 'Orcon', meaning that the originator retains control of the intelligence that has been passed to another nation and has set restrictions on what use may be made of it. Respecting such caveats is another key cooperation principle linked to trust.

Partners enter into relationships expecting there to be mutual benefits. It is easy to talk in general about being in favour of a win–win deal. But to get to a win–win position, a genuinely strategic partnership is needed. Both parties need to satisfy themselves they understand that there will be times when one side has to make some sacrifices to help a partner that is struggling. If firmly within a long-term relationship built on trustworthiness then they will know that at some point in the future the circumstances will be reversed and they will be the one that is glad to receive help. There will be times when one party suddenly has an urgent requirement that the other could help to meet by temporarily giving it priority, but only by accepting that there would be times when the positions would be reversed. Success only comes when all parties are successful.

When one partnering organization is much smaller in scale than the other, tensions are bound to arise if the larger throws its weight around and the smaller feels put upon. But equally great care is needed to ensure there is enough evidence of the value of cooperation to the larger partner. I used to joke with my counterparts in the very much larger US agencies that the post-war UK intelligence community was like Savile Row tailoring, beautifully fitted, hand-cut and hand-sewn suits that would last a lifetime but were so expensive that only a very few could be bought on a British budget. The US on the other hand could afford to think in terms of mass production using the very latest machinery to cut serviceable suits of every weight and style, at a cost low enough to own a full range of them. The combination of both niche quality products (the work of the GCHQ mathematicians comes to mind) and full coverage (the overhead satellite constellation of the US for example) was very powerful during the Cold War. As Sir Joe Hooper, then Director of GCHQ, wrote to his opposite number, General Pat Carter, after the US had joined in a major investment in sigint exploiting a British innovation: 'Between us, we have ensured that the blankets and sheets are more tightly tucked around the bed in which our two sets of people lie and, like you, I like it that way.'[17]

Crises are best managed through partnerships

'Why don't we run this crisis the way we would run the response to a terrorist incident' was my whispered advice to the Home Secretary, Jack Straw, after a dispiriting meeting of the then government's Civil Contingencies Committee of which he was the chair and I, as his Permanent Secretary, was Deputy Chair. It was September 2000 and reports had come in overnight of blockades outside oil refineries by protesters. The Committee meeting had been held in a historic Cabinet Office conference room, with stern portraits of past grandees looking down as ministers told each other what they thought was happening in their constituencies, but with no suggestions as to what to do. The official who acted as secretary would within twenty-four hours circulate an elegant record, no doubt setting down what she thought ministers would have wanted to have decided. But by then events could have got out of hand: fears of a national fuel shortage were already being carried in the media, together with speculation about the dislocation hospitals and the health service would suffer, the difficulties for commuting and the ability of industry to keep functioning. Hence my suggestion to Jack Straw.[18]

We had all had been through exercises on how to handle terrorist incidents such as hijackings and hostage-taking using a 24/7 situation centre known as Cabinet Office Briefing Room A (COBRA, as the media call it rather dramatically). My hope (which proved correct) was that the operational working practices would rub off on those managing a civil emergency, such as maintaining a 'battle rhythm' with meetings at set key intervals during the day so that those down the command chain could prepare intelligence and operational briefs in good time; and sharing that sense of single purpose that every organization involved in such crisis circumstances has. National security is a strategic partnership.

Such use of COBR is now openly acknowledged, with reassuring press briefing in any emergency that COBR has been activated, as it was for COVID-19 in 2020, with footage of determined-looking ministers entering the Cabinet Office clutching their briefing folders. A key lesson is the need for accuracy and truthfulness in conveying information about a situation that affects the public. That learning applies just as much in the commercial world as in the public sector. If there is suspicion that the picture is being 'spun', then credibility is lost, and it will take a long time to recover. One of the lessons I learned was that the first reports from the scene of an emergency are always wrong in significant respects. Sometimes waiting for additional information on the situation is the best course, but often the imperative is to understand the limitations of the information that exists and be open and honest about its limitations.

In the case of the 2000 fuel crisis, forging partnerships proved key. Representatives of the oil companies, equipped with laptops connected to their distribution systems, were brought together under the direction of a chief officer of police in part of the COBR complex, and provided real-time information on the supply situation as well as being able to redirect what supplies there were to priority users, including some major hospitals that were about to run out of fuel. In this way, time was bought for the political strategy to be resolved while the dispute was hammered out.

On becoming aware of a disruption to supply, such as that caused in 2020 by COVID-19, you are faced with the 'prisoners' dilemma' caused by ignorance about how others will behave. Do you rush out and stock up even if you can manage for the moment without, or are you socially responsible and hold back so that those who really need supplies can get them? But you know that everyone else faces the same dilemma. If you hold back and so does everyone else with non-essential needs, then that creates the best outcome for everyone. But if you hold back and they do not, then you suffer from their selfishness. If you do rush to the store, and the others do not, then you will at least enjoy a selfish benefit. If everyone does that of course then everyone suffers but at least you are all worse off. When you review all four outcomes from the individual's point of view, it becomes clear that holding back is not 'rational' benefit-maximizing behaviour. And since most people will reason the same way, inevitably we end up with long queues at the supermarkets and petrol pumps and everyone equally worse off.

Today, social media increase our vulnerability to rumour in crisis (as we saw in Chapter 7). I had already learned that lesson about public awareness of a developing situation as Permanent

Secretary of the Home Office, when a new requirement for passports for children coincided with delays in the introduction of a new IT system. After newspaper headlines highlighted the delay, families rationally thinking ahead to the next summer holiday sensibly put their passport renewal applications in early. That flood of applications caused further delays, and the bad publicity simply triggered even more applications – and more chaos was then caused when inevitably there were some who had to ask for their passports back in a hurry for pressing family emergencies. My boss, the Home Secretary, Jack Straw, later described the passport problem as 'the single most career-threatening issue I ever handled'.[19]

What is clear is that there are no wizarding wands for government to magic away such disruptions to everyday life. So much will depend upon trust in what central and local government and the relevant critical infrastructure companies advise the public to do. And that in turn may well hinge on the relationships previously formed with the media, and the new media, and with civil society groups to which the public will turn in a crisis. Partnerships would be too strong a word for these relationships, but the principles in this chapter identified for sound partnerships are those that lie behind good relationships too.

Looking to meet the threats of the digital future

Retaining public confidence in government is now central to national security. I suspect most of us still think of national security primarily in terms of the territorial defence of our country and of its interests. The armed forces and the NATO Alliance are the necessary embodiment of that defence. Today our thinking also has to widen to cover the direct safety and security of the public at home and when abroad. National security needs to be considered in the twenty-first century from the point of view of the online citizen faced with many global threats, and how we protect our democratic institutions from subversion. I like to describe national security as a psychological state. It is *a state of confidence* that the major risks facing people, such as terrorism, cybercriminality, cyberattacks and digital intimidation, are being managed satisfactorily – so that people can make the most of their lives, freely and with confidence, even knowing that a threat will always remain from hostile states, terrorists and criminals intent on harming our interests.

No nation, however powerful, can manage the digital threats of tomorrow from its own resources alone. The huge value of the 5-eyes relationship today in digital intelligence has been described. But wider partnerships will also be needed between the democracies, not least between North America and Europe. For intelligence and security agencies we know from experience that having trusted international partners with whom it is possible to share advances and conduct peer review of plans and assessments will improve the quality of intelligence produced. Joint training of intelligence officers through a European Intelligence College is just beginning. Today, across Europe after every terrorist attack or massive cyber-breach of personal data there are demands for more cooperation to identify the perpetrators and prevent further outrages. On top of which are now added the increasing demands for intelligence cooperation to counter Russian Internet-based subversive activities in Europe and in the US that are exacerbating populist tensions over race and immigration and interfering with democratic elections. Exceptional results are more and more likely to come from partnering between different organizations so that they can generate together more security for the citizen than they could separately.

Conclusions: trustworthiness and lasting partnerships

Partnerships underpin all of our interactions. At a macro level, when big organizations join together, to a micro level, when people build friendships, or become colleagues, or fall in love. Few nations have succeeded in creating genuine domestic intelligence communities in which different agencies (including the relevant parts of law enforcement) freely come together to cooperate on operations and to share the results. The global world of secret intelligence is one in which rivalries and a degree of mistrust are rife. Even when cooperation takes place it is often on the basis of deals whereby the value of sharing intelligence is weighed case by case. The need to combat terrorism after 9/11 has led to more productive international partnerships on that subject. But the major conclusion is that trustworthiness needs to be built to create strategic partnerships. The lessons learned about building trustworthiness from the successful partnership we see in the 5-eyes international intelligence community hold true when building strategic partnerships everywhere. If we want to build strong partnerships, we should:

- Seek positions of mutual advantage where all parties to the relationship are likely to benefit.
- Build safe spaces where the potential partners can expose their concerns privately to each other.
- Match the specific strengths of one partner with the different strengths of another to generate results well beyond the capacity of either working alone.

- Expose the values and legal context of the potential partners and ensure they are compatible.
- Trust that each partner will be willing to support the priorities of the other and provide help when needed.
- Celebrate the fact that success comes only when all parties are successful.
- Ensure that there are ways in which gains will be shared equitably.
- Establish trustworthiness to move from informal cooperation to coordinational models in which underlying structures remain largely unaltered, to integration models where joint teams are created for operations carried out in partnership, and finally to leadership models.

10

Lesson 10: Subversion and sedition are now digital

A narrative from 2027

It is a cold New Year's Eve in 2027. Snow settles gently on the revellers in their polar bear masks in London's Trafalgar Square. They salute the speech of a young firebrand politician as she promises that if elected Prime Minister in the forthcoming General Election hers will be a new style of environmental peace activism to save the planet. She commits her new political movement to use direct democracy through frequent digital referenda on social media. Her programme includes cleaning up the environment, an immediate zero-carbon emissions policy, introducing punitive taxation on polluters, banning private non-electric motor cars from all town centres, phasing out Britain's nuclear weapons (responding to a Russian offer to host bilateral nuclear disarmament talks) and cuts in defence accompanied by withdrawal from NATO's military structure. At the end of her rousing speech, she receives the cheers and raised clenched fists of the masked crowd.[1]

Her supporters had adopted the polar bear mask as a symbol of their rebellion to save the planet and its disappearing species by leapfrogging the stasis of conventional politics. It was a sideways homage to the dystopian film *V for Vendetta* (2006)[2] that described how, in 2027, an oppressive British government could be destabilized by a radical resistance move-ment – whose symbol was the Guy Fawkes mask. He had tried to blow up Parliament; they would simply bypass the 'deep state' through digital referenda. 2027 had now arrived, but it was the year when the British, on a wave of environmental populism and rejection of conventional representative democracy, elected by a slim majority a revolutionary administration.

The turnout for the election had been one of the lowest ever, reflecting public cynicism over the political class and their parliamentary antics that had gridlocked Parliament for years over Europe. The ebullient Conservative leader had been humiliated by a video uploaded on to YouTube apparently showing him engaging in extreme sexual activity during an overseas trip. The Conservative Party had in any case been split down the middle by leaked emails that revealed a plan to rejoin the reformed European common trade bloc, leading to a mas-sive number of spoiled ballot papers. The left-of-centre Labour Party vote had collapsed after its new leader and his chief of staff had been forced to stand down during investigations into material from a child pornography ring found on their House of Commons computers, a charge they vigorously denied. Social media were full of conspiracy stories that a secret group of senior oil and mineral extraction company executives had contributed handsomely to Liberal Democrat funds in return for promises to shelve plans to increase taxation on their industries.

All this came at the end of a year in which the public had been both entertained and sickened by leaks on social media of emails that seemed to reveal corrupt deals to secure overseas defence contracts, expenses fiddles, and illicit affairs and mis-behaviour by prominent parliamentarians. It was already evident that the restoration of the Palace of Westminster would cost at least three times as much as estimated. To cap it all, a giant oil tanker had released over 100,000 gallons of crude that had drifted into an area of special scientific interest off the Shetlands: a cyberattack on the control system was suspected. And a relaunched Wikileaks site had exposed the security arrangements for the transportation of nuclear waste with emails which showed that safety procedures were being ignored to cut costs and that ministers were turning a blind eye. Enraged environmental protestors – boosted by horror stories on social media sites about the risks of pollution and of nuclear accidents – had joined forces with nuclear disarmers in massive demonstrations and created a new political move-ment. At least for those who did vote, the election of a youthful, uncorrupted, anti-war administration that wanted genuinely to tackle climate change promised hope of a better future.

The first encounters with the NATO heads of government were bruising for the young Prime Minister, and Washington had already yanked on the chain of intelligence cooperation by restricting the flow of American satellite imagery to the UK. By contrast, the reception in Moscow for the first round of nuclear disarmament talks was warm. But evidence was com-ing to light of hidden hands that had been active in the election campaign, shaping public perceptions. The video clips of the Conservative leader at play showed evidence of having been manipulated by 'deep-fake' software. The child pornography that brought down the Labour leader and his chief of staff now appeared to have been planted on their computers and the log of internet access digitally altered using clever software that was installed, MI5 suspected, by a parliamentary intern. Many of the apparent revelations about the private lives of politicians could be tracked to a series of hacks into email systems by criminal groups overseas and had surfaced first through obscure social media news sites owned by front companies. The Russian welcome for bilateral nuclear disarmament talks had turned out to be not all it seemed, since the only reductions contemplated on their side were in ageing tactical nuclear weapons that the Russian General Staff had long wanted rid of because they could not afford replacements.[3]

The assessment of the Joint Intelligence Committee was that the Russians had deliberately pitched their offer of talks as a ploy to influence the outcome of the UK election. The JIC warned, on the advice of the National Cyber Security Centre, that it was likely that Russian groups were behind many of the hacks and other malicious cyber-activity on social media that had affected the Opposition parties. The 'digital honey trap' into which the Conservative leader had been placed was a classic Russian tactic, but the JIC was careful to say it could also have been carried out by several other intelligence agencies from countries with interests in embarrassing the UK. The JIC noted the denials from Moscow but highlighted the stream of English-language propaganda coming from RT and other Russian outlets in the UK against the US and NATO. The JIC pointed to the past record of election interference by Russia, but stopped short of concluding that the recent election outcome had been decisively affected by foreign government interference.

'The election was rigged and is invalid,' nevertheless cried the Leader of the Opposition: 'we were beaten by foreign subversion, not the honest opinion of the British public.' But the Prime Minister's spokeswoman was uncompromising: 'It was a free election and we must respect the will of the people.' Meanwhile, a Conservative who lost his marginal seat launched a case for a judicial review of the failure of the independent Electoral Court to intervene and annul the result. But there was no hard evidence that the substantial funding behind the Prime Minister's new party had come from anything other than individual activists and sympathetic small registered UK companies (although a number did have overseas interests). Rumours circulated that, before the election, the new party had encouraged the hacking of social media accounts and contributed to the tide of 'fake news' that had so soured public attitudes to politics, but there was no actual proof of collusion. In any case, legal opinion was deeply divided about what constituted subversion in the twenty-first century, and what could be held to be an unfair election result in such circumstances.[4] A Supreme Court hearing looked inevitable, with the possibility of a major constitutional crisis if unelected judges overturned the result of what, on the face of it, was the people's choice.

By the end of 2028, the government was down to a tiny working majority in the House of Commons for its domestic agenda. But the value of sterling against the dollar had fallen to a historic low and inflation and unemployment were rising. Painful talks in NATO about dismantling the British contribution dragged on. Moscow's offer to scrap many old weapons was used as justification by the Treasury to insist on an immediate halt to the building of the new Trident ballistic missile submarines and the suspension of deterrent patrols, causing acute concern in the Ministry of Defence and alarm in Washington and Paris. Apparently to divert attention, the government announced to uproar in the House of Commons that following a recent social media poll it would sponsor a series of public focus group meetings on the future of the monarchy, and hold a national referendum to test support for its replacement by a republic.

That evening, a private dinner party was coming to its close in a discreet Mayfair mews house. The host, a media magnate, dismissed the waiter and proffered malt whiskies around the table, at which were seated the retired chair of a global oil major, several senior City financiers, a former right-wing newspaper editor now in the House of Lords, a long-retired senior officer from UK Special Forces, and a retired senior politician and former Guards officer, who was at this very moment holding forth:

' . . . those serving today will, I guarantee you, remember their oath: "to be faithful and bear true allegiance to the Crown and defend it against all enemies". That includes this bunch of revolutionaries in the Cabinet. The majority of the public want rid of them by any means, even if it comes to a fight.'

The host turned with a raised eyebrow to a burly, slightly dishevelled man sitting slightly apart from the table who had not spoken up to now. 'Count us in,' he contributed in an Indiana drawl, 'but force will not be needed. You have friends on the other side of the Atlantic with good connections to Big Tech, so do not be concerned over money or technical support. If there is dirt to be found we can uncover it, and if not we can sure as hell make it up. We were not the first to start that game.'

A tap on the door announced a late arrival, the elegantly suited Principal Private Secretary to the King. Refusing the proffered whisky, she listened intently to the host's summary of the dinner discussion and stood up. 'Gentlemen, this is treason and I can have no part in it. We are a democracy and it is sedition to overthrow an elected government – even if it is intended to safeguard the constitutional position of the monarch. I will not betray your secrets – but,' she added with a shrug, 'all my master and I can do is wait on the sidelines for the verdict of history.'

Fact or fiction?

Fiction, of course. And you would be right to say that such a combination of circumstances makes that scenario unlikely. My political fiction does nevertheless showcase the range of methods of modern warfare as practised today by Russia, and in future very probably by other nations, including China, in relation to their spheres of interest. Often labelled 'hybrid warfare' or warfare in the 'grey zone', for many strategists that is how war itself will be redefined in the first half of the twenty-first century.[5] The underlying lesson for us is that all the individual elements which could contribute to such a crisis already exist.

We have seen how revealing are the traces that we all leave as we choose, share and comment online. We have seen personal data used to target political messaging, including disinformation, at groups of voters who are likely to be the most susceptible. We have seen fake websites pushing extremist messages that open up rifts already apparent in society. Malinformation attacks have taken place in which genuine but compromising material is stolen by hacking or by covert recording then released anonymously; all capitalizing on populist fears and concerns emerging unwittingly from the political interior of the target nation. And all potentially additional to the more traditional old Soviet repertoire of covert 'dirty tricks' that Warsaw Pact intelligence agencies engaged in through entrapment, offering drugs or sex in what were known as 'honey trap' operations. In the future digital world, however, there will be no need to go to those elaborate lengths to ensnare an opponent directly. Compromising material can easily be faked. Sound recordings can be manipulated to make the target appear to be giving vent to damaging views in coarse or racist language. And with the latest deep-fake technology, available video footage of the victim can be manipulated to make them appear to be in highly compromising positions and in deeply dubious company.

A specific lesson from the last few years is that our own personal digital data can be used to target political messages more precisely at us in ways comparable to the marketing of products and services. The same advertising technology (ad tech) drives the placement of political advertising. It provides the advertiser (and the political party) with the ability to infer what it is that the consumer wants through access to the searching, viewing, sharing, liking and spending patterns of the individual on the Internet.

One consequence is to increase polarization in political life, with groups on different sides of key issues listening only to those who know how to enter their echo chambers. It becomes too easy then for politicians simultaneously to convey one message to one group of voters while sending different messages to other groups. It involves understanding what messages key groups of voters in swing constituencies want to hear, and then providing them to amplify their beliefs. The populist politician runs behind his supportive crowd watching which way they want to go, then darts in front and shouts, follow me. As Tim Berners-Lee has argued: 'Targeted advertising allows a campaign to say completely different, possibly conflicting things to different groups. Is that democratic?'[6] The Internet thus shapes reality and is not just a reflection of it.

Even subject to subversive influences we may well still feel passionately that we are exercising our free will as autonomous citizens. In the same way people will maintain that they made their consumer choices themselves, while subconsciously their spending decisions may reflect the subliminal dictates of fashion of which individuals may be only dimly aware. In reality today our choices and our voices and our votes may reflect the deliberate manipulative reshaping of the prevailing narrative, one that has provided us with a different explanation of what is important in the world. Social media messages that have political content have to be accepted as part and parcel of modern democratic debate in a free society, but we also need to know who is behind them, and when these techniques are being employed cynically against us by autocracies such as Russia and China, and by extremist groups with harmful agendas.

We would be wise therefore to re-read the scenario that opened this chapter and ask ourselves what is it that would prevent such events from arising in future, perhaps based on a different cause that generates strong emotions and that can be manipulated by populist politicians (it could be the pressures of climate change – I hesitate to even suggest fears over immigration might be such a cause, and the sort of government that would bring).

Subversion and auto-subversion in the modern digital space

There is a major difference between this chapter and those that preceded it. In earlier parts of the book I drew on experiences from the worlds of defence, security and intelligence to illustrate lessons that I believe we can by extension apply in everyday life. This chapter is different because the worlds of defence, security and intelligence now enter our daily lives directly via the Internet. We do not need to infer relevance: we experience it directly. I prefer to label this troubling internet activity directed against us by an old term: subversion.

A foreign state can advance its interests outside its borders these days, not by kinetic war, or engineering a coup, assassination or fomenting insurrection, but by recognizing an opportunity to exploit genuine domestic concerns in its target and manipulating the democratic process towards an outcome it prefers.

Subversion can be simply thought of as external interference in a nation's affairs to overthrow the existing order of things, whether by forcing a change in policy or a change in the regime itself, on terms favourable to the aggressor. We can think of subversion as an outside-in process, a form of outsider-to-insider threat, for the most part involving a foreign state taking advantage from the outside of vulnerabilities that provide an opportunity to influence opinion in the political interior of its target. It is a different concept from terrorism, sabotage or cyberattacks, although all of those methods of intimidation may form part of a subversive campaign. It can be conceptually distinguished from sedition, another longstanding concern of governments, defined as internal dissent inciting rebellion against the constituted authority in a state. Subversion and sedition nevertheless often appear together when a hostile power exploits 'fellow travellers' inside the target nation to assist in its subversive activity and when a 'home-grown' domestic movement seeks covert financial, military or other form of overseas support for a seditious purpose. Such measures (in Russian, *aktivinyye meropriatia*) became a speciality of the Cold War Soviet KGB and today that tradition is carried on by the Russian intelligence agencies.

The key lesson I want to convey in this chapter is that the modern digital space provides new and effective means for promoting subversion and sedition.[7] These are covert attempts to influence our politics through digital means. When they are directed at us from those outside our democratic realm, we can see that they are dangerous to our autonomy as a democracy. And offensive to our values. But they can also come from within. I term this auto-subversion, by analogy with the medical term auto-intoxication, whereby our bodies are poisoned by a toxin originating within the body itself. We all carry, for example, unconscious fears about others who appear different. This instinctive xenophobia is the result of our evolutionary history as a species. That virus is usually dormant and kept in its place by the immune system that is the culture of civilization. But that can fail, and the virus is wakened into destructive activity inside the body politic. It may not require foreign interference to set it in motion, only domestic neglect of the dangers of stoking extremism.

If that is the case, then to be consistent we have to be prepared to call out the same types of hidden manipulative digital activity when they are being carried out against the public as part of our own domestic politics, as well as by extremist and special interest groups. What is most troubling is that we have only recently become aware of the extent of the potential for hidden manipulation, following scandals such as that of Cambridge Analytica, which in 2018 was exposed as having harvested personal data from the Facebook profiles of millions of people without their consent with the intention of the data being used for political advertising purposes.

We are complacent in allowing both external subversion and this auto-subversion of our own society and its democratic values to continue in part because we enjoy the benefits of targeted marketing every time that a search returns information about products and services of interest to us; we freely use the services of the internet giants because they are useful to us (all the more so since most are free at the point of use). Since we approve of the right to privacy, we also tolerate anonymity on the Internet, which as we have seen encourages digital bad behaviour such as trolling and cyberbullying. We fail nevertheless to put all these developments together to see where the trends are leading and what might be the long-term consequences for society of such a journey.

You are the target

Data from our internet use and digital life is now routinely used by advertisers to target marketing material at us as individuals with known characteristics. Our browsing history may show an interest in scuba diving, our online purchases show the likely level of our disposable income so we should not be surprised to find advertisements in the web pages and sites we visit for tempting holidays in suitable locations, diving equipment and courses, special offers on flights and so on, attractive offers calibrated to cost just slightly more than we had thought of spending. In Chapter 2 we met Bayesian inference, the scientific method for bringing new evidence to bear on the degree of belief we should have in the likelihood of a proposition being true. The same method is what lies behind the training of the artificial intelligence (AI) algorithms that can analyse the large number of data points available on each of us and make informed inferences about our preferences. Such iterative Bayesian learning can produce very powerful selection algorithms. These algorithmic techniques are also now applied by political parties and interest groups using data on consumer behaviour in order to identify from these characteristics the groups of voters in key marginal areas who would be most likely to be receptive to a personalized marketing pitch (or the opposite, in which case the analysis saves wasting effort on those who are unlikely to be persuadable).

Most recently we have seen a disturbing feedback loop emerge in politics. That same personal data from ad tech, along with more traditional polling data, is being used to personalize the political message itself and the way it is expressed in order to maximize the likelihood of garnering maximum support from that specific group. Groups of voters with identifiable characteristics can therefore have crafted political messaging directed at them. Those messages are known in advance to be likely to find approval from that group. Old-style political campaigning involved leaflets, billboard advertisements, and TV and radio spots that everyone could see, and that imposed limits on how far political parties could try to attract different groups of voters with different – and not necessarily consistent – appeals. Now, different directions of spin can be put on a political message for different micro-segmented groups of voters. Those crafting these messages know what to say to maximize the response and the technology provides detailed numerical feedback (click-through rates, dwell time, and so on) to enable messages to be continuously fine-tuned. The emotional charge of the message to the hard-up voter in the small town struggling with job insecurity can be fear of globalization and of free movement of labour and capital, while that directed to the educated young urban voter can be of widening horizons and opportunities offered by less government regulation, with no need to reconcile the policy implications of the messages.

Micro-targeting of political messaging is just part of the way that ad tech has shaped the working of social media so that the user is fed material customized to the characteristics of the individual.[8] News feeds (even the BBC News app) can be set by the user to highlight future items on subjects of interest. Such preferences can be picked up by the algorithms that govern what other material on social media reaches a user. That can result in what has become known as filter bubbles filled largely with material predicted to suit the world view of the user and echo chambers where such users only communicate with others of like mind. That effect can be gamed for malice or subversion to feed existing prejudice and deepen misunderstanding. One result is the risk that society increasingly separates into self-regarding groups that do not realize how the information that is reaching them has already been filtered to suit their preferences. Such groups – including the political parties in the US – have little incentive to intercommunicate and share information.

With this warning that we are all the target, it is time to conduct a systematic SEES analysis of these digital dangers that we face.

Stage 1 of a SEES analysis: situational awareness

A good place to start when looking at what digital information operations can involve is the well-documented and painstaking work of Robert Mueller, the former Director of the FBI who conducted an investigation as a Special Counsel for the Justice Department that reported on Russian interference in the 2016 US Presidential campaign. As I know personally from my time as UK Security and Intelligence Coordinator after 9/11, he is a man of complete integrity. What he uncovered is deeply disturbing about the Russian actions but also about the potential for such activity on the part of others in the future. It comprised hostile action on several fronts: a social media campaign against Hillary Clinton (even before she announced she was a candidate) and subsequently one in favour of Donald Trump conducted largely by the Internet Research Agency in St Petersburg; Russian hacking and weaponizing stolen emails conducted by Russian military intelligence (the Main Directorate known as the GU, or more popularly the GRU); cyber-intrusions into US electoral voting systems, also the work of the GRU; and finally Russian attempts to establish collusive contact with the Trump campaign conducted in secrecy using unofficial intelligence-related intermediaries.[9]

Preparations for the offensive campaign started in the US in 2014 with reconnaissance and the building of a social media infrastructure inside the US focused on Facebook, YouTube and Twitter (Tumblr and Instagram were added later).[10] According to a former employee of the Internet Research Agency, 'our goal wasn't to turn the Americans towards Russia. Our task was to set Americans against their own government: to provoke unrest and discontent.' Staff were therefore trained on the nuances of American social polemics on tax issues, LGBT rights, the gun debate and more.[11] Internet Research Agency employees posing as US activists operated social media accounts and group pages designed to attract US voters. Internet Research Agency Facebook and Instagram accounts had hundreds of thousands of US participants. These accounts addressed divisive social and political issues, including immigration (a Facebook group, 'Secured Borders', was set up) and racial tensions (with groups such as 'Black Matters', 'Blacktivist' and 'Don't Shoot Us'). The objective of the attackers was not to promote one ideological view over another – often both sides in the argument were backed – but to sow dissension and exacerbate divisions in society. By early 2016 as the campaign proper got under way, political advertisements were being bought by Russia in the US in the names of US persons and entities claiming to be engaged in grassroots politics disparaging Hillary Clinton and later favouring Donald Trump. An example was the Twitter account @TEN_GOP purporting to be connected to the Tennessee Republican Party. Dozens of political rallies were staged inside the US where those attending had no idea that they were being manipulated by the Russians; nor, it appears, did the local Trump campaign officials with whom the timing and staging of the rallies was coordinated.

The size of the Russian operation was such that by the end of the election the Russian Internet Research Agency could reach millions of US voters through their social media accounts. Subsequent investigation by Facebook revealed 470 Russian-controlled accounts that collectively made 80,000 posts between January 2015 and August 2017 reaching some 126 million persons. Twitter was also used, and has now identified 3814 Russian-controlled Twitter accounts that were in contact with some 1.4 million people. The Russians operated a network of 'bots' programmed to spread the Twitter messages. 3500 political advertisements were purchased by the Russian Agency to run on Facebook, including one that depicted Clinton and read: 'If one day God lets this liar enter the White House as a president – that day would be a real national tragedy.' As the Russian campaign shifted to being pro-Trump as well as anti-Clinton, an advertisement for its Instagram account purporting to be 'Tea Party News' even asked Americans to help them 'make a patriotic team of young Trump supporters by uploading photos with the hashtag #KIDS4TRUMP'.

While the Russian social media campaign was progressing inside the US, the specialist cyber-attackers of two separate GRU units were hacking into networks being used by the Clinton campaign, including the Democratic Congressional

Campaign Committee and the Democratic National Committee (DNC). That gave the hackers access to email accounts and documents of Clinton campaign volunteers and employees, including the campaign chairman, John Podesta. Hundreds of thousands of documents were stolen from the networks. In the summer of 2016 at the height of the Presidential campaign the GRU began releasing its stolen material through fictitious online personas that they had specially set up to try to disguise their role (the site 'Guccifer 2' pretended it was all the work of a lone Romanian hacker, and 'DC Leaks' aimed to help journalists by indexing different tranches of stolen material arranged by victim). Additional releases were made through Wikileaks, leading Trump notoriously to comment publicly about Clinton's use of her private email server, adding: 'Russia, if you are listening, I hope you will be able to find the 30,000 emails that are missing. I think you will probably be rewarded mightily by our press.' That contrasts adversely with the later statement by the then Director of the CIA (Mike Pompeo) that he considered Wikileaks as a hostile intelligence service, commenting that it walks like one and talks like one. Within approximately five hours of Trump's statement, GRU officers targeted, for the first time, Clinton's personal office. The Russians had indeed been listening.

In a third arm of their campaign, officers from one of the GRU units that hacked the DNC also used spearfishing emails to access computers belonging to state boards of elections, secretaries of state and US companies that supplied software and other technology related to the administration of the 2016 Presidential election. That potentially gave them access to voter registration software and electronic polling stations, especially in 'swing' states. Such attacks could, in the event of a Clinton win, have provided the basis for a legal challenge to the result since the fact of the penetration would have been made evident. Such challenges to the legitimacy of a victory would have tarnished her first 100 days.

The final form of Russian interference was a series of contacts between Trump campaign officials and individuals with ties to the Russian government who offered assistance to the campaign and invitations to Russia. The Trump campaign believed it would benefit electorally from Russian assistance in providing 'dirt' – material damaging to Clinton – in the form of the anonymous release of stolen emails. In return a Russian contact suggested to Trump's campaign manager, Paul Manafort, that he deliver to Trump a Russian peace plan for Ukraine that would have helped Russia consolidate control of eastern Ukraine. Manafort in turn caused internal polling data on the campaign to be shared with the Russians. Several of the individuals associated with the Trump campaign later were found by the Mueller investigation to have lied and deleted relevant communications to conceal the extent of these contacts.

A pernicious example of the ease with which social media spread false stories was the 'Pizzagate' conspiracy.[12] The rumour was spread on social media alleging that the emails hacked from the Democratic Party contained coded messages which revealed that an associate of Hillary Clinton was involved with a covert child abuse sex ring of senior Democrats abusing children in the basement of a pizza parlour. The story went viral, and of course included allegations that it was being covered up by the 'deep-state' authorities. Images on social media showed Hillary Clinton with her photograph juxtaposed and overlaid with other images, including that of the pizza restaurant, to create guilt by association. Tweets and other postings by alt-right Trump supporters added fuel to the fire by referring to the alleged scandal; the volume of such references appeared to add credibility to the story, which was needless to say a manufactured fake from start to finish. The episode almost had a tragic ending, which does demonstrate the powers of such social media stories, when a man armed with a gun rushed into the pizza parlour to rescue the alleged victims of abuse. There was of course no basement, and there were no children to be rescued.

The lesson of the Pizzagate episode is that constant repetition in different news outlets, blogs or other social media channels creates in the viewer a feeling of familiarity with the story that adds to credibility. Even after debunking, that familiarity persists. And for propaganda purposes the story can be revived, again and again, for example by Novosti, the Russian online news outlet, a year later in September 2017 with the hook of a story about child abuse in the US. Their broadcast ended with:

> By the way, the overwhelming majority of the accused are supporters of the US Democratic Party. And here it is appropriate to recall: only at the end of last year the whole of America thundered at 'PizzaGate', the scandalous theory that on the side of Hillary Clinton (then – the presidential candidate) is an influential organization of paedophiles. Headquartered in one of the metropolitan pizzerias, hence the name. The mainstream media hastened to ridicule and forget this story. Now, in the light of new data on the secret life of the mayor-democrats, it is time to take this theory much more seriously.[13]

We can see many of the same tactics being employed by Russia to try to influence French internal politics at the time of the 2017 French Presidential election.

Just before the French Presidential election a large volume of stolen data was dumped on an anonymous file-sharing site, including private emails of the En Marche political party of the Presidential candidate Emmanuel Macron.[14] But in that case the hackers seem to have learned from their experience with the US Presidential campaign that the public is becoming inured to exposure of the indiscreet language common in email exchanges between people who know each other well. The hackers therefore altered some of the emails before release to create an impression of electoral and tax fraud. The lesson for us is how easy it is for hackers that have covert access to emails or documents to add compromising details. The Macron campaign reduced the impact of the email hack with a rapid announcement that it had been attacked, along with an explicit public warning that some of the released emails had been faked. It may well also be the case that the French public was simply not as Internet-addicted and thus vulnerable to online manipulation as that of the US, a lesson for all of us picked up in the final chapter.

The Russian subversion efforts included online black propaganda to try to give the false impression that the Macron campaign was being secretly funded by Saudi Arabia and even more disgracefully that the candidate himself was engaging in a disreputable liaison. Tactics included faking and publishing an online version of the popular Belgian newspaper *Le Soir* voicing allegations. We should not be surprised by this. The faking of documents published online is simply a modern form of the classic technique of black propaganda, the use of forgery that we saw with the Zinoviev letter in Chapter 7.

There is now also a substantial body of reliable information on Russian disinformation operations directed into Europe to alter attitudes to the conflict in Ukraine. Common themes identified by the special EU cell that is monitoring this disinformation activity include the allegation that Ukraine is to be invited to join the EU and NATO, that Ukraine was responsible for downing the Malaysian airliner MH17, that there are fascist roots to the government in Kiev, that COVID-19 was covert bio-warfare by the US against China, and that NATO is planning aggression against Russia.[15] Germany has also been the target of continuous Russian disinformation operations – for example, presenting distorted reports of Chancellor Angela Merkel's policies to fan conspiracy thinking about the impact of Muslim immigration on traditional German society. As we saw in Chapter 6, such stories even when debunked are hard to kill off.

This first part of the SEES analysis gives us the ability to achieve situational awareness. We have assessed a variety of sources of information, including by means of intelligent searching of the web. Some sources we can judge more reliable than others. Caution is needed especially over anonymous or second-hand reports and rumour. The SEES approach reminds us that intelligence is incomplete, fragmentary and sometimes wrong. Nevertheless, as Chapter 1 showed, careful use of Bayesian reasoning leads us to the most reliable picture of what is going on given the available evidence. In the case of the digital domain, the picture shows worrying levels of deceptive, malicious and subversive activity, some of which is directly aimed at us.

Stage 2 of a SEES analysis: explanation

The Russian plans hatched as early as 2014 for interference with the US 2016 election are best explained as a deliberate campaign to prevent Hillary Clinton from becoming US President because of her known hardline views on sanctions on Russia (the Clinton policy being in sharp contrast to what was seen as the approach of the Trump campaign). The attacks on her record and character may have been designed tactically more to sway supporters of her Democratic rival Bernie Sanders from coming out to vote for her, than to win over new undecided voters. What then emerged was determined multifaceted disinformation and malinformation operations to help get Donald Trump elected. In France the Russian objective seems to have been to slow down Macron's candidacy campaign and enhance the vote of the far-right candidate, Marine Le Pen, so that she made it into the final run-off for President (as she did). A strong showing for her far-right movement in France, as with the Alternative für Deutschland party in Germany, and other populist parties in Europe, lessens the risk perceived by Russia of a stronger EU challenging residual Russian influence in Ukraine and elsewhere, or even contemplating further enlargement of the EU.

There is a further lesson for us here. Covert information operations such as those during the US election can be designed to try to achieve a specific shift in public attitudes towards a person, party or policy. We can also see a deeper rationale behind such operations. The Russian leadership appears to have concluded that it is in their interests to undermine public confidence in the traditional Western democratic political order. Propaganda and disinformation operations have therefore simultaneously been supporting extreme left and right, and extreme libertarian and repressive, points of view with the aim of provoking discontent and social unrest. A common theme is to undermine confidence and trust in democratic governments. In the words of Robert Mueller:

'The IRA conducted social media operations targeted at large US audiences with the goal of sowing discord in the US political system.'[16]

That creates a more pernicious danger. The importance of finding out the truth about what is going on – for example, in areas of Russian involvement such as Syria and eastern Ukraine – is swamped by a torrent of different narrative explanations and by the opposing currents of contradictory narratives. Much of the disinformation seen over the last few years has been used to spread rumours rather than to make a convincing case. The pro-Kremlin media in Russia, for example, suggested that cyanide might have been found in tear gas used against 'yellow vests' protesters in France. The expectation is that conventional media will then carry the disinformation and it will be widely recirculated on social media. The objective of such stories is to undermine confidence, detect cracks on populist issues and widen them.

There are two complementary explanations for such wider deception operations by Russia. The first is strategic. A fundamentally weak Russia (in economic and demographic terms) must be expected to continue to want to exercise the place held previously by the Soviet Union at the international top table. Russia will see the US-led NATO (especially with the Baltic States) with the EU and its members as thwarting its ambitions, including to secure sufficient influence in the nations surrounding its homeland. Moscow would therefore see it as to its advantage, especially given the EU attitude to sanctions over Russian actions in Ukraine, to exacerbate tensions within the EU by covertly pushing out stories that raise the political temperature and are designed to inflame right-wing fears as well as leftist fears of the populist right. Distracting key European leaders to deal with such domestic problems can serve a useful strategic purpose for Moscow.

The second explanation reflects more tactical thinking on the part of the Russian authorities, and that is to divert attention from Russian actions that are attracting international criticism. The stream of stories pushed out openly on Russian media and by social media posts after some incident are intended to create such doubt in Western minds over what can be considered true that the public gives up on any attempt to establish what really happened. A chilling example was the attempts to explain away the attempted murder in 2018 by agents of the GRU, the Russian military intelligence service, of the former GRU officer and MI6 agent Sergei Skripal and his daughter, Julia, in the English cathedral city of Salisbury that resulted in the death of an innocent bystander, Dawn Sturgess. A Russian state media and internet propaganda counter-attack injected 'fake-news' stories to distract and confuse, deploying denials, counter-accusations and 'alternative facts' to promote conspiracy theories in order to leave the impression that there is no truth that can be found.[17]

In President Putin's first public response to the news coverage of the attack in Salisbury he denied Russia's culpability while carefully injecting a note of menace. 'If it was military-grade agent,' he said, 'they would have died on the spot, obviously.' He had already told state television that traitors would 'kick the bucket' and 'choke' on their 'pieces of silver'. The theme was later taken up by the Foreign Minister, Sergei Lavrov, saying that the attack on the Skripals was not 'sophisticated', and if it had been the victims would have died immediately. Russian officials and the state media then claimed variously that 'novichok' never existed, then they told the media that it did exist from Soviet times but they had destroyed the stocks, then they claimed that the stocks had escaped to Sweden or the Czech Republic or Slovakia or the United States (in order, it was said, to destabilize the world). A common Russian counter-attack theme is to assert victimhood at the hands of the West and thus reflect responsibility away from itself. In this case, Russian spokesmen went on the offensive against the UK for having dared to claim Russian involvement, accusing Theresa May and British secret agencies of a plot to undermine Russia in the eyes of the world.

In response to the Russian use of a nerve agent on British soil many governments then expelled a large number of Russian intelligence officers. At that point, the Moscow media put out stories claiming variously that Sergei Skripal took an overdose (because he was said to be addicted to novichok), that he attempted suicide (and therefore presumably tried to take his daughter with him), that his attempted murder was revenge for Britain's supposed poisoning of Ivan the Terrible, or that the UK was responsible for the attack so that they could have something to blame Russia over and thus spoil the World Cup. Salisbury, where the Skripals were attacked, is the nearest railway station to the UK defence research establishment Porton Down, where the identification of the nerve agent as novichok took place: unsurprisingly this fact too was wound into a conspiracy theory that the British MOD had manufactured the agent and somehow it had escaped laboratory confinement to drift over Salisbury (and by coincidence target the Skripals). Sergei Lavrov, speaking in Moscow, argued that British intelligence agents could have been involved to create a distraction from Brexit. He suggested the attack was 'in the interests of British special forces who are known for their abilities to act with a licence to kill'. The Russian Embassy in London was at the same time suggesting that the UK had its own stores of novichok agents and questioning why hospital staff in Salisbury happened to have an antidote to the novichok nerve agent used in the attempted murder (reality check: there is no antidote to such an advanced nerve agent – the patients would have been treated with atropine, which is on the World Health Organization's list of effective and safe medicines needed in a health system and is used for treating insecticide poisoning and conditions such as slow heart rate).

To cap it all, the Russian Embassy in London used its Twitter account to send sarcastic messages, including a photograph of Hercule Poirot, Agatha Christie's famous fictional Belgian detective, with the message: 'In the absence of evidence, we definitely need a Poirot in Salisbury.'

This second stage of the SEES method adds causality to the factual picture of situational awareness, so we can explain what is motivating what we see. We know that facts on their own may not have unambiguous meaning, and that we have to connect them with a reliable explanatory narrative. In the case of the malicious activity we see on the Internet, much originates in Russia and is directed against the Western democracies. Robert Mueller uncovered strong evidence of deliberate interference with the 2016 US Presidential election. A test of alternative hypotheses led him to no other credible explanation than that there was a deliberate Russian campaign to prevent Hillary Clinton becoming President and to promote Donald Trump as the candidate most likely to benefit Russian interests.

Stage 3 of a SEES analysis: estimates and predictions

When we try to estimate in stage 3 of the SEES analysis how the threat of deception operations against us may evolve, we should remember that Russia is not the only nation conducting digital information operations. Their digital subversive activities have been widely reported and it is inevitable that other nations and extremist groups will deploy such methods. We saw the use of sophisticated social media communications by the so-called Islamic State in its heyday to promote its global insurrection to young Muslims, including in Europe, North America and Australasia. It used modern advertising methods to seek recruits to take part in its campaign to try and establish a caliphate under extreme Sharia law. Other groups in the future will see the digital medium as well suited to their modus operandi. We must therefore expect to experience more, and more varied, information operations directed against our interests over the next few years. Three factors will drive this trend: opportunism, vulnerability and susceptibility.

Opportunism

When a society continues to offer tempting opportunities to an adversary, whether a nation state or hostile group, to advance its interest we must expect more often than not they will be taken. Russia, for example, did not create the movement in the United Kingdom to leave the European Union. To suggest that would be to fall into the trap of imagining 'monster plots' as we saw in Chapter 6 with the imaginings of the CIA's Angleton and MI5's Peter Wright. But when an opportunity arose to weaken the political cohesion of the EU, it would be surprising if Russia had not considered how it might find ways of nudging the process, whether by covert funding, agents of influence or exploitation of useful idiots (or, more likely, the modern equivalent with social media postings and trolls). In the same way, the Le Pen phenomenon in France and Chancellor Merkel's policy on immigration in Germany have offered opportunities to create difficulties and advance Russian objectives. That will be true for other nations and non-state actors in the future in their perceived spheres of influence.

Vulnerability

As we have seen, the digitization of so much of what goes on in everyday life creates specific weaknesses that will be exploited. The complexity of the computer coding required for sophisticated digital applications leaves plenty of room for human error and thus vulnerability to hacking. The fundamental protocols that are the basis of the Internet and the World Wide Web were themselves not written with security in mind. They were originally written to enable connections between a small number of trusted defence research institutions and university departments on the US West Coast. What became the Internet was not initially designed for the 4 billion netizens now online and connected. There is no check of identity (at least of the kinds of proof of root identity required to set up a bank account) before setting up websites or posting material or opinions on social media. An individual can have multiple personas, such as was the case with the young people employed by the Russian Internet Research Agency and paid to pose as US citizens with strong opinions on race, immigration or politics. Trolls therefore flourish without any inherent requirement for the true identity of the user behind an internet communication or a transaction to be known. The 'dark web' continues to provide an anonymous unpoliced space where hacking tools and illegal information material inciting violence and race hate can circulate, as was described in Chapter 1.

Our critical infrastructure, including that which supplies us with power and communications, is increasingly vulnerable to cyberattacks that can create the basis for intimidation and ransom demands. An example was the 2017 Russian hack that temporarily closed down much of Kiev's electrical supply. The explanation in that case appears to have been not to cause physical damage to the systems per se but to use the cutting off of electricity to emphasize Ukrainian vulnerability to Russian power, and signal displeasure at moves by the Ukrainian government to privatize enterprises in which important Russians had significant stakes and whose interests needed to be safeguarded. Computer attack is increasingly a tool of subversion.

Susceptibility

As individuals, we suffer from a different form of vulnerability, which I call here susceptibility. This is a consequence of the business model of the Internet that provides services free at the point of use funded by the digital advertising that ad tech provides. Such are the genuine advantages of connectivity that most of us swallow any qualms we might have about our personal information being collected for that purpose, including data on our internet use itself (collection that is often through an implied general consent rather than an explicit given agreement for specific purposes). That personal information is the essential feedstock for the personalized marketing to us of products and political views. The pull of the web as the medium for so much social interaction is strengthened by the way that we increasingly take for granted that we will use the Internet for digital access to essential travel and other useful information about commercial, local and central government services.

We saw earlier how platforms like Twitter made it easy for the fake 2016 election messages to be shared and cascaded to others of like mind. We receive the tweets from those we have chosen to follow, and those who follow us will get them too. This is now such second nature for those who use these kinds of platforms that we may not fully recognize its implications. A single tweet from President Trump today will be seen almost instantaneously by all those he might hope would see it through the retweeting actions of thousands of people executing their independent decisions, as well as, we have discovered, by bots that share content automatically, a technique used extensively by the Russians in the US 2016 election campaign. It is also probably true that false information will be shared faster than the truth, particularly where it is packaged in a vivid, or controversial or even salacious form. As Tony Blair once remarked: 'Impact is what matters. It is all that can distinguish, can rise above the clamour, can get noticed. Impact gives competitive edge. Of course, the accuracy of a story matters. But it is often secondary to impact.'[18] There is an asymmetry of passion between the engaging, readily understood fiction and the true but necessarily complex account of reality.

Our personal susceptibility is enhanced by the lengths to which ad tech goes to try to increase conversion rates from desire to fulfilment. Internet companies want to make it as easy, in as few steps as possible, to purchase or respond, with the aim of reducing as far as possible the time for reflection before commitment. By providing credit card information in advance all that is needed to complete a purchase is to click on the prominent 'buy now' button. In the case of purchases, consumer protection law provides a safety net to cancel or amend orders, or to return goods, but for political messaging there is no such buffer. Clicks on petitions online reflect this 'thinking fast' ingestion of the message (to use Daniel Kahneman's distinction between thinking fast and thinking slow[19]). Ad tech is designed to push us into making decisions that provide instantaneous gratification – including feeling good about voicing our opinion – and to suppress the normal social and cultural cues that would otherwise give us pause for genuine thought.

President Obama described this sad prospect in his farewell address to the nation on 10 January 2017 when he returned to Chicago:

> For too many of us, it's become safer to retreat into our own bubbles, whether in our neighborhoods or college campuses or places of worship or our social media feeds, surrounded by people who look like us and share the same political outlook and never challenge our assumptions. The rise of naked partisanship, increasing economic and regional stratification, the splintering of our media into a channel for every taste . . . we become so secure in our bubbles that we accept only information, whether true or not, that fits our opinions, instead of basing our opinions on the evidence that is out there.[20]

This third stage of the SEES method uses our explanatory narrative, including the motivations of those involved, to estimate how things are most likely to evolve. These estimates rely on the causal relationships in our explanatory model, together with the assumptions we make about factors we can ignore or that we think will not affect the result. Such estimates cannot be certain, and they will include warning of some less likely but troubling possible developments. This stage of analysis predicts that malicious activity on the Internet will increase with more nations and non-state actors recognizing the potential for advancing their interests by digital manipulation. This trend will be driven by the three explanatory factors of opportunism on the part of more adversaries, the inherent design vulnerabilities of our web-life to deception, and our personal susceptibility as individuals to online manipulation.

Stage 4 of a SEES analysis: strategic notice

In stage 4 of a SEES analysis we look over the horizon for possible developments that may come to challenge us (or offer us opportunities). We can use such strategic notice to decide whether to invest in preparations in case they were to arrive and to keep our eyes peeled for the first signs that this is happening. We can predict with confidence that the number of people connected to the Internet will continue to grow rapidly and thus also the numbers capable of being influenced by digital means. The greatest growth in numbers will take place in the global south, where the technology will hasten social and economic development without these societies having had to go through the long and polluting stages of the earlier industrial revolutions. There is little limit to the applications that will be developed to encourage local markets and social institutions even when much traditional infrastructure is absent. The access to knowledge that comes with internet connectivity will be a great leveller. A connected student, of whatever age, anywhere will access online courses by the very best teachers and deep library resources previously only available to the most privilged. When natural disaster strikes, the web will provide the means, as it did with COVID-19, to map and assess what needs to be done, to harness support from society and to provide a platform for social solidarity extending way beyond the affected region.

Those trends will, sadly, also be likely to bring an increase in the numbers of malign actors attempting to deceive and confuse, or of criminal attempts to use the digital world to defraud. We will all face increasing dangers from malign tampering with data on which everyday life depends. There will be increasing quantities of such data that can be exploited or tampered with from our future *quantified self* (as we adopt more advanced fitness trackers, heartbeat monitors and apps that use our personal information on our mobile devices), from the *smart home* (that will be equipped with voice-responsive loudspeakers, and Internet-enabled locks and heating systems, and with the children having Internet-connected toys), and finally from our life in the *smart cities* of the future (where electricity grids, traffic light systems, office access, driverless cars and all the other innovations to come will rely on 5G internet access).

As authoritarian regimes come increasingly to fear the liberating effects of internet connectivity on their societies there will be long-term pressure from them to carve up the Internet along national lines, We see this already with China and Russia. More countries will want to follow suit, even if that means fragmenting the essential global promise of the Internet that came with the vision of the West Coast internet pioneers and their protocols. Such steps reduce the added value the technology is capable of delivering by restricting the spread of knowledge and trade. Milan Kundera set his novel *The Unbearable Lightness of Being* during the 1968 Prague Spring, whose brutal suppression we saw in Chapter 3. He writes prophetically of a photographer who takes photos of protestors in the hope that she will inspire more to join their ranks, and who feels happy that she is helping to bring about societal change. But during the subsequent crackdown, those same photographs are used to identify protestors, who are then imprisoned and tortured. We can already see repressive regimes around the world trying to acquire and misuse the most advanced internet surveillance technology for just such a purpose, creating what has been termed 'WMC', weapons of mass control.[21]

Populism has always been present in politics, but the future reach of social media into the global population, and its stickiness as a source of social interaction, makes it a much more effective medium than the pamphlets, newspapers and traditional television appearances of populist leaders of the past. Social media can provide a sense of direct authentic contact on the part of the leader with 'the people'. The impact of those social media interactions is likely to be heightened by comparison with the staid structures and processes of representative democracy. Traditional politicians themselves will increasingly be seen as captives of the old system. Demagogues thrive on simplification. It is not just 'fake news' we have to fear but fake history and fake science peddled by so-called social influencers. We already see vloggers on YouTube and other platforms building up large followings for their video diaries of their every minute and for their insights into what they consider to be the latest fashion – but that can be accompanied by their instantaneous views on matters of moment. YouTube encourages this, and once over the thresholds of 1000 subscribers and 4000 hours watched the producer of video content (the vlogger) is eligible for a partner programme that entitles them to a small cut of the money made from advertising accompanying their videos.[22] Those who follow such vloggers characterize themselves as active, risky and fast by comparison with the followers of traditional TV or print media. And, unlike traditional broadcasters, the vloggers themselves will get paid by the social media platform for attracting attention even were they to do so by proclaiming the Earth is flat.

Digital technology will be more widely available to forge and fake material to achieve a desired effect. An individual will find their image apparently present in a compromising faked photograph. Sound can easily be doctored, as in the 2019 video of the House Speaker, Nancy Pelosi, in which her voice was altered electronically to make it appear she was drunk. Uploaded, this video went viral and was seen millions of times. Video-editing technology has advanced even to the point (so-called 'deep fakes') where existing video clips of leading political figures can be altered imperceptibly and a soundtrack added so that they appear to be speaking the opposite of what they believe, or to be admitting to dishonest or disreputable acts.[23] The latest advanced artificial-intelligence text generator allows software to generate content in a style that matches a given original, and with passages that are invented but make perfect sense, that are close to indistinguishable from genuine news.[24] This for me opens the grim prospect of computer-generated false but eminently plausible information flooding the Internet from multiple sources.

We have from this stage of the SEES analysis ample strategic warning that the abundant digital coinage of the future will enable us to acquire many things of great value to our society, but at the same time will be capable of funding developments that bring great harm. All we can say with confidence today is that if democratic societies do not invest very heavily in understanding these harms and building resilience against them, then there will be nothing to prevent them causing great trouble for us and for democratic society.

Conclusions: the danger of digital subversion and sedition

There is a reason why this chapter on digital dangers comes at the end of this book. First, I wanted in Part One to set out a structured way of thinking to make sense of a confusing world, through the four stages of the SEES model of intelligence analysis as we have just seen applied to digital-information threats. You know therefore how to acquire situational awareness of what is going on around you. You can explain why that is what is being observed. You can make estimates and predictions of how events may unfold. Finally, you will be less vulnerable to future surprises by having strategic warning of what we may all have to face next emerging from over the horizon. Then I drew out in Part Two lessons in how to understand the inevitable unconscious biases we all experience in such thinking, how to avoid being sucked in by obsessions and conspiracies, and how to be aware of when manipulation, fakery and deception are being directed at us. Finally, in Part Three I have wanted to persuade you that to manage our future sensibly we all need effective partnerships based on trust and the ability to establish constructive relationships with those with whom we have to deal. If you have taken on board the lessons embodied in those nine chapters, then I believe you now are successfully equipped, like an intelligence officer, to understand the subversion and sedition being waged online.

Subversion and sedition are very old forms of challenge to the authority of a state. The human motivations behind them will not change. But the means through which they are expressed have already changed radically with the advent of digital technology, particularly the Internet. Digital subversion is already with us as a threat. We are on notice that there are further developments in information warfare capabilities over the horizon that will further damage us, unless we start to prepare now. We already have had plenty of strategic notice of these developments that threaten representative democracy itself. There are two deeper consequences of our digital lives for our democracy that may creep up on us and that particularly concern me. So much so that I have devoted much of the last chapter to examining them in more detail. The first is the implication that in the long term there may prove to be lasting psychological effects of our immersion in a digitized world on ourselves as functioning social beings. The second is a consequence of the first: the risks to retaining a healthy democracy if the worst prognostications about the impact on individual human behaviour turn out to be the case.

Drawing on the lessons in this book we should at the least:

- Learn from the Russian covert campaigns to influence both US and French elections in 2016 the dangers of the different dimensions of digital subversion.
- Be alert to the existence of fake websites and bots being used covertly to spread messaging.
- Understand how the techniques of ad tech are being used to micro-target political messages.
- Recognize the potential for hostile digital messaging to intensify existing splits in society.
- Plan for a future in which more nations and extremist groups use digital subversive methods to advance their interests at our expense.
- Watch out for signs that deep-fake technology is becoming easier to acquire and use.
- Support work by the tech companies to reduce the dangers from anonymous political and other messaging.

- Exercise caution in allowing data from our quantified selves, smart homes and smart cities that would increase our vulnerability to external exploitation and pressure.
- Reduce our personal vulnerability by improving our day-to-day cybersecurity.

In the final chapter I will strike a cautiously optimistic note, based on my belief that we can make good use of these and all the other lessons I have set out in each chapter, learned from the world of security and intelligence, and that I can summarize in telegraphic form:

Lesson 1: Our knowledge of the world is always fragmentary, incomplete and sometimes wrong.

Lesson 2: Facts need explaining.

Lesson 3: Predictions need an explanatory model as well as sufficient data.

Lesson 4: We do not have to be so surprised by surprise.

Lesson 5: It is our own demons that are most likely to mislead us.

Lesson 6: We are all susceptible to obsessive states of mind.

Lesson 7: Seeing is not always believing: beware manipulation, deception and faking.

Lesson 8: Imagine yourself in the shoes of the person on the other side.

Lesson 9. Trustworthiness creates lasting partnerships.

Lesson 10. Subversion and sedition are now digital.

PART FOUR

II

A final lesson in optimism

The intention of this concluding chapter is to draw on the lessons in this book to show how we can make ourselves more resilient to the long-term dangers arising out of our dependence on the Internet and exposure to digital technology. I start with what in the long term may prove to be the lasting psychological effects of our digitized world on ourselves as functioning social beings. Then I examine a consequence of the first: the risks to retaining a healthy democracy if the worst prognostications about the impact on human behaviour turn out to be the case. I intend that the lesson of this chapter should be one of optimism. Thus forewarned and forearmed, we can manage the risks that accompany the benefits of our digital life.

Understanding the lure of a consensual hallucination

A consensual hallucination was how the sci-fi novelist William Gibson first referred to what he went on to term cyberspace.[1] As with any strong narcotic, we can become addicted to experiencing ourselves in cyberspace, playing computer games and engaging deeply in social media. Over time we will find that our brains have accordingly rewired the neural circuits that lead us to feel pleasure. In this immersive environment we lose any sense of time. We experience anxiety if we are not always connected and we endlessly check our mobile devices for incoming communications from others. We become more sensitive to visual clues rather than to the written word. In short, there are implications for the human interactions on which society depends if, as we are beginning to, we live our lives umbilically connected to, and sometimes even for long periods inside, cyberspace. The first step in protecting ourselves is to recognize there is no such place as cyberspace: it is a consensual hallucination. And it is not good for us to spend too long in it.

The citizen has certainly already come to recognize its addictive nature. We expect that the digital experience will be continuously entertaining, diverting and above all engaging. It mostly is. At a trivial level, we may not be too concerned at 'news' items appearing in our feeds that are deliberately interspersed with links to celebrity gossip or fashion, or cat videos. The latter are all forms of 'clickbait', a term that has entered the *Oxford English Dictionary* to describe content whose main purpose is to attract attention and encourage visitors to click on a link to a particular web page. Clickbait is engaging. In that respect our expectations of cyberspace seem very different from what its digital adherents dismissively call 'meatspace', the daily grind of life in three dimensions constrained by the physical laws under which humans evolved over millennia. But these are not separate spaces: what we do in cyberspace does bleed back into the real world. When cybercriminals defraud us, it is real money they steal. When the infrastructure is hacked, it is real lights that go out. When cyberbullying takes place, it is real children who are harmed. As patterns of behaviour develop online, they will come to affect our everyday lives. Nor is it true that what is done online stays there.

It is evident that the younger generations have for some time now relied on social media platforms for interactions with family and friends and making new contacts and relationships. At the same time, they use a host of more specialist sites for connections to likeminded individuals who share their tastes and opinions, including political outlook. As they become senior citizens, I see no reason for them to change those ingrained digital habits. Today, almost 80 per cent of US citizens use social media in some form. This pull of the web as the preferred medium for everyday social interaction is strengthened by our increasing dependence on it for digital access to necessary financial, travel, commercial and government information.

Already in the US, mobile-device screens have come to replace traditional curated outlets such as TV news broadcasts and local and national print media that for previous generations would have been where they derived awareness of what was happening in the world around them. TV news use is already dramatically lower among younger adults, who prefer websites. As of 2018, just one in five US adults often get news from print newspapers, the percentage falling to only one in twenty for 18- to 29-year-olds.[2] A similar trend is likely to be seen in Europe as mobile devices proliferate that are affordable, are always on and allow us to be seamlessly connected. That connectivity leaves no excuse for individuals to avoid the expectation by their peers (and their bosses) that they will be online and thus effectively on-call all the time. As early as 2010 it was noted that 93 per cent of Americans will check their mobile phones while talking to friends and family or while watching TV.[3] This always-on, always-connected phenomenon is a compulsion. It is why, as we saw in the last chapter, messages on social media will reach their intended audiences quickly, and with impact.

The individual Western citizen is thus already, and will be for the foreseeable future, the recipient of digital information of all kinds and most are now active uninhibited participants in social media. Inevitably, all that digital immersion makes the citizen vulnerable to exposure to deliberately misleading, false or malicious information put out by unscrupulous actors, some of whom can legitimately be described as engaged in subversion or sedition. It could be argued that there is a precedent in the early sixteenth century, when the new technology of printing led to sensational pamphleteering in which the novelty of the new medium, combined with lurid atrocity stories, enhanced the call to action in favour of the Reformation and later to promote the Counter-Reformation. Perhaps so, but it is easier and cheaper to achieve the desired effect today if done digitally. Together with the 'digital echo chamber effect' described earlier, such developments will leave the public more open to information manipulation than ever before.

The more time we spend online the more our traits become exaggerated, as we see with disinhibition. This is not all a bad thing. Natural feelings of compassion and altruism are heightened. We see this with online donations to good causes. Crowd funding helps small start-up businesses and those seeking funding for class actions against over-mighty corporations. But the digital medium does encourage 'thinking fast' and reacting accordingly. We have to preserve our reflective, creative time as well.

Digital immersion alters the way we perceive others. One example is the disinhibition that anonymity encourages, leading too many people to be rude and abusive to others in their social media posts. That is already coarsening the tenor of political debate and media coverage of politics, which is beginning to look more and more partisan. The phenomenon has been likened to the modern equivalent of superhero invincibility and invisibility in which individuals feel they can exercise power over others without responsibility.[4] It used to be said that online rants used language that people would not be prepared to use in face-to-face encounters. That is becoming less the case, as real-world street behaviour is demonstrating.

Another example of disinhibition is the growing habit among the young (and some not so young) of 'sexting' and being persuaded to send intimate pictures of themselves online that end up widely circulated, leading to distress, self-harm or even suicide, a phenomenon for which the term 'sextortion' has now been coined. Most users of email and social media are careless about how they exchange uninhibited views and personal details. As we have seen in Chapter 10, our online communications are vulnerable to hackers, who can break in and steal and then 'weaponize' such information. Such material in the wrong hands can be turned into a source of manipulation, ridicule, character assassination or even blackmail.

What needs to be better understood for our own protection is how this constant exposure to the rapid flow of information and raw opinion is altering individual behaviour itself and changing mental processing, including perceptions of reality. The way that Internet users learn of events of interest and the difficulty of separating news from opinion (just as for the media the traditional trade of the reporter has largely morphed into that of the journalist) creates fertile ground for influence operations. The results are for the most part bad for democracy.

Understanding the impact on democracy

The success of the fictional 2027 polar bear movement, my account of which opened the previous chapter, was based in my assessment that we are seeing increasing susceptibility of the public to digital manipulation. We have evidence, not least from the 2016 US Presidential election, of a readiness uncritically to recirculate realistic fakes, hoaxes and lurid exaggerations. We can expect to see more hyper-partisan populist views and conspiracy-laden arguments on social media. Accompanying those trends will be a further decline in the intellectual standards of political argument, a coarsening of debate, a failure to defend scientific reasoning, and an unwillingness to apply evidence properly to policymaking. Voter cynicism about the motives of politicians and resulting low election turnout is with us now. If such indicators worsen then this will not be an accident. It will be because we have passively accepted that reason no longer holds the sway it once did. The subversion of rationality as a guiding principle of statecraft and domestic policy will have come largely from atrophy inside our body politic. That deplorable development has been cynically encouraged and taken advantage of recently by Russian propaganda and disinformation activities. Making ourselves more resilient in the face of these threats is the call to arms that animated me to write this book.

For some, politics will be pleasingly narcissistic, where everything reflects their preconceptions, and anything that might disturb their outlook can be ignored as unreal or uncertain. It is hard to satisfy those who refuse to accept the outcome of rational examination of the facts. We saw in Part One that an important aspect of rationality is inference, the ability to draw supportable conclusions from evidence even when not certain. That is what intelligence officers do. They know that there is rarely absolute certainty and that inferential judgements short of that can still be hugely valuable in helping people make better decisions. We must all do the same. As we saw in Chapter 2, with Bayesian inference we can rationally recalibrate our degree of belief in the opinions that guide our decisions as new evidence arises. We do not have to end up endlessly trapped into the twisted loop of conspiratorial thinking where we dismiss what we do not want to acknowledge.

As a general rule, users are more likely to embrace highly targeted appeals – even if based on false information – as long as they appear to reinforce their core beliefs. This is exploitation of a form of the confirmation bias that we explored in Chapter 5. 'It might have been true' too easily morphs into 'It should have been true', and that becomes, with frequent repetition, 'I want it to be true', and finally 'It is as good as true.' A good example was the slogan on the side of the red battle bus promoting Vote Leave for the 23 June 2016 UK Brexit referendum. 'We send the EU £350m a week. Let's fund our NHS instead'. The independent UK Statistics Authority criticized Boris Johnson for repeating this slogan as 'a clear misuse of official statistics'. The real, net, figure was more like £250m a week. In any case the impact on the economy from changes to trade after leaving the EU is estimated as likely to be far bigger than savings from the UK's membership fee.[5] But for those predisposed to be distrustful of EU membership that £350m-a-week-wasted slogan is as good as true.

Leading that journey into a new form of deception politics are political leaders, such as Donald Trump, who are openly disdainful of experts and the factual accuracy that is their stock in trade, and behave in ways that make clear they do not care whether statements are false or not, but only whether they have the desired emotional impact in conveying a sense of what might be true. On 22 January 2017, only two days into the Trump presidency, Kellyanne Conway, senior counsellor to the President, said that the White House had 'alternative facts' to justify how Donald Trump could have come to the view that his inaugural crowd was the largest ever when photographic evidence showed otherwise.[6] The idea that there are factual statements which are no longer to be considered as capable of being proved or disproved but merely asserted is deeply unsettling. As Hillary Clinton's predecessor as US Senator for New York, Daniel Moynihan, rightly stated: 'Everyone is entitled to his own opinion, but not their own facts.' The sixteenth-century philosopher and statesman Francis Bacon is credited with the tag 'ipsa scientia potestas est' – knowledge is power. In my first book, *Securing the State*, I acknowledged that 'if knowledge is power then secret knowledge is turbo-charged power'.[7] But that statement, although justified, here is trumped by the Trumpian lesson that power is simply what power can do, including change the facts and the meaning of words. The emotional themes of immigration, Islamophobia and xenophobia segue into chants of 'Build the wall' and 'Lock her up.'

Part of the explanation lies in the populist context of the times. The emotional appeal is to groups of voters who may be justified in believing that traditional politics has excluded them, feelings that are exacerbated where such voters are experiencing economic hardship with decay in social structures as a result of factory closures and urban decline. This feeling can be tinged with a false nostalgia, since in that remembered past, despite its privations, life was experienced as being simpler, living with values important to those communities.

People who then find themselves unable to determine simple causes for the complex adverse circumstances in which they find themselves now are more likely to turn to populist explanations. In such circumstances, unresponsive elites that are seen to be practising and benefiting from representative politics can be too easily portrayed as looking after their own interests at the expense of those left behind. The stage is then set for encouraging conspiracy thinking, as we saw in Chapter 6, seeing the authorities – regarded as the embodiment of the 'deep state' – as frustrating the popular will. Social media outlets that promote conspiratorial thinking will then claim that what they report is information and points of view that the mainstream media do not care to – or that have, according to the conspiracy, been suppressed. The twisted loop of conspiracy is thus completed. We could add, with George Orwell, that such politics of chaos is connected to a decline in the precision with which language is used, divorcing words from their meaning. In the hands of an unscrupulous populist leader the dark triad of narcissism, Machiavellianism and psychopathy lead the flight from rational argument. It is what the RAND Corporation called 'truth decay'.[8] That decay can be spotted by four signs of intellectual corruption:

- Increasing disagreement about facts and analytical interpretations of facts and data.
- The blurring of the line between opinion and fact.
- The increasing relative volume, and resulting influence, of opinion and personal experience over fact.
- Diminished trust in expertise and formerly respected institutions as sources of factual information.

Opposing such fashion in ignorance is the tradition of rational inquiry that Francis Bacon exemplified 500 years ago and that seventeenth-century Enlightenment thinkers like David Hume and Adam Smith represented. Their values are embodied in the tradition of observation and rational analysis leading to impartial policy judgement that insists upon integrity of thought.

The evolutionary biologist Robert Trivers has concluded that a distinct strategic advantage may lie in a capacity for self-deception since it enhances the ability to deceive others.[9] If so, there is a disturbing negative feedback between the arguments made by a manipulative politician and the intrinsic merit of those arguments. A growing feature of political debate already reflected on social media, for example, is the over-ready dismissal of expertise as being itself politically motivated, especially when it comes to scientific knowledge. The US Union of Concerned Scientists has complained of the evidence that rolls in daily that the Trump administration is undermining long-established processes for science to inform public policy.[10] It is often not the science itself to which people object, but to how its implications affect their world view. There are precedents. It was not Galileo's predictions from his heliocentric model of how the heavenly bodies moved that so upset the Vatican (God could have so arranged things as to make them appear thus to man) but his insistence that, as he muttered under his breath during his inquisition, *Eppur si muove*, that is how in reality the planets do move.

It is often today not the scientific inquiry itself to which people such as anti-climate change activists object but to how its implications affect their world view and ideology. But here I can only echo Galileo again in saying that 'I do not feel obliged to believe that the same God who has endowed us with sense, reason, and intellect has intended us to forgo their use.'[11]

The exercise of genuine democracy requires both the flow of informed opinion (including criticism of the regime) and engagement in a genuine debate on the issues. The good news is that there is experimental evidence that it is possible to counteract the spread of disinformation.[12] Two approaches are possible.

There is topic rebuttal where misinformation is countered by presenting established facts; and technique rebuttal where the techniques that the deniers are using are unmasked and used back against them. The latter method exposes tricks such as cherry-picking isolated papers or facts out of context that are used to bolster a conspiracy theory. The former method has also been shown to be effective in experiments, although there is the acknowledged risk of reinforcing the conspiratorial mindset on the grounds that the very attempt to convince shows how deep the conspiracy runs.

The appeal to reason will be stronger if there is an emotional resonance with what those concerned care about most. There is perhaps a parallel with dealing with terrorists. Most hardened PIRA terrorists in Northern Ireland eventually went along with the views of their leadership during the long peace process that the surest route to their goal of a united Ireland did not lie in the murder of innocents but by engaging in politics and building cross-border institutions. They had not given up on their goal but recognized the power of the arguments that their terrorist campaign would not get them there.

Fending off digital subversion

A traveller to York in 1538 would have seen the body parts of the plotters of the Pilgrimage of Grace, who dared to challenge Henry VIII, hanging from the castle walls; those visiting Carlisle in 1745 likewise would have seen the severed heads of followers of the Jacobite rebellion stuck on pikes. The French aristocracy fared no better during the revolutionary terror of the 1790s. Historically, there was only one overriding rule of engagement for those promoting subversion and sedition and those attempting to defend the status quo: to the victor, the spoils; to the loser, the gibbet. There may be the semblance of a trial for the loser, like the drumhead court martial of the Romanian communist dictator Nicolae Ceaușescu and his wife, Elena, in 1989, but their death sentence was a formality.[13] That Romania is now a full member of both the European Union and NATO, on the other hand, is testament to the power that democracy can bring even to peoples that have been traumatized by many decades of authoritarian leadership. A realist view of international relations leads democratic governments to feel morally justified in using their power to resist interference with their sovereignty.

One of the options open is investing in gathering and using secret intelligence to gain an advantage over the adversary. In modern times, the protection of the democratic institutions of the state was the justification for the twentieth-century activities of the FBI or MI5. Today's mission is, as the MI5 website explains: 'to keep the country safe. For more than a century we have worked to protect our people from danger, whether it be from terrorism or damaging espionage by hostile states.' Modern digital subversion can, nevertheless, be well hidden and may take careful investigation to determine who is responsible and whether the potential threat is serious enough to merit a determined response.

Combined with the impact, global coverage and speed of transmission, the anonymity inherent in the design of the Internet makes counter-measures much harder to deploy, at least in a free society. Combating modern subversion and sedition must nevertheless be a properly funded component part of national security effort for the democracies. More authoritarian regimes, such as those currently ruling in Russia, China and Iran, have recognized the power of the Internet and invested in the capabilities needed to take advantage of it to promote their external policies. They also know to fear the domestic power of the Internet and are determined that their populations should not have unrestricted access to it.

The right of individual self-development can only be exercised by those who have sufficient control over their lives. That will not be the case for those whose lives are regulated by authoritarian regimes. An example under development is using the 'big nudge' of Internet-based social-credit scores. China is engaged in a huge experiment to see if monitoring internet behaviour and acting on the results can nudge its vast population into socially desirable behaviour (as defined by the Chinese Communist Party) with, at the same time, antisocial behaviour being penalized and thus redirected into more acceptable channels. The giant Chinese internet companies are cooperating in the development and trialling of algorithms to do just that by logging financial activity, online interactions, websites sought and visited, energy use, traffic infringements and much more. The resulting score will then allow the authorities to apply incentives such as job access to the public sector and access to the best educational opportunities for children. Sanctions can also be calibrated. At the most extreme this might involve compulsory re-education in secure training or re-indoctrination centres, as is happening for the members of the Uighur population judged to be not showing sufficient respect for Chinese (that is, Han) values and culture. Such exploitation of the digital world will be an attractive option for many countries around the globe that fear social upheaval or inter-communal tension. It will certainly appeal to autocratic leaders everywhere. The individual liberties we see indissolubly linked to liberal democracy are going to be traded for social cohesion and economic progress.

Countering sedition has always raised difficult ethical problems since it involves questioning the loyalty of the domestic population to the idea of the nation itself. As Chapter 6 illustrated, governments have to take care in conducting surveillance on their own citizens. At one extreme was the East German Stasi with its methodology of keeping the entire population under close surveillance to establish what was normal behaviour for each family and thus creating the ability to spot and investigate any deviations that might presage antisocial activity. At the other extreme is the unreasonable peril in which citizens would be placed if concerns over domestic surveillance prevented effective investigations of suspected suicide bombers intent on committing a terrorist crime.

A government concerned with foreign subversion need, nevertheless, have no ethical qualms about wanting to take steps to defend itself. The presence of foreign agents can be detected, and the individuals arrested and deported in accordance with the law. Things get trickier in the cyber-domain where the hostile activity, be it hacking, trolling, covert financing of seditious movements or other active measures, is remotely generated from another jurisdiction that will not cooperate in efforts to uncover what is going on. The surveillance that is needed to uncover those responsible and to detect malware – for example, by bulk access to internet data – can appear highly invasive of personal privacy. I do not believe we have any alternative for the protection of society from those who mean us harm other than to allow our intelligence and security agencies to use such powerful tools. However, these could, in different hands under different governments, become tools of repression. We are right therefore to regulate and oversee their use under the rule of law.

In nations that believe in the value of free speech (and protect it through constitutional and statutory provisions) there will always be among the swirl of competing ideas and ideologies some material that is harmful to the public interest. Child pornography, incitement to violence, hate speech and racial abuse have no place in a civilized society and there are strong legal sanctions against them in most democracies. In the past, any material of this kind that escaped prosecution would nevertheless be hard to find and unlikely to come to the attention of those who were not seeking it. But the vast, unpoliced oceans of digital material create new problems, not least the ever-present risk that harmful material can be easily accessed by anyone seeking it. We should, however, not confuse the right to freedom of speech with a right to algorithmic amplification of our views.[14] The spreading of Salafist–jihadist imagery and propaganda is one case in point. Russian interference at the time of the US Presidential election of 2016, by setting up deceptive websites and spreading disinformation on the Internet as described in the previous chapter, provides a different example of algorithmic amplification for the purpose of subversion.

Rules of the digital byways

The net social and commercial benefits of the Internet are too great to imagine any significant restrictions being tolerated in the democracies in terms of access to overseas networks and platforms. National laws apply to content, however, and companies will in most jurisdictions be required to remove material deemed to represent hate speech or incitement to violence. Such material is likely to offend in any case against the conditions of service of the operator or platform. Editorial control of internet material inevitably involves fine judgements between material that some may find highly objectionable but in a free society is covered by 'the right to be offended' and material that is actively harmful to the public interest and would be unlawful. For profit-seeking commercial companies (especially when foreign-owned and based) to exercise the duty of choosing what is to be allowed on the Internet is itself a controversial proposition. More censorship of political views that some would consider seditious is likely to be resisted in the democracies on freedom of speech grounds. There is therefore an asymmetry between Western democracies and more authoritarian regimes such as China and Russia that seek to limit public access to external sites which contain what they regard as a much wider class of content deemed politically subversive to the regime.

Of course, living in a free society means that we should all be open to influence. When some of that information is then revealed to be knowingly false, and maliciously spread, confidence in democratic processes and institutions slowly ebbs. Such considerations still leave considerable scope for the circulation, in a free society, of opinions that many would find not just distasteful but unacceptable and would wish to see suppressed. The first hurdle to be overcome is the self-regarding view on the part of the owners and operators of the social media platforms that they are only technical providers of communications pipes with no responsibility for what flows through them, even when the material is poisonous. They are clearly not publishers in the printed book or printed paper sense of that term.[15] This is a case where our old language leads us into a false binary choice. These companies exhibit both characteristics depending upon the context – just as light shows itself as a particle or a wave depending upon how the observer chooses to see it. No perfect solution has been found that reconciles these competing considerations. There has to be an inevitable balancing act between them.

There are core principles that must inform our understanding of what is at stake and the struggle we face. Those who protest against the status quo must confine themselves to peaceful means – which rules out the use or threat of violence and terrorism; they must use democratic means – which confines the legitimate changes to those that can be achieved within a democratic system of government; and they must come from within – which rules out cases of external subversion. A settled constitution (even if it is unwritten, as is the case in the UK) helps define the boundaries of sedition by setting the rules for constitutional change.

The modern rule of law requires transparency of legislation and the regulation of secret activity in accordance with the law. Some essential defence and intelligence activities must necessarily be conducted away from the public gaze. But governments that argue one thing to their publics, yet covertly promote some other policy entirely, are these days going to find the going hard. And today the chances of keeping anything secret beyond the immediate tactical needs of an operation seem more remote than ever. Secrecy, in the era of social media, Wikileaks and citizen journalists, is not what it was.[16]

What can be done?

It is a warm spring day in Trafalgar Square in 2028. A small number of core activists wearing their polar bear masks have gathered to support their revolutionary movement in its annual march down Whitehall to protest outside Parliament, but there are very few journalists to watch them and no crowds.

The recent election resulted in a decisive rejection of their radical brand of direct democracy. Contrary to the worst fears of the pundits the election turnout had been high. Representative democracy seemed to be enjoying a come-back with Members of Parliament using social media responsibly to connect with all their constituents, not just those that voted for them. The electorate had kicked out those politicians they held responsible from the traditional parties for the slow recovery from deep recession that had followed the global COVID-19 pandemic. A new crop of younger Members of Parliament had arrived and were competing with each other to be more open, direct and honest with their electorates. All the political parties had championed the need to tackle climate change (the few climate change deniers had lost their seats) and this had provided a unifying theme for what could be achieved by the nation working together healing the divisions the recession had caused.

The May 2028 edition of the *Economist* newspaper devoted an extended multi-page editorial to explaining why the future for democracy was looking brighter. The editor identified three themes that were changing the political climate for the democracies, 'the rays of sunshine', she called them, breaking through the clouds of pessimism. These are the active defence of liberal democracy; reducing the online vulnerability of the citizen; and achieving stronger cybersecurity and cyber-deterrence.

The first theme was tracked in the editorial back to the far-sighted decision in 2022, after careful preparation, to launch in all schools a major five-year programme to strengthen the roots of liberal democracy and teach critical thinking for the digital world. The result was a more confident young generation but one much more censorious of the sloppy thinking and false promises of the old politicians. The by now annual national sixth-form rebuttal competition had humiliated the worst offenders of political spinning: being with justification branded a liar by young people was becoming a bar to progress as a politician. The results of advanced AI fact-checking software were routinely broadcast alongside media appearances of pundits and politicians alike with a similar effect. All digital paid political content had, by law, to be tagged with the name and address of the originator, which had cut down the 'fake-news' stories that had so disfigured earlier elections. A welcome innovation had been the extension of the remit of the independent Office of Budget Responsibility to provide objective examination of new policies, including responsibility for publishing the factual analysis underlying government decisions.

The second welcome development that the *Economist* identified was the marked reduction in the vulnerability of the public to online manipulation and disinformation. There was praise for the leadership of the new US President in calling a 2025 global conference on internet norms that had brought together democratic governments, civil society groups, the major internet companies and the global advertising industry. She had emphasized the value to democracy of a free press and praised the role of investigative journalism in keeping politics honest. The final communiqué pledged a restoration of truth-telling in government and an end to the promotion of 'alternative facts'. Major investment had been announced in the automated detection and removal of illegal content and material offending against the guidelines of the social media companies. The results were already being seen in cleaning up the digital world. The *Economist* called this a win–win since advertisers and their clients were delighted that their brands would not be tarnished by appearing alongside dubious content. News websites now carried independently verified kitemarks to show their reliability. A consortium of tech companies had launched a secure Internet within the Internet, access to which required biometric identification. This was proving highly popular for social media use, especially by schoolchildren, cutting down on trolling, sexting and online bullying since offenders could be traced. The result was an upsurge of innovation and profitable internet activity. Those who still used the Wild West of the original Internet knew they did so at their own peril.

Finally, the *Economist* pointed to the cumulative gains in cybersecurity following the top priority given to countering subversion as an intelligence requirement. There had been corresponding additional investment in the UK National Cyber Security Centre, working in partnership with the private sector and in close cooperation with its counterparts overseas. The public was much more security-savvy. The critical infrastructure was now much more resilient to any attempts to disrupt it. A small number of highly targeted offensive cyber-operations (which, the editor reminded readers, the *Economist* had always backed) had demonstrated that the UK and US were prepared to defend themselves from cyber-coercion. The UK cyber-domain (.uk) was now protected by active cyber-defences that identified malware in bulk traffic, and removed bad websites and fake internet addresses to which criminals and hacker groups tried to lure unsuspecting citizens. Not only had this hugely cut down on fraud but subversive activity from overseas had become much harder. Hacking in to steal emails to weaponize was a thing of the past. No longer was 'fake news' being directed at the most vulnerable by bots. Regrettably, Russia still pumped out its propaganda through RT and Sputnik (just ignore it, concluded the editor loftily, and recognize it for what it is), but the days of Russian election interference in the West were over. Their last attempts had been thoroughly exposed by Western intelligence penetration of the offending state agencies, and international warrants had been issued for the arrest of those responsible.

It was just a pity, concluded the *Economist*, that these three themes had not received this level of international backing a decade or so earlier. How much trouble the democratic world would have been saved.

If democratic governments and those that work with them in the years to come keep these lessons in mind we can be similarly optimistic about the digital health of our nation, the future of our democracy and the integrity of our elected leaders. We will slow down and even reverse the present erosion of trust in politics and restore confidence in rational debate. And foreign adversaries will no longer have a free run to deploy the techniques of modern digital subversion and manipulation against us. The science fiction writer Isaac Asimov complained of those who have been 'nurtured by the false notion that democracy means that my ignorance is as good as your knowledge'. Our civilization and our security are built on demonstrating that falsity and celebrating its inverse. In so doing we should recall the advice of the philosopher and central figure in the eighteenth-century Scottish Enlightenment, David Hume: 'there is a degree of doubt, caution and modesty, which in all kinds of scrutiny and decision, ought for ever to accompany a just reasoner'.[17]

Acknowledgements

This book draws on sources from a variety of disciplines. I have tried to provide clues in the notes for those who want to follow up these ideas but I can only offer my apologies to the many friends and colleagues whose work I have not had space to reference. There are also many still in government service on both sides of the Atlantic, including those in the secret intelligence world who must remain nameless, on whose ideas I have drawn. They will know how much this book owes to them and how much I admire the way that they are riding the digital wave. The safety and security of all of us depend upon our continuing to adapt to new developments in digital technology and learning the lessons of tracking COVID-19.

I have drawn much inspiration from discussions with the Master's degree students at King's College London, PSIA Sciences Po in Paris and the Norwegian Defence University. They have provided responsive, and helpfully critical, audiences for the ideas in this book as they have evolved in my teaching. For the last twelve years with Professor Michael Goodman I have run the King's Intelligence Studies Programme (KISP) for young analysts from the British intelligence community, now extended to analysts in law enforcement and the major government departments, and have explored with them how the advent of the digital world is transforming their work and will continue to do so in the future. My own experiences and the anecdotes that embody my memories, some of which are included in this book, are mostly from another age, but I have been gratified to find they still resonate with young analysts since they illustrate timeless dilemmas.

I owe specific thanks to Lars Nicander and his colleagues at the Centre for Asymmetric Threat Studies (CATS) in Stockholm for the opportunity to participate in the international seminars they have organized to explore many of the issues that are covered in this book, and to Matti Saarelainen and his team for sharing their pioneering work at the Helsinki Centre of Excellence for Countering Hybrid Threats.

My agent, Toby Mundy, has been a constant source of encouragement and inspiration, for which I am very grateful. I could not have wished for a more imaginative editor than Jack Ramm at Viking, who guided me in how best to introduce my ideas to a wider audience. My thanks to my copy-editor Mark Handsley and to Tom Killingbeck and the production team at Viking, who ensured that the resulting book was delivered as I would have wanted. Finally, to my family, as always, with my appreciation of their great patience during the gestation of this book.

Notes and further reading

Introduction

1   The story of these intercepts and the decision to launch the Task Force to recapture the Falkland Islands is recounted in Sir Lawrence Freedman's official history of the Falklands campaign and vividly in memoirs by Sir John Nott and Admiral Sir Henry Leach, First Sea Lord at the time. Lawrence Freedman, *The Official History of the Falklands Campaign*, vol. 1, London: Routledge, 2005, ch. 19. John Nott, *Here Today, Gone Tomorrow*, London: Politico, 2002. Henry Leach, *Endure No Makeshifts*, London: Pen and Ink Books, 1993.

2   One of the best short descriptions of the nature and use of secret intelligence is included as Chapter 1 of the Butler Report into the failures of intelligence before the invasion of Iraq in 2003. It was written by the adviser to the inquiry, the late Peter Freeman, a former senior colleague at GCHQ. Robin Butler, *Review of Intelligence on Weapons of Mass Destruction*, London: HMSO, 2004, ch. 1.

3   It is, in the formal language of the Joint Intelligence Committee, 'the process of taking known information about situations and entities of strategic, operational, or tactical importance and characterizing the known and the future actions in those situations'.

4   The ethics of secret intelligence is the subject of a dialogue between the political scientist Professor Mark Phythian and myself, as a former practitioner, in our book, *Principled Spying*, Oxford: Oxford University Press, 2018.

5   I am using the term negative capability here in the way that the twentieth-century British psychoanalyst Wilfred Bion adapted

Keats's term to illustrate an attitude of openness of mind and the capacity to be in uncertainty, which he considered of central importance, not only in the psychoanalytic session, but in life itself. See Diana Voller, 'Negative Capability', *Contemporary Psychotherapy*, vol. 2, no. 2, Winter 2010.

6 A feeling for the challenges faced at that time can be found in Richard Aldrich, *GCHQ*, London: Harper Press, 2010, ch. 24, and in the authorized history commissioned by GCHQ to celebrate its 100th anniversary: John Ferris, *Behind the Enigma*, London: Bloomsbury, 2020.

7 Ringu Tulku Rinpoche, *Living without Fear and Anger*, Oxford: Bodhicharya, 2005.

Part One: An analyst SEES

1. Lesson 1: Situational awareness

1 Some of the valuable material provided by Penkovsky was collected together by the CIA and published as a way of getting recognition for what was described as the most successful CIA agent of the era: Frank Gibney (ed.), *The Penkovsky Papers*, New York: Doubleday, 1965. A biography of the CIA officer George Kisevalter who, with the legendary MI6 case officer Harold ('Shergy') Shergold, ran Penkovsky contains a vivid account of the whole case. Clarence Ashley, *CIA Spymaster*, Gretna, La.: Pelican Publishing, 2004, ch. 10. A detailed British account that rings true is Gordon Corera, *The Art of Betrayal*, London: Weidenfeld and Nicolson, 2011, ch. 4.

2 To mark the fiftieth anniversary of the crisis, the National Security Archive at George Washington University in Washington DC assembled a series of briefing books containing original documentary material (including from the Soviet side) that chronicle

the events, available at https://nsarchive2.gwu.edu/NSAEBB/NSAEBB400/, accessed 24 December 2019.

3 For an account of the disputes between statisticians over the validity of Bayesian inference, and of the rediscovery of the method by Alan Turing at Bletchley Park, see Sharon Bertsch McGrayne, *The Theory That Would Not Die*, New Haven, Conn.: Yale University Press, 2012.

4 The classic text on analysis is that of Richards ('Dick') J. Heuer, a long-term CIA officer recruited at the time of the Korean War. In 1999 the CIA released a book based on his classified articles written between 1978 and 1986 intended to improve CIA analytic tradecraft. I have over the years drawn heavily on his ground-breaking work. Richards J. Heuer, Jr, *The Psychology of Intelligence Analysis*, [Washington DC]: CIA Center for the Study of Intelligence, 1999, available at https://www.cia.gov/library/center-for-the-study-of-intelligence/csi-publications/books-and-monographs/psychology-of-intelligence-analysis/PsychofIntelNew.pdf, accessed 24 December 2019.

5 *A Tradecraft Primer: Structured Analytic Techniques for Improving Intelligence Analysis*, Langley, Va.: CIA, 2009, available at https://www.cia.gov/library/center-for-the-study-of-intelligence/csi-publications/books-and-monographs/, accessed 24 December 2019. An excellent compilation of lessons from the CIA's experience of analysis, and of the problems of managing analysts, is Bruce E. Pease, *Leading Intelligence Analysis*, Los Angeles: CQ Press/Sage, 2020.

6 As quoted in Gregory Bergman, *Isms*, London: Adams Media, 2006, p. 105.

7 Donald E. Moggridge (ed.), *The Collected Writings of John Maynard Keynes*, London: Macmillan/Cambridge University Press, 1936, vol. VII, p. 156.

8 Michael Nielsen, *Neural Networks and Deep Learning*, free online book at http://neuralnetworksanddeeplearning.com/, accessed

24 December 2019, provides an insightful step-by-step introduction to how computers learn from observational data using simple coding.

9 The task of the human analyst can be considerably aided by automated visualization tools to show different aspects of the situation, so that key features and trends are more easily detected. A promising development is that of the interactive 'Seeing Spaces', where the room itself is a tool for assisting decisionmakers. See Bret Victor, 2 May 2014 talk on https://vimeo.com/97903574, accessed 24 December 2019. It is not hard to imagine all the four stages of the SEES model being linked together for such interactive presentation to the analyst.

10 Bellingcat has an instructive website with details of its investigations and resources for open-source investigators; see https://www.bellingcat.com/, accessed 24 December 2019.

11 A revealing introduction to the extraordinary people and states of mind to be found on the 'dark web' is Jamie Bartlett, *The Dark Net*, London: Heinemann, 2014.

12 A useful site is the Wayback machine that has archived over 300 billion web pages since 1996, accessible at https://archive.org/web/web.php, accessed 24 December 2019. Another useful site is the Web Archive, which has been storing UK websites on behalf of the six UK legal deposit libraries since 2004 and provides thematic and subject collections of relevant websites; accessible for free at http://www.webarchive.org.uk/ukwa, accessed 24 December 2019.

2. Lesson 2: Explanation

1 The former US Ambassador to NATO, Ivo H. Daalder, has described for the Brookings Institute how he saw the evolution of US and Western policy towards the conflict in Bosnia as the

role of Mladić in Bosnian Serb war crimes became clearer. See article of 1 December 1998 at https://www.brookings.edu/articles/decision-to-intervene-how-the-war-in-bosnia-ended/, accessed 24 December 2019. For the mission to warn Mladić that he had gone too far, see Col. Robert C. Owen (ed.), *Deliberate Force: A Case Study in Effective Air Campaigning*, Maxwell Air Force Base, Ala.: Air University Press, 2000, p. 26.

2 Edward H. Carr, *What is History?* Cambridge: Cambridge University Press, 1961, p. 23.

3 David Omand, *Securing the State*, London: Hurst, 2010, p. 168.

4 I am grateful to Stephen Marrin for that description; Stephen Marrin, 'Analytic Objectivity and Science: Evaluating the US Intelligence Community's Approach to Applied Epistemology', *Intelligence and National Security* (forthcoming).

5 The UK Biobank survey, for example, covers 500,000 individuals, each providing hundreds of data points on their health, diet and way of life over a period of many years.

6 A powerful examination of the problem of inductive reasoning can be found in David Deutsch, *The Fabric of Reality*, London: Allen Lane, 1997, ch. 3.

7 There is much more to the problems that black swans give rise to than their rarity. See Nassim Nicholas Taleb, *The Black Swan*, London: Penguin Books, 2007, ch. 1.

8 A telling example in the cyber-domain is to be found in Ben Buchanan, *The Cybersecurity Dilemma*, Oxford: Oxford University Press, 2017, ch. 1.

9 Michael Goodman and Ian Beesley, *Margaret Thatcher and the Joint Intelligence Committee*, The History of Government Blog, 1 October 2012, available at https://history.blog.gov.uk/, accessed 24 December 2019.

10 Richard Rorty and Pascal Engel, *What's the Use of Truth?*, New York: Columbia University Press, 2007, p. 44.

11 Professor Sir Lawrence Freedman developed the idea of 'strategic scripts' to describe the rules of thumb commonly used as shorthand in political debate, such as the appeasement script or the Vietnam script. Lawrence Freedman, *Strategy: A History*, Oxford: Oxford University Press, 2013, p. iv.

12 There have been a number of comparisons made between intelligence analysis and medical diagnosis, discussed by Mary Manjikian, 'Positivism, Post-Positivism, and Intelligence Analysis', *International Journal of Intelligence and Counter-Intelligence*, vol. 26, no. 3, Fall 2013, p. 563.

13 The ACH (Analysis of Competing Hypotheses) method was popularized by Heuer in his work for the CIA; see Richards J. Heuer, Jr, *The Psychology of Intelligence Analysis*, [Washington DC]: CIA Center for the Study of Intelligence, 1999, pp. 95–110.

14 The story originated on the 'I love Hillary Clinton' Facebook page in 2005. It has been debunked: see https://checkyourfact.com/2019/04/26/fact-check-trump-republicans-dumbest-group-voters/, accessed 24 December 2019.

3. Lesson 3: Estimations

1 The CIA released a large collection of documents on the 1968 Czech crisis as *Lessons Learned from the 1968 Soviet Invasion of Czechoslovakia: Strategic Warning and the Role of Intelligence*, Washington DC: US Government Bookstore, 2010. See also Jaromir Navratil (ed.), *The Prague Spring 1968*, Budapest: Central European University Press, 1998, which documents the events from both Soviet and Western sources.

2 Michael Goodman, *The Official History of the Joint Intelligence Committee*, vol. 1, London: Routledge, 2015, p. 269.

3 Jonathan Swift, 'A Voyage to Brobdingnag', *Gulliver's Travels*, London: Benjamin Motte, 1726, ch. 4.

4 The full 1990 US NIC assessment, 'Yugoslavia Transformed', is available at https://www.cia.gov/library/readingroom/docs/1990–10-01.pdf, accessed 28 July 2019.

5 An entertaining account of the problem of balancing false positives and false negatives is Bill Wisdom, 'Skepticism and Credibility', in Michael Shermer (ed.), *The Skeptic Encyclopedia of Pseudoscience*, vol. 1, p. 455, Santa Barbara, Calif.: ABC-CLIO, 2002.

6 The European Parliament Research Service has published a comprehensive guide to the issues that arise when applying the precautionary principle: Didier Bourguignon, 'The Precautionary Principle', Brussels: European Parliament, 9 December 2015, available at http://www.europarl.europa.eu/RegData/etudes/IDAN/2015/573876/EPRS_IDA%282015%29573876_EN.pdf, accessed 24 December 2019.

7 The medical profession is furthest advanced in trying to find measures to assess the adequacy of results generated by algorithms, such as those applied to distinguish malign from benign tumours. A detailed introduction is Thomas G. Tape, 'Interpreting Diagnostic Tests', University of Nebraska Medical Center, available at http://gim.unmc.edu/dxtests/ROC1.htm, accessed 24 December 2019.

8 Eli Wiesel, speech at the dedication of the Holocaust Memorial, Washington DC, 22 April 1993, https://www.ushmm.org/information/about-the-museum/mission-and-history/wiesel, accessed 24 December 2019.

9 Quintus Smyrnaeus, *The Fall of Troy*, New Haven, Conn.: Loeb Classical Library, 1913, p. 525.

10 Keynes adopted the subjective view of probability in asserting that the state of the future market would reflect the animal spirits of

the investors. As he wrote: 'Is our expectation of rain, when we start out for a walk, always more likely than not, or less likely than not, or as likely as not? I am prepared to argue that on some occasions none of these alternatives hold, and that it will be an arbitrary matter to decide for or against the umbrella. If the barometer is high, but the clouds are black, it is not always rational that one should prevail over the other in our minds, or even that we should balance them, though it will be rational to allow caprice to determine us and to waste no time on the debate.' John Maynard Keynes, *A Treatise on Probability*, London: Macmillan, 1921, p. 30.

11 Dan Coats, 'Statement for the Record: Worldwide Threat Assessment of the US Intelligence Community', Washington DC: Senate Select Committee on Intelligence, 29 January 2019, p. 7, available at https://www.intelligence.senate.gov/sites/default/files/documents/os-dcoats-012919.pdf, accessed 24 December 2019.

12 'National Strategic Assessment', London: National Crime Agency, 2019, p. 2, available at https://nationalcrimeagency.gov.uk/who-we-are/publications/296-national-strategic-assessment-of-serious-organised-crime-2019/file, accessed 24 December 2019.

13 DNI, 'Intelligence Community Directive 203', Washington DC: DNI, 2 January 2015, p. 3.

14 Isaac Asimov, *Foundation*, New York: Gnome Press, 1951.

15 An interesting example is how far it is possible to predict genetic changes; see Troy Day, 'Computability: Gödel's Incompleteness Theorem and an Inherent Limit to the Predictability of Evolution', *Journal of the Royal Society*, 17 August 2011, https://royalsociety-publishing.org/doi/10.1098/rsif.2011.0479, accessed 28 July 2019.

16 A term I was introduced to by Professor Greg Treverton, formerly chair of the US National Intelligence Council, the closest US parallel to the UK Joint Intelligence Committee. Wilhelm Agrell and Gregory F. Treverton, *National Intelligence and Science*, Oxford: Oxford University Press, 2015, p. 33.

17 In some circumstances, experts may do less well than the average of amateur forecasters. Tournaments to test this 'wisdom of the crowds' effect have been run by the Good Judgment Project of the Intelligence Advanced Research Projects Activity (IARPA) within the US Directorate of National Intelligence, and reported in Philip Tetlock and Dan Gardner, *Superforecasting: The Art and Science of Prediction*, New York: Crown, 2015.

18 In Edgar Wind, *Pagan Mysteries in the Renaissance*, London: Peregrine Books, 1967.

4. Lesson 4: Strategic notice

1 A description of this 2010 volcanic eruption and its implications for aircraft jet engines has been provided by the British Geological Survey, see https://www.bgs.ac.uk/research/volcanoes/icelandic_ash.html, accessed 24 December 2019.

2 The precautionary principle requires that, if there is a strong suspicion that a certain activity may have harmful consequences, it is better to control that activity now rather than to wait for incontrovertible scientific evidence.

3 This counter-terrorism exercise in 2003 was the largest ever conducted in the UK; see https://www.telegraph.co.uk/news/uknews/1440619/Blunkett-fears-suicide-bomb.html, accessed 24 December 2019.

4 The terms of reference of the UK JIC include giving early warning of the development of direct and indirect threats and opportunities in those fields to British interests or policies and to the international community as a whole. See https://www.gov.uk/government/groups/joint-intelligence-committee, accessed 24 December 2019.

5 Cynthia Grabo, *Anticipating Surprise: Analysis for Strategic Warning*, Washington DC: University Press of America, 2004. Originally

written for the US intelligence community and later published. The useful idea of setting out to reduce vulnerability to uncertainty, rather than just uncertainty itself, can be found in Yakov Ben-Haim, Policy Neutrality and Uncertainty: an info-gap perspective, Intelligence and National Security, 2016, 31:7, pp. 978–992.

6 The IMF Global Financial Stability Report 2018 concludes that the IMF's capital-flows-at-risk analysis suggests that with a 5 per cent probability, emerging market economies (excluding China) could face debt portfolio outflows in the medium term of $100bn or more over a period of four quarters (or 0.6 per cent of their combined GDP), broadly similar in magnitude to those at the time of the global financial crisis. A long-tail risk therefore still exists. See https://www.imf.org/en Publications/GFSR/Issues/2018/04/02/Global-Financial-Stability-Report-April-2018, accessed 24 December 2019.

7 I described how risk management underlay the CONTEST counter-terrorism strategy in David Omand, 'What Should be the Limits of Western Counter-Terrorism Policy?', in Richard English (ed.), *Illusions of Terrorism and Counter-Terrorism*, London: British Academy Scholarship Online, 2016, ch. 4.

8 The probabilistic basis of layered defence is that at each layer a proportion of the threat can be removed, so that the resulting total likelihood of the threat crystallizing (the product of the probabilities for each layer) can be kept acceptably small. The UK Health and Safety Executive has studied its application to reducing the risk from industrial hazards; see Andrew Franks, 'Lines of Defence/Layers of Protection in the COMAH Context' [COMAH: Control of Major Accidents Regulations], London: HSE, 2017, available at https://www.hse.gov.uk/research/misc/vectra300-2017-r02.pdf, accessed 24 December 2019.

9 A description of the scenarios used by Shell to examine different futures can be found at https://www.shell.com/energy-and-innovation/the-energy-future/scenarios.html, accessed 24 December 2019.

10 *Global Strategic Trends: The Future Starts Today*, London: Ministry of Defence, 2016, available at https://assets.publishing.service.gov. uk/government/uploads/system/uploads/attachment_data/file/ 771309/Global_Strategic_Trends_-_The_Future_Starts_Today. pdf, accessed 24 December 2019.

11 Sir Mark Walport, 'Distributed Ledger Technology: Beyond Blockchain', London: Government. Office for Science, 2016, at https://www.gov.uk/government/news/distributed-ledger- technology-beyond-block-chain, accessed 24 December 2019.

12 According to research by the University of Ottawa there have been over 50 million scientific papers published since 1665, to which some 2.5 million are being added each year, see http:// blog.cdnsciencepub.com/21st-century-science-overload/, accessed 28 July 2019.

13 An example was the publication of a paper by three GCHQ math- ematicians demonstrating that the quantum-resistant algorithm based on cyclic lattices on which they had spent several years of research, codename SOLILOQUY, had in the end not resisted a reasonably efficient quantum attack; see https://docbox.etsi. org/workshop/2014/201410_CRYPTO/S07_Systems_and_ Attacks/S07_Groves_Annex.pdf, accessed 28 July 2019.

14 This is the conclusion of F. H. Knight's major work, *Risk, Uncer- tainty and Profit*, Boston and New York: Houghton Mifflin and Co., 1921.

15 *Global Trends: the Paradox of Progress*, Washington DC: National Intelligence Council, January 2017, https://www.dni.gov/files/ documents/nic/GT-Full-Report.pdf, accessed 8 May 2019.

16 The process is described in a briefing note for the UK Parliament, 24 April 2019, available at https://researchbriefings.parliament. uk/ResearchBriefing/Summary/POST-PB-0031, accessed 9 May 2019.

17 'UK National Security Strategy', London, Cabinet Office, 2018.

Part Two: Three lessons in checking our reasoning

5. Lesson 5: It is our own demons

1   The material in this section is taken from the account by the CIA's senior officer for Europe, Tyler Drumheller, *On the Brink*, New York: Avalon, 2006, and from Bob Drogin, *Curveball: Spies, Lies and the Con Man Who Caused a War*, London: Random House, 2007. The then Deputy DCI, John McLaughlin, has said that he did not receive warnings about Curveball's reliability at the time. The DCI, George Tenet, has added that doubts 'should have been immediately and formally disseminated as a matter of record in a report that would have alerted intelligence and policy officials to the potential problem with Curveball. A second, corresponding formal report should also have been instantly sent across the intelligence and policy community to analysts and policy makers who had received previous Curveball reporting. The transmittal of those two reports would have immediately alerted experts doing the work on Iraq WMD issues across the intelligence community to a problem requiring resolution. No such report was ever disseminated, nor was the issue ever brought to my attention.' George Tenet, *At the Center of the Storm*, New York: HarperCollins, 2007, p. 377.

2   Interview reported by Martin Chulov and Helen Pidd, 'Curveball admits', *Guardian*, 15 February 2011.

3   Cited by the former chair of the US NIC, Tom Fingar, in *Reducing Uncertainty*, Stanford: Stanford University Press, 2011, p. 33.

4   Tenet, *At the Center of the Storm*, p. 333.

5   Richards J. Heuer, Jr, *The Psychology of Intelligence Analysis*, [Washington DC]: CIA Center for the Study of Intelligence, 1999, ch. 3, available at https://www.cia.gov/library/center-for-the-study-

of-intelligence/csi-publications/books-and-monographs/
psychology-of-intelligence-analysis/PsychofIntelNew.pdf.

6   As described by Eyal Pascovich, 'The Devil's Advocate in Intelligence: The Israeli Experience', *Intelligence and National Security*,
33:6, 2018, pp. 854–65.

7   Such as the pioneering work of Dr Wilfred Bion, DSO, who, following distinguished service with the tank corps during the First World
War, went on to provide innovative group therapy to hospitalized
soldiers during the Second World War. Wilfred Bion, *Experiences in
Groups*, London: Tavistock/Routledge, 1961, pp. 11–26.

8   The experimental literature on cognitive biases is vast. The Wikipedia entry lists well over 100 separately defined cognitive biases
plus social and memory biases. A starting source with references
is M. G. Haselton, D. Nettle and P. W. Andrews, 'The Evolution of
Cognitive Bias', in D. M. Buss (ed.), *The Handbook of Evolutionary
Psychology*, Hoboken, NJ: John Wiley & Sons Inc., 2005, pp. 724–46.

9   Cognitive dissonance has been held to be associated in particular
with rigid or authoritarian traits, themselves most likely linked to
early childhood experiences. A series of historical case studies of
decisions showing how British military and naval commanders
tragically fell victim to such resistance to accepting they might be
wrong is examined in Norman F. Dixon, *The Psychology of Military Incompetence*, London: Jonathan Cape, 1976.

10 Nicoll examined seven cases: the Soviet invasion of Czechoslova-
kia (1968); the Egyptian/Syrian invasion of Israel (1972–3); the
Chinese attack on Vietnam (1978–9); the Soviet invasion of
Afghanistan (1979); the Iraqi attack on Iran (1979–80); the Soviet
attack on Iran (1980); and Soviet intervention in Poland (1980–81).
The Nicoll report has been examined by the official histor-
ian of the UK Joint Intelligence Committee, Professor Mike
Goodman of King's College London; see Michael Goodman, 'The

Dog That Didn't Bark: The Joint Intelligence Committee and Warning of Aggression', *Intelligence and National Security*, 7:4, 2007, pp. 529–51.

11 Goodman, 'The Dog That Didn't Bark', p. 1.

12 BBC1, *The Thatcher Years*, part 2, broadcast 13 October 1993 (as pointed out to me by Lord Hennessy).

13 Ted Morgan, *Valley of Death*, New York: Random House, 2010, p. 641.

14 Patrick Porter, *Military Orientalism: Eastern War through Western Eyes*, London: Hurst, 2009, p. 198.

15 The intelligence foundation of Operation Fortitude is authoritatively set out in *British Intelligence in the Second World War*, vol. 5: Michael Howard, *Strategic Deception*, London: HMSO, 1990, p. 103, and colourfully in Ben Macintyre, *Double Cross*, London: Bloomsbury, 2012, p. 173. Antony Beevor, *D-Day: The Battle for Normandy*, London: Viking, 2009, gives a military historian's assessment of its impact on D-Day and beyond.

16 Robin Butler, *Review of Intelligence on Weapons of Mass Destruction*, London: HMSO, 2004, p. 159.

17 Dixon, *Psychology of Military Incompetence*, pp. 164–6.

18 Charles S. Robb and Lawrence H. Silberman (co-chairs), *The Commission on the Intelligence Capabilities of the United States Regarding Weapons of Mass Destruction*, Washington DC: US Government, 31 March 2005, p. 47, available at http://govinfo.library.unt.edu/wmd/about.html, accessed 24 December 2019.

19 Reginald V. Jones, *Reflections on Secret Intelligence*, London: Mandarin, 1989, p. 134. R. V. Jones credits this saying as 'Crow's Law'.

20 Available at https://www.youtube.com/watch?v=vJG698U2Mvo, accessed 24 December 2019.

21 This is the basis of the ancient Greek memory trick of being able to remember all the points to make in a long oration by associating each of the ideas in turn with highly striking or memorable

objects or places such as the furniture or pictures in the rooms of your house. A mental walk round the house then allows the items to be remembered one by one (and would also allow the speech to be delivered from back to front by walking round the rooms of the house in reverse order). Rediscovered during the late Renaissance as part of neo-Platonist thinking this method took on cabbalistic significance for astrologers and magi. Frances Yates, *The Renaissance Art of Memory*, London: Peregrine Books, 1969, ch. 5.

22 Butler, *Review of Intelligence on Weapons of Mass Destruction*, p. 125.

23 CIA, 'Report of a Seminar on Bias in Intelligence Analysis', Langley, Va.: CIA Library, 1977, available at https://www.cia. gov/library/readingroom/document/cia-rdp80-00630a0003000 30001-4, accessed 24 December 2019.

Lesson 6: We are all susceptible to obsessive states of mind

1 I have drawn on a number of sources for this section that paint both a favourable and a critical picture of Angleton. Most agree on his growing paranoia about penetration agents in the light of the Philby affair. Tom Mangold, *Cold Warrior. James Jesus Angleton: The CIA's Master Spyhunter*, New York: Simon and Schuster, 1991. David C. Martin, *Wilderness of Mirrors: Intrigue, Deception and the Secrets That Destroyed Two of the Cold War's Most Important Agents*, Boston: Lyons Press, 1983. Jefferson Morley, *The Ghost: The Secret Life of CIA Spymaster James Jesus Angleton*, New York: St Martin's Press, 2017. David Wise, *Molehunt: The Secret Search for Traitors That Shattered the CIA*, New York: Random House, 1992. Ray S. Cline, *Secrets, Spies and Scholars*, Washington DC: Acropolis Books, 1976, p. 198.

2 Chaired by the Oxford historian J. C. Masterman, the Twenty Committee (for XX = double cross) authorized the release

through German double agents of a skilful admixture of real intelligence (which they had calculated the Germans would already know or easily derive) and important falsehoods that they wanted the German High Command to believe.

3 Philby's action led to the highly embarrassing flight to Moscow of Donald Maclean, Head of Chancery in the Washington Embassy, with fellow diplomat Guy Burgess, under the nose of the authorities, the first two of the Cambridge spies to be exposed.

4 Ben Macintyre, *A Spy among Friends*, New York: Random House–Crown, 2014, ch. 10, describes the relationship with Angleton from Philby's perspective.

5 Some of Angleton's colleagues maintained to the end that Nosenko had to be a plant. Tennent H. Bagley, *Spymaster*, New York: Skyhorse, 2013, ch. 14, sets out a list of discrepancies in Nosenko's story. These have been explained as errors, misunderstandings or translation errors. See the declassified CIA compilation of internal reports, CIA, 'A Fixation on Moles', *Studies in Intelligence*, vol. 55, no. 4, December 2011, declassified 21 August 2013; Clarence Ashley, *CIA Spymaster*, Gretna, La.: Pelican Publishing, 2004, chs. 10–15; and Michael J. Sulick, *American Spies: Espionage against the United States from the Cold War to the Present*, Washington DC: Georgetown University Press, ch. 6.

6 See Richard H. Rovere, *Senator Joe McCarthy*, Berkeley and Los Angeles: University of California Press, 1959, and Ellen Schrecker, *The Age of McCarthyism: A Brief History with Documents* (2nd edn), New York: Palgrave Macmillan, 2002.

7 Wright justified his own role in his autobiography. Peter Wright, *Spycatcher*, New York: Viking, 1987, ch. 14.

8 Notably in Chapman Pincher, *Their Trade is Treachery*, London: New English Library, 1981.

9 Vasili Mitrokhin and Christopher Andrew, *The Mitrokhin Archive*, London: Allen Lane, 1999, pp. 528–9. The account of the Driberg case is at pp. 522–6.

10 This was the famous speech in which a profusely sweating Gaitskell had vowed in opposing the disarmers to fight, fight and fight again to save the party he loved.

11 Michael Shermer, 'The Conspiracy Theory Detector', *Scientific American*, vol. 303, issue 6, December 2010.

12 The conspiracy was started by a 1974 memoir by Group Captain Winterbotham, *The Ultra Secret*, in which he misremembered that Enigma had revealed Coventry to be the target. In fact, the Enigma messages (now in the UK National Archives) had not mentioned the target, which the Air Staffs had assumed would be London. The facts about the intelligence on the raid are set out in F. H. Hinsley et al., *British Intelligence in the Second World War*, vol. 1: *Its Influence on Strategy and Operations*, London: HMSO, 1979, pp. 316–17, and examined again by Martin Gilbert, Churchill's biographer; see https://winstonchurchill.org/resources/myths/coventry-what-really-happened/, accessed 24 December 2019.

13 The Wikileaks article on 9/11 conspiracies cites 284 references. The summary by Michael Powell, 'The disbelievers', *Washington Post*, 8 September 2006, cites a 2006 Scripps Howard/Ohio University poll of 1010 Americans which found that 36 per cent suspect the US government promoted the attacks or intentionally sat on its hands; 16 per cent believe explosives brought down the towers; 12 per cent believe a cruise missile hit the Pentagon.

14 An engineering rebuttal of these claims is Thomas W. Eagar and Christopher Musso, 'Why Did the World Trade Center Collapse? Science, Engineering and Speculation', *Journal of the Minerals, Metals and Materials Society*, 53(12), 2001, pp. 8–11, available at https://www.tms.org/pubs/journals/JOM/0112/Eagar/Eagar-0112.html, accessed 24 December 2019.

15 John le Carré, *Tinker Tailor Soldier Spy*, London: Hodder and Stoughton, 1974, pp. 216–18.

16 Robin Butler, *Review of Intelligence on Weapons of Mass Destruction*, London: HMSO, 2004, p. 153.

7. Lesson 7: Seeing is not always believing

1   The classic account of this era of British naval intelligence is Patrick Beesly, *Room 40: British Naval Intelligence 1914–1918*, London: Hamish Hamilton, 1982. For the story of the Zimmermann telegram, Barbara Tuchman, *The Zimmermann Telegram*, New York: Ballantine Books, 1958, and John Johnson, *The Evolution of British Sigint 1653–1939*, London: HMSO, 1997.

2   Malinformation, disinformation and misinformation are defined in Claire Wardle and Hossein Derakhshan, *Information Disorder: Towards an Interdisciplinary Framework for Research and Policy*, Council of Europe report DGI(2017)09.

3   The biography of Chelsea (previously Bradley) Manning is recounted in Denver Nicks, *Private Bradley Manning, WikiLeaks, and the Biggest Exposure of Official Secrets in American History*, Chicago: Chicago Review Press, 2012. The connection to Wikileaks is described by David Leigh and Luke Harding, *WikiLeaks: Inside Julian Assange's War on Secrecy*, London: Guardian Books, 2011.

4   For the background to the Snowden leaks see Luke Harding, *The Snowden Files*, London: Guardian Books, 2014, and Edward Lucas, *The Snowden Operation: Inside the West's Greatest Intelligence Disaster*, London: Kindle Single, 2014.

5   Cited in Mark Urban, *UK Eyes Alpha*, London: Faber and Faber, 1996, p. 67.

6   Antony Beevor, *D-Day: The Battle for Normandy*, London: Viking, 2009, p. 148.

7   Gill Bennett, *The Zinoviev Letter: The Story That Never Dies*, Oxford: Oxford University Press, 2018, ch. 7.

8   Vasili Mitrokhin and Christopher Andrew, *The Mitrokhin Archive*, London: Allen Lane, 1999, pp. 318–19. The KGB's own efforts are described in Boris Volodarsky, *The KGB's Poison Factory: From Lenin to Litvenenko*, London: Frontline Books, 2009.

9   Key documents relating to the ARCOS raid can be found in the Warwick University Modern Records Centre, available at https://warwick.ac.uk/services/library/mrc/explorefurther/digital/russia/arcos/, accessed 24 December 2019.

10 Ian Beesley, *The Official History of the Cabinet Secretaries*, London: Routledge, 2017, p. 320.

11 Ibid., p. 321.

12 See the 2017 briefing paper by the House of Commons Library, https://researchbriefings.parliament.uk/ResearchBriefing/Summary/SN04258, accessed 24 December 2019.

Part Three: Three lessons in making intelligent use of intelligence

8. Lesson 8: Imagine yourself in the shoes of the person . . .

1   Gordievsky's own memoir, written after he was exfiltrated by MI6 from the Soviet Union to the UK, is Oleg Gordievsky, *Next Stop Execution*, London: Macmillan, 1995. A gripping account of the Gordievsky case that benefits from interviews with those involved in MI6 is Ben Macintyre, *The Spy and the Traitor*, London: Viking, 2018.

2   Charles Moore, *Margaret Thatcher*, vol. 2, London: Allen Lane, 2015.

3   Cited in Macintyre, *The Spy and the Traitor*, p. 200.

4   The way Project Ryan was regarded within the KGB is described in Christopher Andrew and Vasili Mitrokhin, *The*

Mitrokhin Archive, vol. 1, London: Allen Lane, 1999, pp. 512–13 and 565–6.

5 Examples can be found in the EU Stratcom reports of Russian disinformation, such as #DisinfoReview from the EU East Strat-Com Task Force of 28 March 2019.

6 The title of a Pentagon publication by Reagan's Secretary of Defense, Caspar Weinberger, designed to persuade Congress that additional funding was needed for US force modernization.

7 Thatcher to Reagan, note released to UK National Archives, January 2014, cited in Macintyre, *The Spy and the Traitor*, p. 340.

8 Reported in the National Security Archive file on Able Archer, https://unredacted.com/2013/07/09/president-reagan-meets-oleg-gordievsky-soviet-double-agent-who-reported-danger-of-able-archer-83/, accessed 24 December 2019.

9 Frederick Kempe, *Berlin 1961*, New York: G. P. Putnam's Sons, 2011, pp. 184–6.

10 Peter Taylor, *Brits*, London: Bloomsbury, 2001, p. 164. This book provides one of the most detailed and incisive accounts of the activity of the British government behind the scenes, leading eventually to the peace process in Northern Ireland.

11 How the peace process was then advanced is described in Jonathan Powell, *Great Hatred, Little Room*, London: Vintage Books, 2009.

12 The idea of BATNA as a strengthening of negotiating psychology was introduced by Roger Fisher and William Ury, *Getting to Yes: Negotiating without Giving In*, New York: Random House Business Books, 1981, as part of the Harvard Negotiating Project (rev. edn with Bruce Patton, 2011); see https://www.pon.harvard.edu/daily/batna/translate-your-batna-to-the-current-deal/, accessed 24 December 2019.

13 Simon Horobin, 'How one proverb became a recurring part of the Brexit debate', *Prospect Magazine*, 7 March 2018. See https://

www.prospectmagazine.co.uk/arts-and-books/cakeism-brexit-linguist-have-your-cake-eat-it-too, accessed 24 December 2019.

14 Trump's co-author, Tony Schwartz, has commented: 'I wrote *The Art of the Deal* with Trump. He's still a scared child', 'Opinion', *Guardian*, 18 January 2018, https://www.theguardian.com/global/commentisfree/2018/jan/18/fear-donald-trump-us-president-art-of-the-deal, accessed 24 December 2019.

15 John Stuart Mill, *On Liberty*, London: Longmans, Roberts and Green, 1869, ch. 1, 'Introductory'.

16 Ethical scenarios form a central part of training for the finance profession. To be accredited in London by the Chartered Institute for Securities and Investment requires the candidate to pass an online integrity test responding to such scenarios; see https://www.cisi.org/cisiweb2/cisi-website/integrity-ethics/integritymatters-product-suite, accessed 28 July 2019.

9. Lesson 9: Trustworthiness creates lasting partnerships

1 Luc, Raphael and Guillaume Bardin, *Strategic Partnerships*, London: Kogan Page, 2014, p. 2. This book by the Bardins is one of the surest guides to strategic partnering, based on the deep experience of Luc Bardin applying this strategy within BP, and I recognize many of its insights in the intelligence world as described in this chapter.

2 Many of the founding documents can now be accessed in the UK National Archives, see http://www.nationalarchives.gov.uk/ukusa/, accessed 24 December 2019, amplifying earlier accounts such as Jeffrey T. Richelson and Desmond Ball, *The Ties That Bind: Intelligence Cooperation between the UKUSA Countries*, London: Allen and Unwin, 1985.

3 The story was uncovered by the historian Jim Beach in his article 'Origins of the Special Intelligence Relationship? Anglo-American

Intelligence Co-operation on the Western Front, 1917–18', *Intelligence and National Security*, 22(2), pp. 229–49.

4   A biography of Denniston, the first Director, was launched in 2017 at GCHQ: Joel Greenberg, *Alastair Denniston: Code-Breaking from Room 40 to Berkeley Street and the Birth of GCHQ*, London: Frontline Books, 2017.

5   Christopher Andrew, *The Secret World: A History of Intelligence*, London: Allen Lane, 2018, p. 643.

6   Cited in Richard Aldrich, *GCHQ*, London: Harper Press, 2010, p. 89.

7   Copies of the original and the 1956 version of the agreement can be found on the NSA website, https://www.nsa.gov/news-features/declassified-documents/ukusa/index.shtml, accessed 24 December 2019.

8   Chester L. Cooper, *In the Shadow of History*, New York: Prometheus Books, 2005.

9   R. Louis Benson and Michael Warner (eds.), *Venona*, Washington DC: NSA/CIA, 1996.

10 I sat with Professor (Dame) Onora O'Neill on a 2015 inquiry commissioned by the UK Deputy Prime Minister examining surveillance in the light of the Snowden affair and have been much influenced by her writing on trustworthiness: Onora O'Neill, 'Linking Trust to Trustworthiness', *International Journal of Philosophical Studies*, 2018, 26:2, pp. 293–300.

11 Michael J. Hayden, *Playing to the Edge*, New York: Penguin Books, 2017.

12 http://www.nytimes.com/1994/11/11/world/president-orders-end-to-enforcing-bosnian-embargo.html, accessed 24 December 2019.

13 Included as letter C-32/1 of 25 February 1942 in Warren F. Kimball, *Churchill and Roosevelt: The Complete Correspondence*, vol. 1: *Alliance Emerging: October 1933–November 1942*, Princeton: Prince-

ton University Press, 2015, p. 371. The letter was first published (from a US copy) in 1989 by Louis Krue.

14 Bradley Smith, *The Ultra-Magic Deals and the Most Secret Special Relationship, 1940–1946*, Novato, Calif.: Presidio, 1992, p. vii.

15 Bardin, *Strategic Partnerships*, p. 2.

16 Presidential Policy Directive PPD-28, Washington DC: White House, 2014, Section 3(c).

17 Cited in James Bamford, *Body of Secrets*, New York: Doubleday, 2001, p. 407.

18 Jack Straw liked the idea of using COBR for civil contingencies and its use became routine; see Jack Straw, *Last Man Standing*, London: Macmillan, 2012, p. 309.

19 Ibid., p. 296.

10. Lesson 10: Subversion and sedition are now digital

1 What follows is a dystopian fiction. Such a combination of events is unlikely to arise at a moment in time but each element is likely to occur at some point.

2 The film *V for Vendetta* was itself an adaptation of an Alan Moore graphic novel, first published by DC Comics in 1981.

3 As at 2018, excluding deployed warheads Russia had 5250 nuclear warheads in storage, retired warheads and warheads awaiting dismantlement. The UK had 120 deployed warheads in total and 95 stored. *SIPRI Yearbook 2018*, Oxford: Oxford University Press, 18 June 2018, available at https://www.sipri.org/yearbook/2018, accessed 24 December 2019.

4 The UK Electoral Commission has stated: 'The grounds for bringing an election petition in the UK are not clearly defined in legislation' in its 2012 report into *Challenging Elections in the UK*, available at https://www.electoralcommission.org.uk/sites/

default/files/pdf_file/Challenging-elections-in-the-UK.pdf, accessed 24 December 2019.

5   A critical examination of the concept, concluding that we are dangerously unprepared for it, is Sean McFate, *Goliath*, London: Michael Joseph, 2019, pp. 179–93.

6   In an Open Letter from the Web Foundation, 12 March 2017, World Wide Web Foundation, 12 March 2017, https://webfoundation. org/2017/03/web-turns-28-letter/, accessed 24 December 2019.

7   David Omand, 'The Threats from Modern Digital Subversion and Sedition', *Journal of Cyber Policy*, 2018, 3:1, pp. 5–23.

8   A guide to this new world of digital marketing and personal data is Dominik Kosorin, *Introduction to Programmatic Advertising*, 2016 Kindle edition, and his more advanced *Data in Digital Advertising*, 2019 Kindle edition.

9   The Russian Internet Research Agency (IRA) is described by the US Director of National Intelligence as an agency of professional trolls in St Petersburg. It works with the Russian intelligence services to create fake internet postings and fake social media groups, using a variety of avatars or false identifities. The likely financier of the IRA is a close Putin ally with ties to Russian intelligence. For the Russian campaign in 2016, see Clint Watts, *Messing with the Enemy*, New York: HarperCollins, 2018, and Luke Harding, *Collusion*, London: Guardian Books, 2017.

10 This section draws on the official US investigations, see DNI, 'Assessing Russian Activities and Intentions in Recent US Elections', Washington DC, 6 January 2017; Senate Select Committee on Intelligence Report, 'The Intelligence Community Assessment: Assessing Russian Activities and Intentions in Recent U.S. Elections', Washington DC, 3 July 2018; and the findings of the Special Counsel Mueller inquiry, 'Report on the Investigation into Russian Interference in the 2016 Presidential Election', Washington DC: Department of Justice, 2019.

11 'Putin's Asymmetric Assault on Democracy in Russia and Europe: Implications for US National Security', Minority Staff Report for the Committee on Foreign Relations, Washington DC: US Government Publishing Office, 10 January 2018, p. 45.

12 The BBC published a full account of the Pizzagate conspiracy on the blog https://www.bbc.co.uk/news/blogs-trending-38156985, 2 December 2016, accessed 24 December 2019.

13 Novosti, 15 September 2017, http://ren.tv/novosti/2017–09-15/vysshiy-eshelon-amerikanskih-vlastey-sotryasaet-pedofilskiy-skandal, accessed 28 July 2019, since removed from the site.

14 The NSA Director testified before the US Armed Services Committee on the hack, see *Wired*, 9 May 2017, https://www.wired.com/2017/05/nsa-director-confirms-russia-hacked-french-election-infrastructure/, accessed 24 December 2019.

15 EU Stratcom, the EU East Strategic Communications Task Force, https://euvsdisinfo.eu/disinfo-review, accessed 24 December 2019.

16 Mueller indictment of IRA and others, District of Columbia District Court, 16 February 2018, 18 U.S.C. §§ 2,371, 1349, 1028A, p. 3.

17 David Omand, *From Nudge to Novichok*, Helsinki: European Centre of Excellence for Countering Hybrid Threats, Working Paper, April 2018.

18 Speech to Reuters by the Prime Minister, Tony Blair, 12 June 2007, available at https://uk.reuters.com/article/uk-blair-speech/full-transcript-of-blair-speech-idUKZWE24585220070612, accessed 24 December 2019.

19 Daniel Kahneman, *Thinking, Fast and Slow*, London: Allen Lane, 2011, p. 13.

20 http://www.latimes.com/politics/la-pol-obama-farewell-speech-transcript-20170110-story.html, accessed 24 December 2019.

21 As used by Kathleen Taylor, *Brainwashing: The Science of Thought Control*, Oxford: Oxford University Press, 2006, p. 61.

22 Emma Grey Ellis, 'The Alt-Right are savvy internet users. Stop letting them surprise you', *Wired*, 9 August 2018, p. 533.

23 The *Washington Post* has a guide to such deceptive techniques; see https://www.washingtonpost.com/graphics/2019/politics/fact-checker/manipulated-video-guide/, accessed 26 June 2019.

24 Given the danger of such malicious use, the software company OpenAI (a non-profit research company backed by Elon Musk) has not released its detailed research findings. Alex Hern, *Guardian*, 16 February 2019, p. 15.

Part Four

11. *A final lesson in optimism*

1 William Gibson, *Neuromancer*, London: Gollancz, 1984, p. 2.

2 Elisa Shearer, 'Social media outpaces print newspapers in the US as a news source', Pew Research Center, 10 December 2018, https://www.pewresearch.org/fact-tank/2018/12/10/social-media-outpaces-print-newspapers-in-the-u-s-as-a-news-source/, accessed 24 December 2019.

3 Amanda Lenhart, Rich Ling, Scott Campbell and Kristen Purcell, 'Teens and mobile phones', Pew Research Center, 20 April 2010, https://www.pewinternet.org/2010/04/20/teens-and-mobile-phones/, accessed 24 December 2019.

4 By Dr Mary Aiken, a leading expert in forensic cyberpsychology; see Mary Aiken, *The Cyber Effect*, London: John Murray, 2016, p. 5.

5 According to the UK fact-checking charity Full Fact, set up in 2017 with the backing of George Soros and Pierre Omidyar, https://fullfact.org/europe/350-million-week-boris-johnson-statistics-authority-misuse/, accessed 24 December 2019.

6   Commenting on the claim by the Press Secretary, Sean Spicer, about attendance figures at the Trump inauguration, recorded at https://www.youtube.com/watch?v=VSrEEDQgFc8 accessed 24 December 2019.

7   David Omand, *Securing the State*, London: Hurst 2010, p. 191.

8   In their report for the RAND Corporation, Jennifer Kavanagh and Michael D. Rich, *Truth Decay*, Santa Monica: RAND, 2018.

9   Robert Trivers, *Deceipt and Self-Deception*, London: Allen Lane, 2011, ch. 1.

10 J. Carter, J. G. Goldman, G. Reed, P. Hansel, M. Halpern and A. Rosenberg, 'Sidelining science since day one: How the Trump administration has harmed public health and safety in its first six months', Union of Concerned Scientists, 2018, online at https://www.ucsusa.org/sites/default/files/attach/2017/07/sidelining-science-report-ucs-7-20-2017.pdf, accessed 24 December 2019.

11 Galileo Galilei, 'Letter to the Grand Duchess Christina of Tuscany, 1615', online at https://web.stanford.edu/~jsabol/certainty/readings/Galileo-LetterDuchessChristina.pdf, accessed 24 December 2019.

12 Philipp Schmid and Cornelia Betsch, 'Effective Strategies for Rebutting Science Denialism in Public Discussions', *Nature Human Behaviour*, 24 June 2019, https://doi.org/10.1038/s41562-019-0632-4.

13 At the insistence of the Council of the Romanian National Salvation Front that had temporarily replaced their dictatorship after the collapse of communist rule.

14 An argument made by Renee DiResta, 'Free speech is not the same as free reach', *Wired Ideas*, 30 August 2018.

15 UK Parliament, report of the DCMS Committee, Disinformation and Fake News, London, 18 February 2019, available at https://publications.parliament.uk/pa/cm201719/cmselect/cmcumeds/1791/179102.htm, accessed 24 December 2019.

16 It is wise to judge whistleblowers who leak information by whether they have a legitimate public interest in their disclosure, have taken all reasonable steps to minimize the harm to others their disclosures will cause, and have exhausted the remedies open to them, including through democratic routes in Parliament or Congress before going public. If they do go public, then ethically they should resign and accept the consequences, not cling to their job by leaking anonymously.

17 David Hume, *An Enquiry Concerning Human Understanding* (1748), Oxford: Oxford University Press, 1999 edn, Section III, p. 102.

Index

He just wanted a decent book to read ...

Not too much to ask, is it? It was in 1935 when Allen Lane, Managing Director of Bodley Head Publishers, stood on a platform at Exeter railway station looking for something good to read on his journey back to London. His choice was limited to popular magazines and poor-quality paperbacks – the same choice faced every day by the vast majority of readers, few of whom could afford hardbacks. Lane's disappointment and subsequent anger at the range of books generally available led him to found a company – and change the world.

'We believed in the existence in this country of a vast reading public for intelligent books at a low price, and staked everything on it'
Sir Allen Lane, 1902–1970, founder of Penguin Books

The quality paperback had arrived – and not just in bookshops. Lane was adamant that his Penguins should appear in chain stores and tobacconists, and should cost no more than a packet of cigarettes.

Reading habits (and cigarette prices) have changed since 1935, but Penguin still believes in publishing the best books for everybody to enjoy. We still believe that good design costs no more than bad design, and we still believe that quality books published passionately and responsibly make the world a better place.

So wherever you see the little bird – whether it's on a piece of prize-winning literary fiction or a celebrity autobiography, political tour de force or historical masterpiece, a serial-killer thriller, reference book, world classic or a piece of pure escapism – you can bet that it represents the very best that the genre has to offer.

Whatever you like to read – trust Penguin.